MADAME TUSSAUD: HER LIFE AND LEGACY

FOR MY SON
who loves interesting facts

MADAME TUSSAUD: HER LIFE AND LEGACY

AN HISTORICAL ACCOUNT

GERI WALTON

PEN & SWORD
HISTORY

AN IMPRINT OF PEN & SWORD BOOKS LTD.
YORKSHIRE - PHILADELPHIA

First published in Great Britain in 2019 by
PEN AND SWORD HISTORY
an imprint of
Pen and Sword Books Ltd
Yorkshire – Philadelphia

ISBN 978 1 52673 408 2

Typeset in Times New Roman 11/13.5 by
Aura Technology and Software Services, India

Printed and bound in the UK by TJ International Ltd, Padstow, Cornwall

Pen & Sword Books Ltd incorporates the imprints of Pen & Sword
Archaeology, Atlas, Aviation, Battleground, Discovery,
Family History, History, Maritime, Military, Naval, Politics, Railways,
Select, Social History, Transport, True Crime, Claymore Press,
Frontline Books, Leo Cooper, Praetorian Press, Remember When,
Seaforth Publishing and Wharncliffe.

For a complete list of Pen & Sword titles please contact
PEN & SWORD BOOKS LIMITED
47 Church Street, Barnsley, South Yorkshire, S70 2AS, England
E-mail: enquiries@pen-and-sword.co.uk
Website: www.pen-and-sword.co.uk

Or
PEN AND SWORD BOOKS
1950 Lawrence Rd, Havertown, PA 19083, USA
E-mail: Uspen-and-sword@casematepublishers.com
Website: www.penandswordbooks.com

Contents

Map of Important Sites

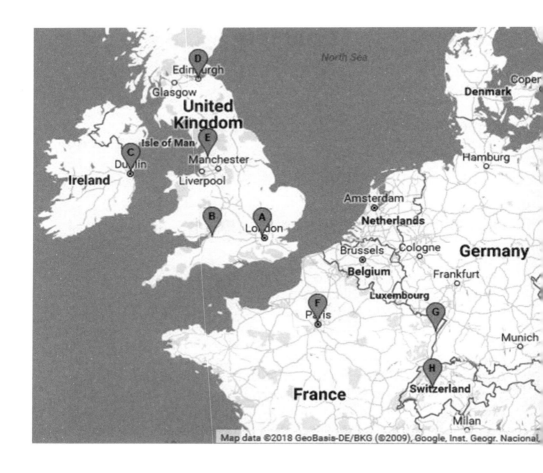

MAP OF IMPORTANT SITES

A. **London**. This is where Madame Tussaud first exhibited her wax figures after moving to England. She later established her museum on Baker Street, and then in the late 1800s, Madame Tussaud's museum moved around the corner to its current location on Marylebone Street.

B. **Bristol**. This is the site of the Bristol Riots in 1831 that threatened Madame Tussaud and her wax figures.

C. **Dublin**. This is one of the regular cities that Madame Tussaud toured in the 1800s with her wax exhibit.

D. **Edinburgh**. This city was one of Madame Tussaud's favorite cities to tour. This is also the city where two infamous murderers – William Burke and William Hare – committed a series of murders for profit.

E. **Lancashire coast**. Madame Tussaud appeared at a Mrs. Farington's home along this stretch of coast after a shipwreck that caused her to lose part of her wax exhibit.

F. **Paris**. This was the location where many of the major events of the French Revolution occurred. It is also the site of the Bastille, the Temple, Dr Curtius' Salon de Cire and Caverne des Grands Voleurs, the Palace of the Tuileries, the Louvre, the Fête de la Fédération and Maximilien Robespierre's 'Festival of the Supreme Being'.

G. **Strasbourg**. This is the birthplace of Madame Tussaud.

H. **Bern**. This is where Madame Tussaud spent the first few years of her life and the location where Dr Curtius began making his anatomical wax figures.

Preface

On December 1, 2017, a location of the world-famous Madame Tussauds wax museum opened in Delhi, India. With over 20 locations in major cities around the world, the Madame Tussauds brand is a household name synonymous with the concept of a wax museum. Moreover, the chain has more than doubled in size over the last ten years, and while revenues for the chain are not publicly available, the Tussaud Group was purchased in 2007 for $1.9 billion. This chain of museums has remained a vibrant, ongoing attraction for well over 200 years, all stemming from the remarkable efforts of one Anne Marie Tussaud née Grosholtz, born into one of the most violent and turbulent times in human history.

This is her story.

PART I

Marie Grosholtz

Spring 1789

Versailles, France

Chapter 1

Boiling Point

'I can boast that the first act of the Revolution began
at my house.'

Dr Phillipe Curtius

Traveling from Paris in the spring of 1789, 28-year old Marie Grosholtz witnessed one of the greatest splendours of her time. It was the Palace of Versailles. In front of her would have been a grand structure comprising a huge gold-trimmed building (the *corps de logis*) that contained the royal apartments, flanked on three sides by colonnaded secondary buildings that thus enclosed the *Cour Royale* (Royal Court). The Palace of Versailles was then the centre of royal influence in France and the home of King Louis XVI and his Queen, Marie Antoinette. In those days, France was one of the most powerful nations in the world, and the Palace of Versailles proudly symbolized France's status. Yet, this world was on the verge of cataclysmic change.

Marie was likely conscious of a looming social upheaval. Just that spring, outside the very gates of the Palace, the French populace had formed a National Assembly and soon after made an oath not to disband until they created a new constitution. There was great unrest over excessive taxation, lack of food, and the perceived ineptitude and moral turpitude of the royals. Moreover, despite France's stature in the world, the French state faced crushing debt. The King had recently reinstated the popular Jacques Necker to stabilize finances, but tensions between the monarchy and the populace continued to heighten.

In those days, Marie's business at the Palace of Versailles likely involved tutoring King Louis XVI's youngest sister, Madame Élisabeth, in the art of making wax figurines. The making of wax creations had caught the eye of Élisabeth several years earlier, just like it had caught the eye of others. Wax creations were extremely popular in Paris in the late 1700s, and representations of fruit and flowers were the frequent results.

Élisabeth supposedly became so enamoured with the artistic potential of wax that she begged to learn wax modelling. To aid in her instructions in

1779, Marie's mentor and uncle, Dr Philippe Mathé Curtius, appointed then 18-year-old Marie to teach her. According to Marie, she was so often at the Palace that Élisabeth became attached to her and requested she live there. While it is unclear if Marie truly resided there, it is known that Élisabeth created many wax figures, including Christ, the Virgin Mary, and other holy figures, which she gave to friends.

Most of what is known about Marie's early life comes from her *Memoirs*, although several scholars have cast doubt on the validity of some of her stories. For example, Marie noted that she served Élisabeth as more than just a tutor. Marie also recounted that the famed Enlightenment philosopher Jean-Jacques Rousseau found himself owing some critical debt, and to solve it, he appealed to Élisabeth. It was rather suspect that the pious Élisabeth, who confessed every Saturday and took the sacrament every Sunday, was willing to help Rousseau, whose theological ideas were at complete variance to her own. However, Marie was supposedly sent off 'to Paris with the sum adequate to relieve Rousseau from his difficulties'.[1]

When not teaching Madame Élisabeth the art of wax making or running errands, Marie could have explored Versailles magnificent gardens. Under Louis XVI, a complete replanting of the gardens had occurred. This included the labour-intensive palisade hedging that was replaced by lime and chestnut trees. In addition, a rockwork grotto, inspired by Hubert Robert, was set in an English style bosquet but what made Versailles's gardens fascinating was not the hedges, trees, or grotto; it was that Marie, or any one of the ordinary public, could stroll in these same gardens and have a chance of meeting the promenading King and Queen.

Louis XVI was a man who never wanted to be king. He looked nothing like a king with his slipshod dress, clumsy gait, and inability to look anyone in the eye. His passions were also not necessarily kingly either. He enjoyed reading, hunting, and locksmithing. Yet, because his grandfather Louis XV died prematurely, he was forced to assume the role of king in 1774.

Queen Marie Antoinette was Austrian and developed a reputation as a fashion trendsetter in France. Women embraced her fashion style, which included her expensive tastes and her high, teetering, and outlandish hairdos. Like her husband, the queen dreamed of a different life, a life without the pressures of being a royal and a life where she could promenade in muslin dresses and floppy hats and avoid court etiquette and all the associated tediousness related to court life.

One tedious aspect of court life that the Queen detested was the nightly dining ritual called *Grand Couvert*, where common people watched the King and Queen have dinner as a form of public entertainment. Thus, every evening Louis — with his untidy, haphazard appearance — dined next to a Marie Antoinette bedecked in feathers and jewels. This was when 'the good, honest people from the country, after visiting the menageries to see the lions, tigers, and monkeys fed, hastened to the palace to see the king and queen take their soup'.[2]

These good, honest people were railed off from the royal family, and almost no one was denied admission, so throngs of people poured through the apartments, such that 'those in the advance [were] crowded slowly along by those in the rear, and all eyes riveted upon the royal feeders'.[3] People could watch the queen sup her soup and the king devour his boiled meat. Although the king hardly noticed the crowd, the queen glared back at the spectators, exasperated at being on stage.

Other people routinely seen at the Palace of Versailles included the queen's dear friend and Superintendent of the Household, the Princess de Lamballe. Her translucent complexion and hair of an indescribable golden hue got her noticed, but it was her noble, generous, and amiable personality that got her loved.

The King's cousin and the infamous womanizer Louis Philippe Joseph II, Duke d'Orléans also frequented Versailles. He was in line for the throne and brother-in-law to the Princess de Lamballe. Marie described the 5-foot 9-inch Duke as stout, and in his youth, dashing, although later his face was covered in oozing pustules and red pimples.

There were many other nobles at Versailles. Many of these noble or elite were very likely part of the circle of influential people that Marie and Dr Curtius cultivated. In those days, they wanted to develop relationships with the French elite, so they could model them in wax for Curtius' galleries in Paris.

These nobles enjoyed the Palace despite the required etiquette that ruled their lives and consisted of inflexible rules and irrevocable decrees. The traditions of the court had long been established and were based on the precedent of earlier courts. Moreover, etiquette ruled a courtier's every word, gesture, and act, and it also regulated French society and governed the French court. Polite behaviour had been particularly important in the seventeenth century. In fact, it was of such importance to Louis XIV that he was able to enforce it with a single look. He could do this because courtiers lived at the palace under his watchful eye, and if courtiers behaved improperly or displeased him, Louis simply singled them out by ignoring them. This disapproval or lack of being 'seen' could affect a person's career and future and was equivalent to being insignificant or inconsequential.

Inflexible etiquette likewise affected courtiers in Louis XVI and Marie Antoinette's time. Courtiers found it an honour to serve at court and wanted to gain their monarch's favour. They also wanted to obtain the highest rank possible because the higher the rank they obtained, the greater the money, prestige, and power they acquired. Of course, this also meant that disagreements and arguments occurred regularly among courtiers as they sought to gain the affection and approval of the King or Queen.

Marie might have found it difficult to believe this style of living, associated with the *ancien régime* that had existed for centuries, could completely collapse in the span of a few years. She was still young then, a thin-framed and pleasant-looking woman. Portraits depict her as having heavy lidded, deep-set brown eyes, thick eyebrows, and a thin upper lip with a prominent cupid's bow. Her neck was long and accentuated by a massive amount of hair that tumbled down from its cap with a natural wave or curl to it. If Marie possessed any less-appealing physical feature it might have been her larger than normal, rather downturned nose. Yet, despite her youth, the forces of change were about to bring a heavy burden on her frail shoulders.

The approach of great social unrest was clear by May 1789 when the Estates General met in a small hotel that Marie likely passed on her way to the Versailles gate. The Estates General was a representative and consultative body formed from three classes – First Estate (nobility), Second Estate (clergy), and Third Estate (common people or bourgeoisie), and many of the people who participated in this convention were soon to become important in Marie's life. The Estates General had not met since 1614 and were summoned by a royal edict dated 24 January 1789 to meet in May. Louis XVI had called the Estates General hoping to solve the fiscal crisis plaguing France, but the leaders from the three Estates had deep and conflicting interests.

The problems stemmed in part from the system of taxation. Although the French people paid fewer taxes than the British at the time, there were major inequities within the French tax system. There also existed many exemptions for the privileged classes. Tax reformation had been attempted in earlier years, but those efforts failed to shift more of the tax burden onto the wealthier classes. In the meantime, France's financial problems continued to grow, which also increased the country's debt.

The calling of the Estates General inspired several people that Marie would be involved with over the next few years. One of them was Honoré Gabriel Riqueti, better known as the Count of Mirabeau. He hoped to be elected by the Second Estate from his district in Provence, but, unfortunately, the nobles rejected him. Instead, Mirabeau was elected in both Aix and

Marseilles by the Third Estate. He accepted the call from Aix and appeared at the meeting of the Estates General on 4 May 1789.

In the Estates General, Mirabeau soon made some important connections and was introduced to several other deputies also representing the Third Estate. One of them was another person Marie would include in her social circle, Maximilien François Marie Isidore de Robespierre. He was a lawyer and politician, and he would eventually become one of the most prominent and influential figures of the French Revolution and the Reign of Terror.

The same rituals that had opened the 1614 Estates General opened the one in May 1789. First, there was a procession that occurred on Monday, 4 May. At the front was a religious processional cross followed by the First Estate decked out in black and white satin with plumed caps. The Second Estate came next, resplendent in purple. The Third Estate brought up the rear, and, in contrast to the finery and sumptuousness of the First and Second Estate, they were unadorned in black with a black and gold overcoat. Royalty closed the procession with the king wearing his coronation mantle and on his head the Regent Diamond. The queen was dressed in silver and gold.

Rain had attempted to dampen spirits, but as dawn broke, the rain ceased. Members of the procession travelled from one church to another in serpentine fashion. The three-hour procession moved from Notre-Dame across the Place d'Armes to the Church of Saint-Louis. Nearly everyone carried a lighted candle, and by the time the head of procession reached Saint-Louis, the tail had hardly left Notre Dame.

Along the way, the streets were lined with French and Swiss Guards and throngs of people. While it is not clear if Marie was there, many people filled windows and rooftops, gaily cheering whenever the Third Estate passed. Some spectators also cheered the king, others pointed out Mirabeau, and a few applauded the Duke d'Orléans. However, when the queen passed by, she was accompanied by a 'belt of silence' that lasted before and after the appearance of her ladies.

At the church, the three Estates sat in importance with the First at the front and the Third at the back. There, they listened to the Bishop of Nancy present a two-hour long sermon. He 'mentioned the barbarities of tax collectors, the extravagance of Queen Marie Antoinette, the iniquity of the writings of the philosophes, such as the late Voltaire … the necessity for religion as the continuing basis of the national life, and the need for voluntary renunciation of exemptions from taxation'.[4] He also rebuked the court for their appalling luxury and received enthusiastic applause.

The following day, the Estates General met in a temporary hall near the Palace of Versailles. It was on the Avenue de Paris behind the Hotel of Menus Plaisirs and was a rectangular chamber spacious enough to hold 1,200 deputies and numerous spectators. At one end was a platform under a canopy of gold fringe that was splendidly decorated, where the king and queen's thrones were placed, with the queen's throne to the left of the king's. Tier seating formed the remainder of the seats. To the right of the thrones were the seats for the Second Estate and to the left, the seats for the First Estate. In front of the thrones at the far end sat the Third Estate.

Strict protocol ensued at the Estates General. The First and Second Estates sat first while the Third Estate stood standing and waiting outside. About an hour and half later, the Third Estate sat. After the three estates were seated, the king entered with his entourage. He was followed by the ill-at-ease queen and her respective entourage.

Louis presided over the meeting. He opened with his speech, presented some reforms, and declared himself 'the best friend of his people'.[5] He was followed by the Keeper of the Seal, who gave a tedious speech. The King's finance minister, Jacques Necker, spoke next on France's economic situation. But Necker further weakened his reputation with the people by talking for hours without offering ideas about how to reform policy to save the nation. Instead, he gave them financial data, which suggested to the people that he thought the Estates General was simply an administrative function rather than a new government.

When the Estates General next met, their meeting quickly turned from finances into a debate about how to vote. The Third Estate was less powerful than the First or Second, but they had twice as many delegates and represented the majority. Therefore, the Third Estate wanted to vote based on headcount, not power. As the First and Second Estate had the power, they did not want any change. Necker supported doubling the representation of Third Estate, but he and the king let the argument go on too long, and by the time they conceded, the Third Estate felt their concession was not very magnanimous.

The three estates met over the next few weeks but were unable to reach a substantive agreement. Unwilling to wait for the others, the Third Estate began passing its own resolutions. Around 17 June, they began calling themselves the National Assembly, led by Mirabeau.

While Mirabeau may have been just one of many deputies in the Estates General, he stood out. His eloquent voice and stupendous speaking abilities rallied the people in time of crisis, despite the problems associated with his early life that included scandalous liaisons, time in prison, and extensive debt.

Moreover, people found he possessed natural abilities of leadership that were enhanced by his logical acuity, intense reliability, and passionate enthusiasm.

On 17 June, Mirabeau's eloquence was one reason the Third Estate decided to call themselves the National Assembly – a few weeks later they would be called the National Constituent Assembly but loosely called the National Assembly. The National Assembly proceeded to elect an astronomer, mathematician, and freemason named Jean-Sylvain Bailly as their first president. Then, because the new Assembly had the most delegates, they decided to solve the financial crisis.

In the meantime, Louis, under the influence of his privy council, decided he would dictate reforms and hold a meeting on 22 June to finalize his reforms. On 20 June, when the National Assembly went to meet at the hall in the Hôtel des Menus Plaisirs, they found the door closed and barred. Historians have long debated why. Was it a royal tactic or was it an accident, as the next scheduled meeting was 22 June? Although it may have been an accident, when the Assembly learned they were locked out, they were furious. They believed that the king had locked them out on purpose and that he would try to force them to disband. So, they moved their meeting to a nearby tennis court, which was, in fact, the tennis court where Louis played tennis. They also decided because they had gathered together to take the following oath:

> 'The National Assembly, considering that it has been summoned to determine the constitution of the Kingdom … decrees that all the members of this assembly shall immediately take a solemn oath never to separate and to reassemble wherever circumstance shall require until the constitution of the Kingdom shall be established and consolidated upon firm foundations; and that the said oath being taken, all the members and each of the individually shall ratify by their signatures this steadfast resolution'.[6]

The oath was a revolutionary act. It was the first time that French citizens stood up to their king. The oath also reflected the Assembly's desires, as its preamble closely resembled America's famous Declaration of Independence that America's Founding Father Benjamin Franklin had helped conceive along with Thomas Jefferson, John Adams, Robert R. Livingston, and Roger Sherman. Moreover, the oath inspired future revolutionary activity and reasserted the power that the Assembly had claimed.

In this way, Marie's life would be thrown into turmoil for the next ten years. Many of the figures from the Estates General and others who would be swept up in the ensuing French Revolution would prove of great interest to her not only in her life but also in her profession as a wax modeler.

The trip back to Paris would have given Marie a visual and sharp contrast, exposing the reason the unrest resulted in the formation of the National Assembly and the taking of the Tennis Court Oath. In contrast to the opulence of the Palace of Versailles, the people were living in squalor. They had also suffered poor grain harvests in 1769, 1776, and 1783. The poor harvests, along with France's continued financial struggles, were exacerbated in 1788 when yet again all hopes of a good grain harvest faded.

The great hail storm of 1788 began with a darkened sky on 13 July and turned into a terrifying ordeal. People heard loud claps of thunder and then saw vivid lightning flashes. Before long, hail stones were pummelling the earth that weighed sometimes as much as half a pound. The hail storm moved fast, probably lasted no longer than about eight minutes, but it was deadly. It killed many animals and damaged buildings. Fruit trees were demolished, grape vines stripped, crops ruined, and gardens destroyed. The loss was incalculable and resulted in a sharp increase in wheat prices.

In Paris, the two most familiar places to Marie were probably the wax attraction venues that belonged to Dr Curtius, her mentor and uncle. The first place was called Salon de Cire (House of Wax), located at number 7 in the Palais-Royal. The Palais-Royal was owned by the King's cousin, the Duke d'Orléans, who had completely refurbished the building and its garden. He had turned it into a commercial money-making machine, and as the Palais Royal was in the heart of Paris, it did not take much for Dr Curtius' wax displays to attract fashionable men and women.

Near the Palais-Royal was the Tuileries Palace, which sat empty on the right bank of the Seine River. Louis XIV and Louis XV had lived in the Tuileries Palace off and on, but since about the 1740s, Louis XV had allowed the Tuileries to remain practically empty as Versailles had become the seat of political power for the French monarchy. Moreover, Versailles was famous not only as a stately building but also because it represented the Ancien Régime and its system of absolute monarchy.

A stone's throw away from the Tuileries Palace, also on the right bank of the Seine, was the Louvre. The Louvre had originally served as fortress in the twelfth and thirteenth centuries before being converted into the main residence for France's kings in 1546. After its conversion, it was extended many times and eventually became the default spot to display the royal art collection.

Beyond the Louvre was the Boulevard du Temple. It was a thoroughfare that housed a row of theatres and entertainment centres. The Boulevard du

Temple was where Dr Curtius' second shop was located, and beyond it, further to the southeast, were the looming walls of the Bastille, the state prison where reputedly the king's enemies were imprisoned without trial and based on his whims.

At Dr Curtius' shop, the wax models were sometimes arranged in scenes. One of these scenes was in fact a representation of the Grand Couvert that occurred nightly at Versailles, apparently for those who couldn't or didn't want to make the 20-mile trek to the actual event. Near the wax museum, people could hear the museum's crier grow hoarse exclaiming, 'Enter, enter, gentlemen, come and see the grand course, 'tis all as at Versailles'[7] Inside, in many ways, the wax museum's version of the Grand Couvert was better than the real thing. It cost spectators just a few sous to gawk continually at the wax replicas of the king and queen dining, and the wax figures would not glare back.

Another event from Versailles that was captured in wax was a tableau with some Indian envoys wearing brilliantly-coloured native costumes and standing under a tent situated at Grand Trianon. The tableau also included several Indian soldiers, known as sepoys, that served under the British. The scene had been set up after an incident occurred involving the envoys and the king and queen in 1788 and was based on a prank which occurred when the king and queen received and entertained envoys from the Kingdom of Mysore, located in the southwest of the Indian subcontinent. Tipu Sultan, also known as the Tiger of Mysor or Tipu Sahib, was hoping to rally support in his opposition to the British. He sent his ambassadors to France to ensure French support.

In France, the envoys attended the opera, and a favourite painter of the queen's, Louise-Elisabeth Vigée-LeBrun, saw them. Through an interpreter she asked if she might be allowed to paint them, but they refused. Vigée-LeBrun then asked the queen to persuade them, which she did because a few days later Vigée-LeBrun visited the envoy's hotel armed with her paints and canvases. She wrote of their meeting:

> On my arrival one of them brought in a jar of rose-water, with which he sprinkled my hands; then the tallest ... gave me a sitting. I did him standing, with his hand on his dagger. He threw himself into such an easy, natural position ... that I did not make him change it. I let the paint dry in another room, and began on the portrait of the old ambassador, whom I represented seated with his son next to him. The father especially had a magnificent head. Both were clad in flowing

robes of white muslin worked with golden flowers, and these robes, a sort of long tunic with wide up-turned sleeves, were held in place by gorgeous belts.[8]

The envoys were there for a time before Louis granted them an audience in August. According to Marie, before their visit to Versailles, the ambassadors allowed her to make casts of their faces. They then visited Dr Curtius' wax exhibition and after that visit, went to the Palace of Versailles where the Queen seems to have devised a prank, as they thought they were going to be shown more wax figures.

The courtiers were already seated waiting behind glass and the queen had forewarned them to remain motionless. So, when the envoys arrived, they assumed the courtiers to be wax figures. Marie wrote that 'the royal family amused themselves in a singular manner with the credulity of the Indians [and] ... were highly amused with the remarks of the Indians, who were much struck with the wax figures, as they imagined them to be, so exactly imitating life'.[9] Such a prank today might be viewed as tasteless. Nonetheless, after the event, Dr Curtius had Marie remove the models to Paris where they were set up in a tableau in the *Salon de Cire* to commemorate the event.

Besides the scenes of Indian envoys or the Grand Couvert, Dr Curtius' wax exhibition had a much more serious tone. Other wax busts included the philosopher Rousseau who was the originator of the notion of social contract between people and state, as well as the finance minister Necker, the king, and the Duke d'Orléans. Additionally, there was a dinner table of distinguished wax guests that always evolved to meet the public's taste.

In 1789, Dr Curtius consolidated his exhibition from the Palais-Royal into one at No. 20 Boulevard du Temple. While he had customarily exhibited wax figures of royals and nobles, Marie found the wax visitors evolving during the turbulent late 1780s to include some of the best and the worst characters of the times. Despite the political changes of his exhibition, Dr Curtius' wax collection remained popular. Also, Dr Curtius himself became political active and spoke out for change, something that Marie could not share with those at Versailles.

By July 1789, the events driving France toward major change began to accelerate. On 11 July, Necker was dismissed, and the following day protestors arrived knocking on Dr Curtius' wax museum door. According to Marie, they wanted a life size figure of the king and two wax busts, the

Duke d'Orléans and that of Jacques Necker, to carry in a protest march. Dr Curtius refused them the king, stating that his bust would fall apart if carried, so they settled for the other two.

Marie also maintained that when the crowd appeared demanding the busts, she was not the least bit apprehensive and reported:

> 'M. Curtius, when he found them coming, gave directions to shut the gate of a railing which was in front of his house, to prevent their rushing into his museum. They, making no attempts to enter, but civilly demanding what they required, and having in part met with compliance, they departed, without offering the slightest outrage'.[10]

The protestors then took the commandeered heads of Necker and the Duke d'Orléans, placed them on pikes, held them aloft, and marched through Parisian streets beating drums. A journalist and dramatist, Louis-Abel, Beffroy de Reigny, was informed about the protests. Curious, he left the safety of his home to investigate, and when he reached the Boulevard du Temple, he reported:

> 'There I saw about five or six thousand men marching fairly fast and without any order, some of them armed, others with sabres, spears, and pitchforks. They triumphantly carried the wax busts of the Duc d'Orléans and of M. Necker, whom they had asked of M. Curtius. Near these busts were placed two black standards bordered with white, as a sign of the sorrow caused by the disgrace of this adored Minister. This little army threatened to burn all the theatres if they were not closed on the spot, saying that the French were not to rejoice in the bosom of public misfortunes. All theatres therefore closed'.[11]

Later that day, the mob arrived at the Place Louis XV where they encountered royal guards. The royal guards staunchly refused to salute their busts. The protestors took offense and insults between the two groups led to a fracas where a royal guard hacked off part of Necker's head. Dr Curtius offered this account of the event in 1790:

> 'I will not retrace the horrors committed on that memorable day. I can say only that the bearer who carried the bust of … Orléans

was wounded in the pit of the stomach by a bayonet thrust and the one who carried M. Necker was killed by a Dragoon … The bust of … Orléans was returned to me without damage, but that of M. Necker was given back only six days afterwards by a Swiss guard of the Palais-Royal; The hair was burned, and the face bore the imprint of several blows of the sabre. So, I can boast that the first act of the Revolution began at my house'.[12]

Unfortunately, two days later, on 14 July, the crowd was not in such a pleasant mood. The medieval fortress and prison known as the Bastille was stormed:

'The storming of the Bastille was more than an attack against the Paris prison with its seemingly impassable wide, deep ditches, and eight inaccessible towers. It was an attack against the monarchy and despotism'.[13]

The king learned about the attack the following morning. He had been hunting, and when he appeared at the Assembly, he was astonished that the Bastille had been taken. This storming against the symbol of the monarchy was the beginning of the end for Louis, and it would change the political landscape of France forever.

Dr Curtius was one of the first to don the uniform of red and blue that represented the citizen soldiers. The day before the attack, he joined a band of eight to nine-hundred soldiers, who became known as the *vainqueur de la Bastille,* and was elected a captain. He was also with the citizen soldiers when they searched for weapons, but he was not with them when they stormed the Bastille, having arrived shortly thereafter.

Marie noted that after the Bastille fell, revolutionaries decried the king's injustice and searched for implements used to torture prisoners in the Bastille. The most exciting thing discovered was a printing press that was mistaken for an instrument of torture. There was also not much to be found in the way of prisoners either. There were only seven.

According to Marie, one of the prisoners was the white-haired Count de Lorges, who had been imprisoned there over thirty years and had a waist-long beard. She claims in her *Memoirs* that he was brought to her and she made a cast of his face. Unfortunately, despite her claims, history shows that he was a fictional character devised and popularized by a French journalist and revolutionary named Jean-Louis Carra, and, so, whoever she modelled, it was not the Count de Lorges.

When the Bastille fell, 21-year-old François-René, vicomte de Chateaubriand was visiting Paris and reported he was present. He wrote about the incident:

> 'In the midst of these murders the people abandoned themselves to orgies similar to those carried on during the trouble of Rome under Otho and Vitellius. The conquerors of the Bastille, heroes of the tavern, road along in hired carriages, in drunken happiness; low women and *sans-culottes* began to reign, and formed their escort. The passers-by uncovered their head with the respect of fear to these heroes'.[14]

Chateaubriand, who was a French writer, diplomat, politician, historian, and considered the founder of Romanticism in French literature, claimed that he saw one man shot through the head and the governor of the Bastille, a man named De Launay, subjected to numerous outrages before he was callously murdered on the steps of the Hôtel de Ville (City Hall), his head severed, and put on a pike. In addition, another gentleman named Jacques de Flesselles was accused of misleading people about the location of arms before the storming. After he was murdered, his head was impaled on a pike too. Marie maintains that after their heads were removed from the pikes, both showed up at Dr Curtius' and she was forced to make casts of them.

She claimed that she dared not refuse, and not wanting to let the mob into the house, she took a chair and placed it in the doorway telling the mob they could watch her work. Unbeknownst to Marie, the English equestrian, circus owner, and inventor, Philip Astley, was in France at the time. He witnessed the event and wrote about it in his diary, noting that he had seen Marie in her doorway taking the bloody heads, placing them in her lap, and making the death masks. Several days later, Astley ordered wax copies of the men's heads, smuggled them across the border, and advertised them in his London circus where they were a 'horrifying' hit with his clientele.

As the crowd walked away satisfied with the work she had done, Marie had just played a part in the opening stages of the French Revolution. While she was likely unaware that in the next few years she would be making wax representations of many influential figures around her, and that many of them would be soon dead, she probably could sense that dangerous times were afoot. She would have wondered, could Dr Curtius' business survive long enough for her to take it over? Would France survive? Would she?

Chapter 2

Marie and Dr Curtius

'Madame Tussaud liked to associate herself with the famous,
in life as well as in wax, but who can tell if this or any other
of her tales were true?'

Pamela Pilbeam

The room was a flickering nightmare of sorts, sombre and dark, lit only by candles. Arms and legs were tossed on shelves, laying in piles, or propped in corners, and in the shadows stood several frozen lifeless figures and a ghastly pair of headless bodies leaned against one wall. Expected at any moment was an anatomist carrying his scalpel and ready to scrape clean a cadaver's bones.

What made Dr Curtius' building even more ghastly was the pervasive deathly silence that seemed as if it was like an eerie warning cry to visitors. Perhaps, the eeriest cry came from the graveyard of pristine heads weirdly featured in well-ordered rows sitting on a shelf against a grey mortared stone wall as if carved headstones. Some heads were toothless, some hairless, and some eyeless, yet their features were still so lifelike that even in their half-finished states they seemed bizarrely real.

For the dozen or so finished heads, the human details and their lifelike expressions were unnerving. When you looked at them, they looked back. When you moved, their glistening eyes seemed to follow you. Their facial expressions were unnerving too; a cadaverous sneer on one, pursed lips of unhappiness on another, and the self-satisfied grin of a toothless, pocked-marked man.

Dr Curtius did not have a separate workshop. He combined his shop with his home, and visitors might have described it as barbaric or something between a freak show and 'Chamber of Horrors'. If Frankenstein had stopped by, even he might have quickly retreated. First-time visitors probably described their visit as disturbing, accompanied by spine tingling chills, wide-eyed uneasiness, and shallow breathing.

Yet, of all the first-time visitors, one impressionable and precocious 6-year-old girl would feel more than tingling chills. Her bright brown eyes envisioned dramatic possibilities not ghastly heads or lifeless bodies. What she saw was the ability to sculpt a historical scene from pliable wax because like pliable wax, she would change from a child named Marie Grosholtz into the famous wax modeler Madame Tussaud.

Marie claims to have been born in 1760 in Bern, Switzerland, but baptismal records from Old St. Peter's Catholic Church give Strasbourg as her birthplace. The baptismal record also shows that on 1 December 1761 she was christened Anne-Marie. However, to differentiate her from her 18-year-old mother, after whom she was named, she was called Marie.

Marie's father was Johann Joseph Grosholtz, a 45-year-old soldier who died two months before her birth. Marie claims her father came from a distinguished family, but the Grosholtz or Grosholz line served as public executioners as far back as the fifteenth century with Marie's grandfather, Johann Jakob Grosholz, filling the role. Marie's father chose not to follow in his father's footsteps. Instead he served as an aide-de-camp to Austrian field marshal General Wurmser and served during the Seven Years' War. Grosholtz was then killed in battle and 'was so mutilated with wounds, that his forehead was laid bare, and his lower jaw shot away'.[1]

With her father dead, support for Marie fell solely upon her widowed mother's shoulders. Her name was Anne-Marie Walder,[2] and she had few talents other than cooking and cleaning. So, to provide for herself and her daughter, Anne-Marie took work as a domestic and began working for her brother-in-law, a bachelor named Dr Philippe Mathé Curtius.

Dr Curtius became both a father and uncle to Marie, and he treated her tenderly and adopted her in every way. Marie claims in her *Memoirs* that Dr Curtius was her uncle, and Marie's great-grandson, John Theodore Tussaud, states that Dr Curtius was the brother of Marie's mother. However, some people have claimed that Dr Curtius may have not been her uncle but rather her father. Dr Curtius is also mentioned prominently in the Tussaud family history, and Marie maintained that he legally adopted her, although no official records show that he ever did any such thing. However, he did serve as a father figure and was almost certainly the most important man in Marie's life.

Dr Curtius had moved from Germany to Bern, Switzerland about 1760. Around this time, a clamour arose across Europe from the medical community demanding to learn more about human anatomy. However, to study human anatomy, the medical community needed corpses, and corpses were not an easy thing to acquire. The public looked down on dissection, and the only eligible corpses for study were the corpses of criminals condemned to death or bodies snatched from graves.

Because it was easier to get a body snatched from a grave than through legal means, body snatching or resurrections (as they were sometimes called) were rife in the 1700 and 1800s; demonstrative of this was a man who claimed to have guarded the body of his relative one night to prevent it from being snatched for dissection. Yet, he was not alone in guarding his loved one's grave. Body snatching became so commonplace by the nineteenth century that worried families began to schedule shifts for their relatives to guard loved one's graves. Unfortunately, even this precaution sometimes failed. It seemed that the moment grave watchers shut their eyes, the body snatcher struck.

Because grave watchers did not solve the problem, more creative solutions were devised to protect corpses. For instance, sometimes two pieces of wood were inserted crosswise at the foot and head of a coffin so that it could not be easily extracted from the grave. Churchyard walls were also raised, and heavy iron, spiked contrivances gruesomely called mortsafes were installed over graves making it impossible for anyone to access the coffin. Spring guns were also set in various configurations around churchyards ready to explode upon the slightest movement. Yet, despite all these precautions, body snatchers were still often successful.

People found that ghoulish body snatchers were highly skilled. In fact, it took a body snatcher practically no time at all to obtain a corpse. There were many stories about the speed in which body snatchers could reach the inside of a grave, acquire the corpse, and rebury an empty coffin. One individual claimed:

> 'I was once told by a Resurrectionist, that he had taken two bodies from separate graves of considerable depth, and had restored the coffins and the earth itself to their former position in the short space of an hour and a half ... Another man proved to me that he had completed the exhumation of a body in a quarter of an hour'.[3]

Besides being quick, body snatchers were also extremely cunning. Generally, body snatchers attacked a new grave soon after a burial, before the grave was tidied up. This made it difficult to determine whether the grave had been disturbed. Body snatchers were also extremely adept in their rifling, which was noted by one nineteenth-century author who stated:

> 'All attempts on the part of friends to detect removal were futile, any marks adopted to ascertain exhumation being carefully replaced to disarm suspicion'.[4]

Over time, body snatchers became more inventive. Instead of disturbing the exact grave site, they disturbed an area about five or six feet away. First, they removed a square of turf and set it aside. Because body snatchers knew that most graves were dug at a specific depth, they would then tunnel on a slant from where the turf had been removed to the end of the coffin. Hooks then wrenched off the coffin's end. The corpse was secured by its feet or head, pulled out of the ground, the slanted hole filled, and the turf returned to its spot. This ingenious method left the coffin unmoved and the family believing their loved one remained undisturbed.

Once a body snatcher obtained the corpse, there were a couple of ways to deal with it. Sometimes it was deposited in a sack, carried to a vehicle, and sent on its way for dissection. Other times, it was bundled into a long square of green-baize cloth with the four corners of the cloth tightly secured. It was then temporarily deposited in a hide away, retrieved the following day, and carried without a hint of concern through busy metropolitan streets to a dissecting room.

Long before there were body snatchers, there was an interest in wax or wax sculpting related to human anatomy. One early collection that began in the seventeenth century was in Florence, Italy, and contained thirty rooms filled with coloured wax parts of the human body. The collection began with a physician named Nones, of Genoa:

> 'Nones ... wished to preserve a human body by embalming it; but not being able entirely to prevent putrefaction, he considered whether he could imitate the body in wax. The Abbate Zumbo, of Sicily, imitated the head so perfectly, under the direction of Nones, that many persons believed the coloured wax to be the real head'.[5]

This Zumbo of Sicily mentioned was the wax modeler named Gaetano Giulio Zumbo. He was self-taught and although he never learned how to chisel stone, he did learn how to model clay. He then began to create paintings out of locally coloured wax. These curious productions were called 'Zumbos' and were created usually with a moral lesson in mind but often included touches of ghoulishness or horror.

Zumbos were also considered highly unusual, and their creator gained the patronage of a Grand Duke who commissioned him to create several morbid models that captured the progression of a decomposing body. One eighteenth-century newspaper described his works in the following manner:

> 'the decomposition of the body through every conceivable stage
> of putrefaction – the blackening, the swelling, the bursting of
> the trunk, the worm, the rat, and the tarantula at work, and the
> mushroom springing up in the midst of corruption'.[6]

In late seventeenth century France, there was also a surgeon named Guillaume Desnoues. He was working at the University of Genoa holding medical lectures. To accompany these lectures, he created productions or preparations injected with wax. One was the body of a pregnant woman with her foetus. However, day-by-day his production wasted away, and he wanted something that could be preserved permanently. That is when he learned about Zumbo and his wax creations.

Desnoues and Zumbo soon formed a partnership. Desnoues dissected the body, and Zumbo created the anatomical form in wax. Zumbo's wax anatomical figures offered several advantages; besides longevity, the wax models were wonderful teaching aids. That was because in decomposing bodies, it was sometimes difficult to distinguish parts. Wax was different, not only were wax parts more distinguishable, veins and arteries could be coloured and therefore made more prominent. Wax figures also helped alleviate the problem of too few corpses, and they provided a permanence that a decomposing body could not.

Although Zumbo's wax figures offered Desnoues advantages, they were often ghoulish. So, when the two men quarrelled over money, Desnoues broke with Zumbo and began using an ivory carver named François de la Croix to create his wax anatomical parts. These skilful reproductions soon garnered the medical community's attention, and, as a result, Desnoues was invited to present his wax anatomical models to the Royal Academy of Sciences in 1711.

Between 1711 and 1740, Desnoues' medical wax anatomical models went on the road to major cities in France and England. The anatomical models were at first only exhibited to the public, but doctors soon came to realize the importance of them, and, so, between exhibitions, Desnoues' wax models were rented out to doctors, surgeons, or anatomists and used for training purposes. An announcement about one exhibition read:

> 'The Sieur Desnoues has lately received from Paris four new Anatomical Preparations in wax-work never seen before … the anatomy of a woman to the waste where all the parts of the brain may be seen, and taken out of their place, and set back again. … two handsome heads [to show], by a new method, the structure of the brain and the first rise of the nerves from it. The anatomy of a newly born, of which the breast and belly are opened [to show] the inward parts and every one of Natural Biggness and colour. This whole performance has been thirty years amaking. … These figures have as fine a prospect by candle as by daylight'.[7]

Like Desnoues, Dr Curtius became interested in providing models for medical students. Dr Curtius began to create miniature anatomically correct flesh-tinted models from wax for anatomical study. These tiny anatomical replicas initially sparked local interest. News also spread about Dr Curtius' realistic wax models and the Prince of Conti, a cousin to Louis XV, who was also a celebrated art collector, became interested.

When the Prince of Conti visited Bern, he decided to see Dr Curtius' models for himself. He was so impressed that he proposed a patronage to Dr Curtius but required him to move to Paris. The offer was appealing enough to cause Dr Curtius to renounce the medical profession, pack up his belongings, and settle in Paris in the Rue St. Honoré.

In Paris, Dr Curtius, now just called Curtius, did well in his new calling. He soon acquired a following that resulted in him obtaining both private commissions and public exhibitions of what were now full-sized wax models of people. In addition, the Prince of Conti's 'liberality and kindness not only equalled but rather surpassed his promises,'[8] and, thus, when Marie was about six, she and her mother joined Curtius in the bustling city of Paris.

Marie and her mother's arrival in the capital occurred around the time Louis XV gifted his mistress, Madame de Pompadour, Petit Trianon, a small chateau, next to the larger Grand Trianon. Ange-Jacques Gabriel designed Petit Trianon, creating a simple, but elegant edifice described as:

'a little square pavilion of the Corinthian order, built in the Italian style, with a single principal story, a basement, and a very low second story, five windows on each side, which were separated on the front by beautiful columns with acanthus capitals, and by four pilasters of the same order on the other facades'.[9]

Besides the wonderful gift of Trianon, there were many other interesting things happening in and around Paris in the late 1760s. For instance, Paris was the centre for Enlightenment, and it was the first city to venture into modern finance by opening a private bank. It was also a city where the nobility was as powdered and bewigged as when Louis XIV reigned. But for all of Paris' enlightenment, finance, and powdered wigs, its streets were little more than a pigsty thick with discarded garbage, vegetable muck, and horse manure.

Traversing Parisian streets was a major and daring feat. The streets were not only crowded and dirty but also narrow with barely a footpath. One man wrote, 'To walk through them was toil and fatigue to a man and an impossibility to a well-dressed woman'.[10] Moreover, persons of moderate means who did not own their own carriages were forced to dress all in black (including stockings), because mud, muck, and mire would splash all over them.

There were also bad smells. Foul and stinking air was claimed to be a common occurrence. One stench that was regularly produced throughout Paris came 'from the fermentation of the various impurities carried off into draining wells, from being driven back, or rising and entering into the lower apartments of a house, so as to render those [buildings] situated underground particularly, almost absolutely uninhabitable'.[11] Men and women frequently braved the streets with handkerchiefs to their noses to avoid the 'miasma' of awful smells generated by breweries, manufactures, and tanners. In fact, near the Bièvre River, the combination of sewage, horse urine and other pollutants was so dangerous, a few sniffs caused people to faint.

Besides the filthy streets and offensive smells, Parisians had to watch for danger when on the streets. One-horse cabriolets driven by reckless and fashionable young men endangered life and limb. Moreover, on more than one occasion, poor pedestrians faced off against a wealthy blazoned carriage that rumbled down the narrow streets at top speed. One person wrote that 'sometimes one or two huge dogs careered in front, and the

Parisians complained that they were first knocked down by the dogs and then run over by the wheels'.[12] The only time a speeding carriage stopped was if a horse was injured.

One visitor to Paris who observed these horrendous driving practices was peg-legged Gouverneur Morris, an American statesman and Founding Father. Such driving appalled him, perhaps more so because he himself had lost a leg in his early youth due to a carriage accident. He provided his view of the dangerous practice in a sarcastic but humorous poem titled 'Paris':

> 'A coachman driving furious on,
> For here, to fly is quite the *ton*,
> Thro' the thick vapors of the night,
> Sees by a glimmering lamp's dim light,
> Some creature struggling in the street,
> Which soon beneath his horses feet
> Is trod, and there in anguish feels
> The crushing of the chariot wheels.
> "Villain!" exclaims the aged count,
> "Stop! ho!" the guard; *bougez*, dismount.
> "The law, *pardieu*, shall have its course."
> …
> (*Au Commissaire*.) "He has killed my horse."
> Had I supposed a horse lay there,
> I would have taken better care,
> But by St. Jacques declare I can,
> I thought 'twas nothing but a man'.[13]

Paris was also bustling in other ways. Everyone was busy. In fact, Morris claimed he was so busy that he could not a have a single quiet moment. Between his business and personal engagements, he was always in a 'perpetual hurry'. He found Paris filled with street vendors who barked, shrieked, and cried as they offered oysters, apples, and coffee for sale. Like London, there were also crossing sweepers who, for a fee, would sweep the path ahead of pedestrians or lay down boards to protect clothing as people walked down the filthy streets.

In the 1760s, fashion was of course fashionable in Paris. The upper classes wore clothes that were rich, colourful, and luxurious having been tailored from satin, velvet, or silk and profusely trimmed with lace. Men were decked out in coats, waistcoats, and breeches, and women were seen promenading in sack-back gowns, known as *robe à la française*. These gowns with their elegant elbow-length sleeves had an exaggerated silhouette with an inverted cone-shaped torso and low, oval necklines. Women were also on the verge of embracing extreme headdresses piled high and made higher by false hair pieces and a gooey paste made from hog's grease, beef marrow, and tallow, called pomatum.

In contrast to this image of mincing gentlemen and prancing ladies was the lower classes. One eyewitness remarked that 'the lowest peasant speaks, moves, dresses, eats, and drinks, as much as a man of the first fashion; but does them all quite differently'.[14] The clothing of the lower classes might have had the same features as the upper classes, but it was more utilitarian and long-lasting versus fashionable and luxurious. Moreover, clothing was regulated, which meant that even if a poor man saved up for a fancy outfit, he could not have worn it anyway because of rules and regulations surrounding court etiquette which had begun with Louis XIV. Part of his reasoning was related to his belief about etiquette and that survival of the monarchy depended on lavish spending to stimulate the French economy. Louis XIV also deemed himself the arbiter of fashion and embraced expensive, colourful, and ornate clothing and accessories. He then ensured that nobility and aristocrats would likewise appear in similar splendid clothing when he imposed etiquette rules at court, knowing that image often shapes perception.

Louis XIV's etiquette rules were not the only thing that locked courtiers into expensive French fashions. He also forbade all French subjects from buying any imported clothing products that could be made in France. Thus, people were forced to wear French textiles and French-made clothing, and that helped France establish a highly lucrative clothing and textile trade which competed effectively against foreign markets. All of this led to an increasing dissatisfaction with the lower class who saw the noble classes as living a life of luxury on the backs of poor starving Frenchmen. Moreover, the nobles more and more seemed to be making the situation worse through their excesses and mismanagement of the government. Vigorous debate emerged across France in many private clubs and homes, and one of those homes belonged to Curtius and Marie.

Chapter 3

The Resort of Talented Men

'The dross wants separating from the gold'.

Marie Tussaud, on Voltaire

Marie described Curtius' Paris house as the 'resort of many of the most talented men in France'.[1] These talented men convened there regularly to debate the serious issues of the times. According to Marie, Curtius was a brilliant conversationalist, which was part of the draw for visitors who reputedly included such illustrious guests as the Enlightenment writer François-Marie Arouet, known by his nom de plume Voltaire. There was also the philosopher Rousseau, the French Revolutionary writer and orator who excelled at the Estates General, the Count of Mirabeau, and later one of the best known and most influential figures associated with the French Revolution and the Reign of Terror, Robespierre. Moreover, Curtius kept wax busts of some of the remarkable people that he had modelled, and these could be seen in his drawing rooms.

Marie claimed to be present when these interesting guests appeared, and as an adult she told many stories about them. One of the frequent visitors was apparently the Duke d'Orleans. Marie deplored his visits and reported that although they began agreeably, they became unpleasant once he became intoxicated. Curtius would then encourage the drunken man to leave and go to a nearby tavern, where he would remain for hours carousing with friends and committing all sorts of excesses.

As France moved toward revolution, Curtius' dining room table became filled with 'fanatic politicians, furious demagogues, and wild theorists, forever thundering forth their anathemas against monarchy, haranguing on the different forms of government, and propounding their extravagant ideas on republicanism'.[2]

Among these controversial figures was Voltaire, a frequent guest, who besides being an Enlightenment writer was also a historian and philosopher. He was particularly known for his witty attacks on the church and for his advocacy of freedom of religion, freedom of speech, and separation of church and state. His wax head was in fact the first one Marie did on her own, accomplishing it a few months before his death. Marie also maintained that many rancorous discussions occurred between Voltaire and Rousseau. She recalled the rivalry between the men was more interesting because of the difference in their physical appearances. Voltaire was tall and thin, shrivelled in appearance, usually clothed in a brown coat with gold lace, a waistcoat with large lappets, striped silk stockings, large shoes, and a long flowing wig that he accented with a small cocked hat. Rousseau, on the other hand, was stout and of medium height with grey eyes, a light complexion, a short round wig, and always dressed in a plain suit cut in the old style.

Often added into the conversational mix was Mirabeau. He was about 5-foot 10-inches tall and stout. His face was pitted with smallpox scars that in certain lights made him appear ugly. He also possessed a profusion of bushy frizzed hair that was highly powdered, and he appeared frequently dressed in a sombre black corded velvet. However, despite his unpleasant appearance, when he opened his mouth all these disadvantages disappeared as he was extremely eloquent and greatly admired for his passion and public speaking skills.

One recurrent topic of discussion at Curtius' table was the romantic idea of liberty. These discussions became more frequent after the arrival of Benjamin Franklin, the noted American statesman who served as ambassador to France from 1776 to 1785. Although funding the American Revolution was one of the causes of France's dire financial situation, the success of the Revolution inspired many people to believe that a life without monarchy was both possible and desirable. Beloved by the French people, Franklin was a powerful voice for what could be, and he was often joined by a French aristocrat and military officer who would soon fight for the United States in the American Revolutionary War. His name was Gilbert du Motier, Marquis de Lafayette, known simply as Lafayette.

Franklin and Lafayette connected and supposedly spent many hours discussing liberty. In fact, Marie later alleged:

> 'Dr Franklin's visit to Paris may be attributed the primary cause of the French Revolution, as La Fayette was not alone in becoming the disciple of the transatlantic philosopher; for the minds of numbers of young enthusiasts amongst the French nobility also became impregnated with the seeds

of republicanism, which, quickly germinating, were soon extended to all parts of France'.[3]

During her early years in Paris, Marie's curiosity about Curtius' waxworks grew. She acquired a love and appreciation for art, and, over time, Curtius taught her his secrets to wax-figure making. Fortunately, Marie was a good student and a quick study. She developed perfection in creating her own wax figures and, in 1777, began working for Curtius. Although Curtius' name remained on everyone lips, Marie worked behind the scenes as his apprentice.

As Marie trained in wax and improved her skills, Curtius opened his first exhibition in 1776. It was located at the St-Laurent fair, near the Temple, a medieval fortress that would be used as a prison during the French Revolution. Curtius' home and workshop were nearby and located on the Boulevard du Temple. A few years later, Curtius moved his exhibition into number 7 at the Palais-Royal and his Salon de Cire became fashionable and popular.

About a year after Curtius opened the Salon de Cire, the queen's older brother, Joseph II, the Holy Roman Emperor paid his sister a visit under the name of Count Falkenstein. Joseph was well-read but was crude, boorish, and opinionated. He also liked to tell embarrassing stories about his relatives or his visits to various courts. He once related a story about his fat brother stating, 'Feasting and fasting produce the same effect [in him]. In wind and food he is quite an adept, puffing, from one cause of the other, like a smith's bellows'.[4]

During Joseph's visit to France, Marie noted that he came to see Curtius' exhibition. She described the 36-year-old Emperor as tall and 'fine-looking'. He had a fair complexion like his sister Marie Antoinette, light hair, and was 'plainly dressed' with a cocked hat. When Marie saw him later at Versailles, she described him as presenting a 'fine appearance' and being 'splendidly dressed'.

Marie claimed that she was the one that usually served as a guide for exhibition tours, but this time Curtius himself took that role and guided Joseph. Joseph was reportedly highly impressed and requested to see Curtius' workshop and studio too. As he was being shown to it, a glorious smell greeted his 'olfactory nerves' and he threw up his hands and exclaimed that he smelled sauerkraut. Thus, Marie maintained the relationship with the Emperor was more than casual because Joseph then joined the family for dinner:

> '[He] seated himself at the table, not suffering an individual to rise
> from it, but joining the group *en famille*, and ate, drank, talked,

laughed, and joked, with all possible affability and familiarity, making himself as much at home as if he had been at his palace of Schöbrusen, and consumed to his own share a large dish of sour krout [sic], and then said, "There! now I have dined."[5]

Curtius, who the French thought of as German and whom they often called Kurtz, did financially well as the public became increasingly fascinated by wax figures. He had opened a second exhibition location by 1787 that included the Cavern of the Grand Thieves (*Caverne des Grands Voleurs*) and was gory and bloody. Because Curtius' exhibits were so life-like and intriguing, one Frenchman wrote that Curtius' skills were celebrated on the boulevards and that you could see among his wax figures the most infamous of thieves, as well as the most royal of kings.

Yet, it was no easy task for Curtius or Marie to generate new wax figures even if wax required less strength and skill to mould than traditional sculptural techniques. It was a time-consuming, labour-intensive, and complex process. To accomplish the task, a person had to sit quietly while his or her face was moulded. Those being modelled had to first endure their face being slathered in oil and pomade so that facial hairs would be flat. Quills were then inserted into the nostrils to allow the person to breathe before a fine layer of plaster of Paris was applied. The plaster was then checked and rechecked to assure an appropriate likeness. From this came a two-piece clay mould that would produce the finished wax head.

The recipe for the wax was composed primarily from bleached beeswax. Beeswax was considered a convenient medium because at ordinary temperatures it could be cut and shaped effortlessly and at slightly higher temperatures it melted easily. Its texture and consistency also allowed for the addition of other media. Molten beeswax also easily took the minutest impression before setting and hardening, so that no 'climatic influences' affected it. Moreover, it readily mixed with colouring and easily accepted surface tints. Beeswax and vegetable tallow (called japan wax) were combined in a three to one proportion. Old wax was also added because it helped to reduce shrinkage and gave colour to the wax. This mixture was then poured into a two-piece clay mould where it cooled and set, and when set, the wax head was carefully removed.

Finishing touches came next. They included adding appropriate coloured glass eyes and flesh tinting, which was perhaps the most important aspect of a figure, as an unnatural flesh tint emphasized the figure's artificiality. Beginning in the early 1700s, artificial teeth for humans were being made from natural teeth, sea-horse and walrus teeth, or the long bones of the ox, which were boiled and bleached in lime. If possible, Curtius used actual human teeth, and when unavailable, he may have used artificial teeth for the wax figures he or Marie created.

Hair, eyebrows, and beards or moustaches also needed to be added. This was tedious work as the hairs were added a single strand at a time and it sometimes took as long as two weeks to finish the hair. When human hair could not be found, hair might also be obtained from thoroughbred horses housed at the royal stables.

To accomplish a wax figure today is somewhat different than it was two hundred years ago. Today, each figure requires between three to four months to complete, and technology is part of the process. At a sitting, 200 measurements are taken, photographs are taken from every angle, and a person's skin, hair, and eye colours are scrupulously matched from samples, to ensure complete accuracy.

The next step is the sculpting process. According to a behind the scenes factoid at Madame Tussauds modern exhibit in London, 'a metal armature is constructed to support the clay mould, which is then built up using meticulous detail. The head is worked on separately and can take between four to six weeks to sculpt and achieve an exact likeness of a famous face'.[6] Once the clay sculpture is completed, it is used to create a plaster cast. Melted wax is then poured slowly into the mould to prevent air bubbles, and, 50 minutes later, the excess liquid wax is poured off and the remainder is left to harden and may sit for up to 170 hours. The result is a hollow head. A person's body is also completed and to ensure durability fiberglass is used instead of wax.

That is not the end of the process. Individual strands of hair are then inserted into the scalp, and ten layers of oil base paints are applied to achieve realistic translucent skin tones. The eyes and teeth are next. Eyes today are created from an acrylic resin, and the teeth, which were moulded during the sitting, are replicated from dental acrylic. Eyebrows, moles, tattoos, scars, or anything else visible are also added to complete the wax figure. Once the wardrobe is added, the figure usually looks life-like.

As mentioned, one of the visitors to Curtius and Marie's dinner table was the enigmatic American stateman Benjamin Franklin. The American Second Continental Congress had adopted the Declaration of Independence on 5 July 1776, and shortly after its adoption, the balding Franklin was dispatched to France at the age of seventy to serve as the first official ambassador for the United States. His goal was to maintain good relations with France and encourage their continued support against Britain. He took his grandson and he remained in France until 1785.

In France, Franklin chose to live in a quaint, but expensive, suburb known as Passy. Passy was situated on a lofty hill on the Seine's right bank and in an area known for its expansive gardens, beautiful parks, and numerous chateaux. Passy was also half way between Paris and Versailles, making Passy a convenient location for Franklin, as he visited these two sites frequently.

The estate Franklin lived on belonged to a wealthy man, the jack-of-all trades Jacques-Donatien Le Ray de Chaumont. Chaumont supported the American Revolution and later become an important supplier to the Continental Army. Soon after Franklin arrived, Chaumont befriended him; Chaumont hoped that if the colonists won America's War of Independence and if he aided Franklin by allowing him to live free at his estate, Congress might grant him land in America after the war. So, he convinced Franklin to reside on his estate, and, for location reasons, Franklin agreed to Chaumont's offer.

While Franklin lived at Passy, he conducted several experiments. One involved Dr Charles Deslon, who was a disciple of the German doctor Franz Mesmer, the German physician from whom the word mesmerize was coined and from whom the idea of 'animal magnetism' originated. Animal magnetism was supposedly a 'subtle' fluid within everyone and everything in the universe. If this magnetic fluid became blocked, Mesmer argued, the blockages could create psychological or physical imbalances, and his cures relied on righting these magnetic imbalances. Deslon also used this animal magnetism upon Franklin 'as well as upon the members of his family, who, notwithstanding … were ladies in delicate health, [but they] were found quite insensible to the whole ceremonial of magnetism'.[7]

Franklin's house at Passy also contained a printing press. The idea for the press likely occurred because he wanted to print government documents and legal blanks. Eventually, he also began printing small numbers (a dozen to fifteen copies) of essays and satires. The nineteenth-century American author, historian, and Unitarian minister, named Edward Everett Hale, noted other things that he printed:

> 'Franklin soon established in his own house at Passy a little printing establishment, from which occasionally a tract or handbill was issued. From this press the pretended "Independent Chronicle," with an account of Indian scalping,

was issued, and the little books published here are among the treasures most desired by the connoisseurs'.[8]

Franklin electrified Parisians. They were eager to get a glimpse of him and meet this ambassador that they had heard so much about. They were also enamoured of his rustic appeal, made more so by his marten fur hat that had protected him from the freezing cold as he crossed the Atlantic and that he regularly wore in France. In addition, Franklin continued to practice freemasonry as he had been initiated into it in 1731 in America at the St. John's Lodge in Philadelphia.

In France, balloons also captured Franklin's attention. Marie never mentioned anything about balloon flight, but she did mention that when Franklin was not attending to political business, presiding over freemason meetings, or looking upward to the sky, he sometimes visited Curtius' abode. Marie's great-grandson wrote about her opinion of Franklin stating:

> 'Dr Franklin [was] an agreeable companion. His personal appearance was that of the most perfect simplicity, and his manners truly amiable. He was a stout man, about five feet ten inches in height; his eyes were grey, his complexion light; he dressed in black; his clothes were cut in the old-fashioned style; he was remarked for having particularly fine legs; his hair was very long and grey'.[9]

At one or more of these visits to the Curtius home, Franklin allowed wax moulds of his face to be created. In fact, wax sculptures fascinated him, and Franklin 'also ordered models of many other notable characters of the day'.[10] These models were displayed in his rooms while he lived in Passy. Franklin's fascination with wax sculpture also resulted in him commissioning Curtius to execute several wax likenesses of him, including some miniatures that he kept for himself. In addition, at least one full-size model of Franklin, executed by Curtius in 1783 and exhibited in the late 1700s, can sometimes be seen today at Madame Tussauds in London.

Voltaire was one of the most important people of the French Revolution and someone Marie met many times. His influence on the revolution arose because his ideas and philosophy (along with the ideas and beliefs of his contemporary, Rousseau) led the way for the Enlightenment. This contributed to the French Revolution as a profound eighteenth century intellectual movement that dominated ideas, centred on reason, advancing such notions as constitutional governments, liberty, and separation of church and state.

Years earlier, Voltaire had been banished from France by Louis XV. Voltaire's writings during his absence did nothing to soften the king's stance and, in fact, only hardened the implacable Louis XV against him. If Voltaire wanted to return to Paris, the advice given him was to stop writing, but he refused. By February 1773, the writer was suffering from prostate cancer, and although he thought the end was near, his health appeared to miraculously improve. His recovery took another step backwards when in March of 1774, his prostate problem seemed to reappear. This time, it was even more troubling because everywhere he looked it seemed as if someone was dying. In fact, Louis XV died on 10 May 1774 from smallpox.

The 19-year-old Louis XVI took the throne to reign with his young bride, 17-year-old Marie Antoinette. Louis' rule meant change and all indications seemed to bode well for France; there would be fresh blood and fresh ideas. Moreover, to get a better grip on French finances, a friend to Voltaire, Anne-Robert Jacques Turgot, was named Controller-General of France in August of 1774.

Turgot had progressive ideas, and everything pointed to an embracement of *philosophies* and acceptance of Voltaire's ideas. Turgot suggested abolishing privilege and taxation and encouraged tight and rigid economics. Another of his goals was to ensure economic liberty and create wealth for all Frenchmen. To accomplish this, he addressed a letter to Louis stating: 'No bankruptcy!' 'No increase of taxes!' 'No borrowings!'[11]

Turgot's fall came in 1776, and even Voltaire thought his ideas too radical. However, that was also the year that Voltaire was viewed somewhat as an idol by Frenchmen. He had been absent from France for over a quarter of a century and now he wanted to go home. To return, Voltaire wrote a play, a tragedy titled *Irène*. It was completed in 1777 and in January of 1778 the Comédie-Française agreed to perform it, although they were not necessarily enthusiastic about it.

Having been slighted by their lack of enthusiasm, Voltaire decided to supervise the play himself. As Louis was not particularly opposed to his return and as there was no official documentation from Louis XV's era banning him from Paris, Voltaire arrived at the custom barrier about 3:30pm on 10 February:

> 'When the officials asked if he was carrying anything "contrary to the King's orders", Voltaire replied: "I think the only contraband is me." At which point one of the officials realized who he was dealing with: "By God, It's Monsieur de Voltaire!"'

With Voltaire's return to Paris came well-wishers and visitors. Turgot dropped by, as did his popular replacement, Jacques Necker. An enthusiastic Franklin stopped by too. He had read Voltaire's works for forty-five years and wanted to meet the writer. There were other visitors, including Louis XV's ex-mistress and enemy to the queen, the squeaky voiced Madame du Barry.

Curtius also sent a dinner invitation to Voltaire. He wanted Voltaire to see his Salon de Cire. Curtius' Salon fulfilled the public desire to see the rich and famous and included such wax figures as Madame du Barry, the king and queen, and a 'young negroe girl ... half black, and half white; or what [was] called a pied colour'.[12] There was also a life-size wax model of Voltaire.

Voltaire accepted the invitation, and it was during this visit that a motivated Marie made her first wax sculpture; it was of the venerable Voltaire. What Marie felt as she created this mould of Voltaire's face, one can only guess. She was always reticent and guarded about talking about herself or her feelings, but she did speak freely about others and her recollections of them. At the time, she was still in training, although eventually, she would develop such skill that it was practically impossible to tell her waxwork creations from those of Curtius.

As a child, she remembered Voltaire fondly. She noted that he was someone who patted her on the cheek and commented she was pretty. She could also provide a fairly thorough description of him physically, but when it came to Voltaire's personality and character, that seemed lacking as demonstrated by what she said about him years later when she was touring England:

> 'His writing contains a considerable portion of wit and general learning, but is not calculated for the perusal of youth, being mixed with much indecency and profaneness. The dross wants separating from the gold'.[13]

Soon after Voltaire's arrival in Paris, he fell ill. While confined to bed and recovering, he continued to work and was working when a bronchial artery burst after which he suffered a coughing fit. Blood poured from his nose and mouth, and his doctor was called. Of course, he bled him further. The doctor also gave Voltaire a strict set of rules: no speaking; no working; no visitors. Voltaire did not follow doctor's orders and three weeks later he was still spitting blood.

Meanwhile, the play debuted. The queen and her entire retinue were there on opening night when the curtain rose, but Voltaire was too ill to attend. With every new performance thereafter came the prediction that Voltaire would appear. He finally did on 30 March and when the frail playwright entered his box, the audience cheered, and the adulations continued until Marie remembered him being crowned with a laurel wreath. After the play and before he departed, there was more cheering and adulation from his adoring fans.

In contrast to this noisy adulation, Voltaire's end came quietly two months later. The infirmities of old age at last embraced him, and he died on Saturday 30 May 1778 in Paris. Voltaire's deist beliefs and his constant criticism of the Church meant there was to be no Christian burial. Instead it was planned that his body would be interred in Ferney, the spot that had been his home for so many years. He would be entombed next to his library in the bathhouse.

The day after his death, a post-mortem was conducted; his corpse was embalmed, his brain retained by the local apothecary, and his heart given to a French writer who was his protégé, Charles Michel, Marquis of Villette. After dark, Voltaire's corpse was dressed to make the journey to Ferney and his brainless and heartless body tied upright to the carriage. Once the carriage got underway, it quickly became apparent his upright embalmed corpse was not up to the journey.

A stop at the monastery at Scellières resulted in the atheist Voltaire receiving a Christian burial after all. It would not have happened if a note prohibiting his burial at the site had arrived earlier. His burial displeased many Christians, and it did not take long for many false rumours to circulate about his death. Included among these claims was that he suffered 'great agonies' and was terrified of his approaching end, screaming and writhing for Jesus Christ to save him. In fact, that could not have been further from the truth as his niece reported that he died 'in great pain, except for the last four days, when he went out like a candle'.[14]

Although Voltaire's physical life might have gone out like a candle, his ideas were a spark that set off a change to the world order. His arguments against religious authority, for freedom of thought, and for a constitutional monarchy opened the door for what was to come. So, Marie's first wax sculpture was of someone who first evangelized key ideas of the French Revolution.

PART II

Surviving the French Revolution

Summer 1789 to 1801

Paris, France

Chapter 4

Mounting Tensions

'Free me from a post which compels me to witness
such horrors.'

Lafayette

What happens to Marie next is elusive. Relatively little is known about her years in France, and almost all of what we do know comes from her *Memoires*, in which she recounted the French Revolution as she remembered it. Many historians have questioned the authenticity of Marie's account, and there could be good reasons for this. First, her account was dictated to a writer about 40 years after she experienced it, and, second, she was a story teller at heart: She loved to talk and over the course of time became an expert at capturing people's attention. She may have also exaggerated some of the details of her experiences to promote her show or improve her reputation. Perhaps over time, she even came to believe these stories herself. But it would be a shame to completely reject her stories because they may be embellished or mis-remembered.

In her memoirs, unlike a traditional memoir, Marie gives few personal reflections on her life. That is, the activities of her daily life are omitted; how she emotionally dealt with the incredible terror and turbulence of the times is not known. Her thoughts are mainly captured in observations of the personal appearances and behaviours of people whom she met who were key figures in the French Revolution. This again makes sense for a highly accomplished wax sculptress – she was highly attuned to faces, clothes, personalities, and relationships with people who would interest her clientele. Thus, we can understand her in part by what she does not recollect.

Other works about her have sought to fill the gap with wax-making details, information about Curtius, or critiques of her authenticity. Often overlooked is the key fact that she was deeply involved in a bloody and cataclysmic period in history. The omission of these personal details of her life and emotions might have been a form of self-protection. Despite her father not serving as executioner, the stigma of being born into a family of executioners still remained. In the Revolution, terror and death abounded. She might have ignored her feelings and pressed on with her shows, as a way of surviving in a gruesome world. As a result, understanding her takes some empathy. We must look at the French Revolution and seek to place ourselves in her shoes, considering how she might have felt and how she might have dealt with it – all without the benefit of her providing her own emotions. Yet, those events must have deeply affected her.

In what follows, her experience in the French Revolution is told, as much as it is known. The facts of events are given based on what is now believed to be accurate, while integrating it with her experience and role in those events. To be sure, she was not a major player. But she was intimately involved, to the point of personally knowing key leaders and handling their severed heads. Thus, if we want to understand her and how she became so successful later in England, we need to understand the major events that happened to her in the French Revolution. It must have been a gut-wrenching, life altering time, even if she does not reflect it in writing. We do know the events of the French Revolution became fundamental to how she positioned her shows and ran her business in England. In many ways, the story of her later success cannot be understood without understanding her experience in the French Revolution.

After the fall of the Bastille, Marie noticed that French society began to crumble as well. While Louis XVI struggled to retain control and restore France to stability, the forces against him strengthened and assailed him on many fronts. Of course, finances and reform of government power were primary issues. But powerful factions in France such as the Estates General representatives including Robespierre and his associate, physician, social agitator, and radical journalist Jean-Paul Marat, began to put forth both conciliatory and very violent competing visions for what role the monarchy and nobility should have in French government and society.

Marat had been born in Switzerland on 24 May 1743 to an Italian father and a French Huguenot mother. He left home at the age of sixteen and went to Bordeaux. Two years later, he moved to Paris and began to study medicine. He then moved to London and informally became a doctor. He was, however, highly ambitious and quickly joined the intellectual scene, publishing some scientific, philosophical, and political works.

When he returned to France in 1777, Marat was appointed physician to the personal guards who served the king's brother, the Count d'Artois (the future Charles X). Around this same time, Marat experimented and wrote several scientific articles. The Royal Academy of Rouen honoured one of his papers on electricity in 1783, which caused him to leave the medical field and concentrate on science. However, when he failed to be elected into the Academy of Sciences, he changed his focus again and went into politics.

Marat had begun to focus strictly on politics after the Estates General was called to convene. In January of 1789, he had published his *Offering to the Nation* (*Offrande à la Patrie*) about the king's capability to solve France's problems, but soon changed his stance and took up the cause of the Third Estate. With his pen as his sword, his *Offering* was followed by another document that criticized Louis. In it, Marat claimed that Louis neglected the people and only cared about financial issues.

Marie found herself supporting the growing clamour for change and harsh criticism of the monarchy and noble classes. This new breed of outspoken writers like Robespierre and Marat were expressing a distrust and suspicion of the monarchy that had been building for decades. While the mistrust was certainly shaped by many events, two stories mentioned by Marie particularly influenced the public in the later years of the monarchy. These were the scandalous life of Duke d'Orléans and the 1785 incident known as the 'Diamond Necklace Affair'. Both are prime examples of events that helped crystalize public opinion that the monarchy was immoral and not to be trusted. The mistrust fostered by such events ultimately shook the monarchy to its core.

The Duke d'Orléans was the epitome of what was wrong with the noble class. His publicly visible lifestyle of excess, privilege, and wanton disregard for those of lower social status was an aggravation to the starving, destitute French populace. He was the son of Louis Philippe d'Orléans and Louise Henriette de Bourbon. Soon after the marriage, Louis Henriette became involved in several scandalous extramarital affairs, and because of these affairs, Louise Henriette's father-in-law refused to recognize the legitimacy of the Duke d'Orléans at his birth. Perhaps, this was one reason that the Duke d'Orléans grew into a provocateur like his mother, but it also may have been because his family decided he needed to be seduced at the age of fifteen because he showed no interest in women.

The seduction worked. Thereafter, he became known as an unrepentant womanizer who constantly sought debauchery and depravity. He also became known for 'a sumptuous temple of prostitution, where his favourites indulged themselves in the most abandoned profligacy'[1], where it was claimed that participants attended a banquet stark naked, supped on the most delicious foods, and drank liberally of the most expensive spirits.

After the banquet, the Duke gave the naked participants a signal, which resulted in each man taking his own pleasure:

> 'Benches, stools, armed chairs, bergères, sophas, and ottomans, in an instant were occupied … [as the Duke d'Orléans strolled] up and down in this motley scene'.[2]

Other stories about the Duke d'Orléans' sexual proclivities and activities also surfaced. For example:

> 'Once, when some wagering enthusiasts proposed he gallop nude on his horse from his stables to his home at the Palais-Royal, [he] countered that he would ride even farther. Then not caring a jot about laws against public indecency, he mounted his horse and rode at a full gallop from Versailles to the Palais-Royal.'[3]

The Duke d'Orléans was also rumoured to be as heartless as he was sexually inspired. One story that freely circulated after his death, and may or may not be true, was about his pregnant spaniel who approached him 'with all the attachment of the most faithful and affectionate of animals. She crouched, licked his feet, and offered him every sign of fondness'.[4] Unfortunately, in doing so she also dirtied his prized white stockings. Livid over this unpardonable offense, the Duke was alleged to have thrown her with the most savage indifference from a window and onto the decorative iron pikes of the railing just outside his door. Moreover, as the poor anguished spaniel lay dying, crying with great anguish, he reputedly 'called to the creature in those words and accents of invitation, which are used when such animals are wanted to approach'.[5]

Marie herself discusses the Duke d'Orléans' shameful involvement in the Battle of Ushant, fought in 1778. The French and the British faced off against one another just west of the island of Ushant, which is located at the mouth of the English Channel off the north-westernmost point of France. The area was famous for not only its superb fishing but also being a key landmark used by ships when approaching the Channel.

The Battle of Ushant was the first major naval engagement between the French and British since France had formally backed the Americans in the American Revolutionary War. Commanding the French fleet was Vice-Admiral Louis Guillouet, better known as the Count d'Orvilliers.

The French possessed three more ships than the British fleet of twenty-nine that were commanded by Admiral Augustus Keppel. The battle ultimately proved indecisive for both sides but that was not the story the Duke d'Orléans told upon his arrival home. He claimed the French were heroes, which 'resulted in him being greeted by enthusiastic crowds who hailed him as a conqueror and gave him a twenty-nine-minute standing ovation at the opera while burning Admiral Keppel's effigy at the Palais-Royal'.[6] However, soon after, rumours began to circulate that the French had not won and that the Duke's participation at the battle was anything but heroic.

Eventually, the story came out that when the action ensued, the Duke turned into a coward. He supposedly 'secreted himself in the lowest recesses of the ship on which he served, and from which retreat no persuasions of duty, honour or self-respect could induce him to emerge till all danger of accident was passed'.[7] Of course, the Duke denied the story, but it permanently damaged his reputation, particularly after the Count d'Orvilliers essentially confirmed the story.

The Duke d'Orléans' disgrace at the Battle of Ushant became a watershed moment between him and the king, a strained relationship thereafter developing between the two. This relationship was then worsened because of another scandalous incident that occurred in 1785, involved a dazzling 2,800-carat diamond necklace, and implicated the queen.

French people like Marie were beginning to see that the nobles were not necessarily to be admired. In so many ways, the Duke distinguished himself not as noble, but as clearly ignoble. He was a cheat, a liar, and a coward. Nobles like him were increasingly viewed as part of the problem.

A second defining incident mentioned by Marie in her *Memoirs* was the 'Affair of the Diamond Necklace'. The story is full of intrigue and a cast of characters that would make any Hollywood executive sit up and take notice,

The story begins with an artful and seductive woman named Jeanne de Valois-Saint-Rémy, known as Countess de la Motte. She became involved with Cardinal Rohan, who was the Roman Catholic Cardinal and a former French ambassador to the court of Vienna. Rohan was also ambitious to make a name for himself in politics. Because the Cardinal had attempted to thwart an alliance between Austria and France, the queen kept her distance, as did the king.

In 1783, the Cardinal met the Countess and began an intimate relationship with her. When he heard that the Countess had a friendly relationship with the queen, he was immediately intrigued because he wanted to improve his relationship with her. The problem was, the Countess had no such relationship, rather she had bribed a gatekeeper so that she could be seen occasionally coming and going from the queen's precious Petite Trianon that Louis had given her.

With the Countess as the Cardinal's lover, the Cardinal attempted to use her relationship with the queen to his advantage. He did so by offering advice to the Countess about how to improve her position with the queen. The Countess saw her relationship with the Cardinal as monetarily advantageous because he began to provide her with money. So, the next step in her plan to further deceive the Cardinal was to have him write to the queen.

Of course, the person the Cardinal was exchanging letters with was not the queen. Rather it was the Countess's lover, who was also a forger. However, the Cardinal was completely deluded and soon he began to press the Countess telling her that he wanted to meet the queen. The Countess did not want the ruse to end and engaged a woman who highly resembled the queen to meet the Cardinal. The ruse occurred late at night, in a dark corner in one of the gardens of Versailles, but it convinced the Cardinal that the Countess had sway with the queen.

Having convinced the Cardinal now that she was close friends with the queen, the Countess's next step in her fraud involved a 2,800-carat diamond necklace. Jewellers who had made the necklace approached the Countess because of her supposed friendship with the queen, hoping that the Countess would act as an intermediary and get the queen to buy the necklace. The Countess initially resisted, but after seeing 647 diamonds of dazzling brilliance, greed overcame her.

The Countess's ruse then involved forging letters of credit, getting the Cardinal to agree to deliver the necklace, and obtaining an agreement from the jewellers to accept four instalments from the Queen to pay off the necklace. When the Cardinal obtained the necklace from the jewellers, he thought he would deliver it to the queen personally. Instead, it was delivered to the Countess and then into the hands of the queen's supposed valet (who was the Countess's lover).

At that point, even though neither the jewellers nor the Cardinal knew it, the diamond necklace was history. The Countess's husband and the supposed valet, immediately removed the diamonds from their setting. They spirited most of them out of France and into England, where they sold them piecemeal.

In the meantime, a few months passed before the first instalment was due, which was when the ruse was finally discovered. It happened after the jewellers approached the queen about her late payment. When the queen claimed she knew nothing, the jewellers were thunderstruck. The Cardinal was soon questioned, and he quickly realized he had been duped and found himself sitting in jail.

Meanwhile, as the plot was imploding, the Countess was busy destroying all evidence related to the ruse and planning her escape, but her escape failed. Her husband, the supposed valet, and the faux queen succeeded in escaping France. However, because the story was international news, they were soon located and arrested.

The queen was adamant that a trial should be held and that her name should be cleared. The verdict cleared the Cardinal and condemned the Countess. However, instead of clearing the queen's name, people continued to believe she had somehow been involved, and it further tarnished her reputation and discredited the Bourbon monarchy. The effect upon the monarchy cannot be underestimated. and it served as a tipping point that proved to people that the monarchy could not be trusted.

Changes were happening quickly after the storming of the Bastille. On 15 July, the first president of the National Assembly Jean-Sylvain Bailly became Paris's new mayor, and Lafayette, recently returned from the America Revolution, was appointed commander of the newly formed National Guard. On the 16th Louis XVI reinstated Necker, and on 17 July, the king visited Paris.

He arrived surrounded by his deputies and was received by Mayor Bailly and Lafayette at City Hall. Curtius and his company were also there. The king was presented with a cockade of blue and red, the traditional colours of Paris. White (the Bourbon colour) would be added soon after to nationalize the design and create the tricolour cockade of the people in blue, white, and red. However, the appearance of the speechless and somewhat sullen king won him no friends among the people.

Something else happened after the fall of the Bastille. That was when Curtius and Marie's neighbour, Joseph-François Foulon of Doué, was appointed minister of the king's household in the new government. Marie remembered Foulon well and noted that his tenure was cut dramatically short. Foulon had long been disliked, even before he was appointed to his new position. In fact, when he served in the *Parlement* of Paris prior to the revolution, he was nicknamed "âme damnée du Parlement", which roughly translates to 'henchman of Parliament'.[8] It did not take Foulon long in his new position to become even more unpopular with the people.

It seemed as if everyone disliked him. The fermier generals who provided outsourced taxes, customs, and excise operations, disliked him because he was too severe. The poor disliked him because he was wealthy and exploited them. There was also an unconfirmed rumour that circulated alleging that Foulon had said during the famine, 'if the rascals have no bread they will eat hay'.[9]

After the deaths of De Launay and Flesselles at the storming of the Bastille, 74-year-old Foulon understood the crowds could be brutal, and he feared for his life. Knowing that he was unpopular and that he was being accused of being treasonous to the revolution, he began to circulate false stories of his own death and then fled to a friend's estate just south of Paris. The ruse that he was dead did not last long. Local peasants discovered him on his friend's estate.

> 'The peasants placed a necklace of nettles on him, a bouquet of thistles in his button hole, and a truss of hay upon his shoulders, and fastening him behind a cart, with his hands tied, they dragged him to Paris. ... He was thirsty; a glass of vinegar was offered to him.'[10]

Adorned with nettles, thistles, and hay, the heavy and fat Foulon mounted the steps at City Hall on 22 July, but there was a problem. Once inside, officials did not know what to do with him but finally decided to incarcerate him at Saint Germain. In the meantime, the Third Estate learned of his capture and an angry crowd appeared at City Hall demanding Foulon. When he was not produced, the crowd went in search of him, and found the 74-year old man. Mayor Bailly and the National Guard commander Lafayette tried to intervene, but the crowd dragged Foulon to a lamp post in Place de Grève outside City Hall where an eyewitness reported:

> A rope is passed around his neck, and he is raised a certain height. ... Twice did the rope break, and twice did the old man fall on his knees, crying for pity. Some of the people, moved with pity, raised their sabres to put an end to this agony. The executioners oppose them ... After a delay of a quarter of an hour, he is hung for the third time, and finally expires. ... A wretch then cut off his head, filled the mouth with a gag formed of a handfull of hay, and ran to carry this horrid trophy through Paris.[11]

In the meantime, Foulon's son-in-law Louis-Jean Bertier of Sauvigny became another target of the Third Estate. Bertier had served as the intendant of the royal army and was tasked with providing food and provisions for the troops. He was charged with having concealed a quantity of flour from the people for military use, and it outraged the Third Estate because they were starving. Bertier was also suspected of speculating and causing grain prices to rise. Although Bertier may have been honest, he was haughty and insolent, which resulted in him having many enemies. Moreover, he was the son-in-law of the unpopular Foulon.

Bertier was retrieved from his country estate in Compiegne by armed horseman to answer for starving the Third Estate. He was taken by cabriolet, and, during the trip to Paris, was noticed by the people because of his escort. Word soon spread that he had been arrested. Unhappy citizens began to surround the cabriolet, and at one point they pulled off the cabriolet's roof, so they could better see him.

It was under such circumstances that Bertier entered Paris on the same day his father-in-law died. Moreover, at the Porte Saint-Martin monument, a cart appeared that had the following accusations written boldly across its planks for Bertier to read:

> 'He has robbed the king and France. He has devoured the substance of the people. He has been the slave of the rich and tyrant of the poor. He has betrayed his country etc.'[12]

Bertier finally reached City Hall accompanied by sixteen-hundred persons. Along the way he had been stoned, beaten, and unceremoniously shown the gruesome head of his father-in-law, 'soiled with blood and dust, on the end of a pike'.[13] The guards ushered him through the milling crowd outside City Hall and he was taken inside, where it was determined he would be sent to prison. However, the crowd was so angry that, when he reappeared, he was shot and hanged from the same lamp post as his father-in-law.

Moments later, a dragoon appeared inside City Hall carrying Bertier's bleeding heart and exclaiming, 'There is the heart of Bertier.'[14] Those inside City Hall were horror stricken. Someone else arrived announcing that soon Bertier's severed head would appear, but he was told that City Hall officials did not want any bloody heads brought inside. Lafayette was so disgusted by the incident, he exclaimed, 'free me from a post which compels me to witness such horrors,'[15] and the following day, he resigned as commander of the National Guard. However, he was induced to resume his post.

In her *Memoirs*, Marie mentioned the murders of Foulon and Bertier matter-of-factly but did not mention how they affected her. She noted that

Foulon was considered obnoxious, that he was humiliated with the nettles, thistles, and hay, and that he was dragged to City Hall where he was killed. She also revealed that when Bertier reached City Hall, he made desperate attempts to get away from the crowd and at one point succeeded, snatching a weapon and attempting to defend himself.

The day after Foulon and Bertier's deaths, on Thursday, 23 July, Curtius resigned his commission. Nevertheless, he remained a member of the guard and politically active. Acceptance of his resignation was obtained at City Hall, along with a letter of gratitude for having served as a valuable member of the guard.

With all the upheaval and the murders of Foulon and Bertier, the king decided to try and calm things. On 4 August, he appointed a reformist ministry to help Necker achieve his reforms. The Assembly also voted to abolish privilege and feudal rights of the nobility. Later in August, Curtius was recalled and when the National Guard and Chasseurs were put under each section, Curtius, who was a friend of Bailly's, received an appointment as a Captain of a local battalion of Chasseurs. His battalion was tasked with guarding the city gates, preventing smuggling, and collecting dues.

After the Bastille fell, visitors flocked to see it, and people told many stories about its fall, some stories more outlandish than others. Curtius and Marie participated in this, perhaps to boost the notoriety of their shows. For example, despite Curtius' non-participation in the storming of the Bastille, Marie would eventually exhibit a gun used in the French army that was presented to Curtius 'by the National Assembly of France, in recognition of his bravery as one of the conquerors of the Bastille'.[16] Curtius also published a thin pamphlet in 1790 about his heroic feats at the Bastille called *Services of Mr. Curtis* (*Services du Sieur Curtius vainqueur de la Bastille depuis le 12 juillet jusqu'au 6 octobre 1789*). It was full of exaggerations and read as if he had seized the prison single-handedly, despite not being there.

Like Curtius, the pretty Marie loved to tell stories, and like him, she sometimes embellished them. Another story she liked to relate was that the king's brother, the Count d'Artois, once flirted with her and that his flirtation resulted in a slap from her. While it seems likely she could have met him at Versailles, historians doubt the flirtation story on the basis it would have been a serious breach of etiquette on his part.

Another story of flirtation involves Robespierre. After the Bastille was stormed, tours were being offered and Marie took a tour with Curtius and Robespierre. While descending some narrow stairs, her foot slipped, and she would have fallen had it not been for Robespierre, who reached out and saved her. Then according to Marie, he said 'in the language of compliment observing, that it would have been a great pity that so young and pretty a patriot should have broken her neck in such a horrid place'.[17]

While we do not know if that is exactly how it happened, we do know Robespierre would soon have a big impact on Marie's life and the history of France. Marie describes Curtius having a friendship with Robespierre, and she once described Robespierre in the following manner:

> 'In dress he was neat, and even elegant, never failing to have his hair in the best order. His features had nothing remarkable about them, unless that their general aspect was somewhat forbidding: his complexion was livid and bilious; his eyes dull, and sunk in their sockets. The constant blinking of the eyelids seemed to arise from convulsive agitation; and he was never without a remedy in his pocket. He could soften his voice, which was naturally harsh and croaking, and could give grace to his provincial accent.'[18]

Robespierre was also a Jacobin, and the Jacobins were the most famous political club of the French Revolution. The Jacobin club originated from the Breton Club, which was composed of a group of deputies from Brittany who had gathered together during and after the time of the Estates General to decide how to vote as a group. After the Tennis Court Oath was taken, other deputies such as Mirabeau, Bailly, and Robespierre also joined the Breton Club, which essentially disbanded after the National Assembly was formed.

The Jacobins were a left-wing group closely allied to the Parisian working-class known as the *sans-culottes*, the common lower classes and their name also referred to their clothing because instead of wearing fashionable knee-breeches, *sans-culottes* wore pantaloons instead. Many of the Jacobins sat in the highest seats within the Assembly, and because of where they sat, they were dubbed the '*Montagnards*' in reference to 'Mountaineers' or 'Mountain Men'. In addition, the Jacobins held significant power within the Convention because of the *sans-culottes* backing, which also resulted in the Revolution coalescing around them.

After the Bastille fell, there was an ongoing debate about whether it should be destroyed. Some people thought it should remain as a permanent monument, but the decision was made to raze it to the ground. A committee was then established to oversee its destruction, and within less than a year, it had been dismantled.

One of the Bastille committee members was an entrepreneur named Pierre-Francois Palloy, who saw the destruction of the Bastille as a way for him to make money. He took charge, and a memorabilia industry grew out of it that Palloy called 'relics of freedom'. These relics included such things as etched or engraved stones the size of sugar cubes, stone busts created of Mirabeau, endless numbers of 'authentic' Bastille keys, inkwells made from metal guaranteed to have come from leg irons, and models of the Bastille carved from its stones.

Curtius bought a piece of the Bastille as a souvenir on 18 January 1790. He wrote to Palloy requesting a certificate of authenticity as he intended on presenting the stone to the Assembly. Unfortunately, after he received the letter of authenticity, he somehow lost it. He then requested a second certificate, which was sent, but the stone never made it to the Assembly. Instead, it ended up on display at Curtius's Salon de Cire.

Chapter 5

Prisoners of the People

'If your head is wax, don't walk in the sun.'

Benjamin Franklin

After the storming of the Bastille, Marie must have felt the combination of fear and excitement which pervaded Paris as apprehension grew in the minds of Frenchmen. Parisians believed that Louis XVI was going to destroy the people's new-found liberty at any moment, while those supporting Louis were worried that the monarchy would be destroyed. During this tumultuous time, Marie observed her former wax making student and the king's sister, Madame Élisabeth, weeping. She also heard about the flight of nobles and their families, including the Count d'Artois, who left France with his family three days after the Bastille fell. The few prisoners found in the Bastille were paraded in the streets so that people could see what the revolutionaries alleged were examples of the king's injustice.

As the revolution roared into full gear, Marie found her associations more important than ever. Suspicions grew everywhere, and it was always uncertain whether someone was friend or foe. People who had once supported the monarchy, now voiced hateful opposition, and 'the great mass of the people, ignorant, degraded, and maddened by centuries of oppression were rising up with delirious energy, to batter down a corrupt church and a despotic throne'.[1]

After the Bastille was stormed, Curtius was poised to take advantage of the fact the monarchy was under siege and politics were being determined by the common person on the street. Plays, newspapers, and journals were being censored, but Curtius was under no such censorship, and he could easily provide up-to-date tableaus of the happenings related to the revolution. Moreover, he could replace the Grand Couvert of Louis and Marie Antoinette with a new table filled with the latest revolutionaries.

Curtius' Salon de Cire had long been popular. Prospective patrons were greeted with, 'Come in, gentlemen and ladies, come and see the large table; Enter, it is just as at Versailles'.[2] Curtius' salon was also endorsed and promoted in other ways. One compiler of almanacs who visited the salon and was impressed, noted in 1782:

> 'This hardworking German produces coloured wax heads of such quality that one could imagine that they are alive ... with an entry fee of merely two sous they attract a mass of fascinated people from all ranks of society ... Curtius does not miss an opportunity to add something new to the show.'[3]

A 1783 etching by Pierre Charles Duvivier, showed Curtius' constant changing of heads. In the engraving, a mesmerized crowd is shown watching people switching in and out heads with the bodies standing beneath the shelf. It was titled *Change moi cette Tête!* and captured the popularity of Curtius' salon, while depicting the ever-changing wax figures that populated his exhibition.

Marie stated that in September 1789, the social agitator Marat became the publisher and editor of *The Friend of the People* (*l'Ami du Peuple*), and she noted that this paper advocated a radical stance in relation to the revolution. Marat, whose writing stemmed from events at the Estates General meetings, continued to call for change and declared the reforms to be nothing more than a plot to 'lull the people'. He was so vocal and so demanding that the revolution should become radical that he established himself as the voice of the *sans-culottes*. However, Marat was not alone in his radical stance.

His call for a radical revolution was joined by Camille Desmoulins, who had also witnessed the procession of the Estates General and written about it. Since then, he found his influence increasing, because Mirabeau was so impressed by Desmoulins' piece that he asked him to write for his newspaper, which in turn strengthened his journalistic reputation.

Days after the storming of the Bastille, Desmoulins started his publication *Free France* (*La France Libre*) and demanded a more radical revolution. Then, after the Assembly decided to give the king the power to veto legislation, Desmoulins spoke out against it and organized an uprising that failed. A few weeks later he published *The Streetlamps' Address to the Parisians* (*Discours de la lanterne aux Parisiens*), a radical pamphlet glorifying political violence and exalting Parisian mobs.

Marie mentions an incident in her *Memoirs* that occurred a few weeks after Desmoulins' glorification of violence. It occurred on 1 October and was a banquet for the king's bodyguards that was held to honour the newly arrived regiment of Flanders. They had come to quell any possible riots and help maintain order in the capital. The banquet was held at the Palace of Versailles with 210 participants. It was a sumptuous affair with decorations surrounding the tables to represent a forest. In addition, an orchestra was provided that included trumpeters from the bodyguards and music from the Flanders regiment.

The banquet began at four o'clock in the afternoon. Besides tables full of delicious meats, vegetables, and delicacies, there was generous amounts of alcohol, mostly wine as the most easily available. Wine consumption was common at the time and people could easily obtain it. Its purpose, as with other forms of alcohol, was primarily for sociability rather than for getting drunk, although people did get intoxicated. This night, the alcohol was as liberal as the toasts, which included one to the king and queen's health and resulted in white Bourbon cockades being thrown into the crowd.

The Bourbon cockade toss increased the patriotic fervour of banquet participants and resulted in a deafening cry from the alcohol-laced crowd. The cry was repeated over and over and asked for the king and queen to appear. Unexpectedly, the royal couple *did* appear, and when they did, the crowd went wild. 'Long live the King,' rang out followed by a thunderous ovation of joy, so thunderous that Louis was unable to contain himself and burst into tears at the show of loyalty.

The next day, the people's press quickly got to work. Rumours spread, altering the banquet into a gluttonous feast, which infuriated starving Parisians. It was also claimed that during the banquet, the people's cockade, the tricolour, had been trodden shamelessly under the feet of the guards and that 'they had sharpened their sabres and sworn to exterminate the Assembly and the people of Paris'.[4]

A clamour arose for the people to march on Versailles, and among those who demanded the march were Marat and Desmoulins. A few days later, hundreds of hungry market women answered the call in what became known as the 'Women's March on Versailles'. The women were led by a rough and fierce looking man, Stanislas-Marie Maillard, whom Marie claimed was the son of a bailiff in her neighbourhood. Behind them came the National Guard headed by Lafayette, who hoped to maintain order.

When the marchers met with the king, they demanded food and change. He agreed to provide them with both, but most of the marchers remained dissatisfied, refused to leave, and stayed the night. It was an unsettling night and things got worse in the morning when, on 6 October, an attack inside the palace threatened the life of the queen.

Marchers became reinvigorated about four in the morning and a group of intruders stole into the palace through an open gate. Supposedly, a royal guardsman fired at them, which infuriated them further and they decided to search for the queen. It seemed fitting to the intruders to blame her for their misfortunes and hunger. She had been nervous all night. At about 2am, she finally retired to bed after being reassured everything was safe. Hardly had she fallen asleep when one of her ladies heard a noise, opened the door, and discovered a guard drenched in blood who screeched, 'Save the Queen.' The lady warned the queen and a mad dash was made by Marie Antoinette and her ladies to the king's room.

They left the queen's bedchambers through a secret door and ran down the hall; when they reached the king's room, they pounded on his door, each pound growing more desperate as they heard the intruders trying to break into the queen's bedchambers. Just as the intruders burst through the queen's door, the king opened his door. The frightened queen and her ladies tumbled in, relieved to have reached safety.

As for the intruders, they stabbed at the bedding hoping to kill the queen. They must have been sorely disappointed to find she had already fled. Lafayette was also now fully aware of what was happening and appeared on the scene. As intruders ransacked and destroyed Versailles, Lafayette gained control, calmed the intruders, and restored order. Among those on the scene to control the intruders was Thomas de Mahy, Marquis de Favras, who came from an impoverished but aristocratic family. At seventeen, he had become a captain of the dragoons and later served as a first lieutenant in the Swiss Guard for Louis's younger brother, the Count of Provence (the future Louis XVIII). However, an inability to meet the expense of his rank caused Favras to retire in 1775. He married a year later and then travelled to Vienna and Warsaw, returning to Paris in 1789.

Favras' return in 1789 resulted in him being at Versailles when the women's march occurred. Accordingly, he was fearful for the King's safety and formed a 'bold resolution' proposing to courtiers 'to collect a few faithful solders, and to go, sword in hand, and endeavour, if possible to disperse the multitude, but at any rate to bar its way to the palace'.[5] Favras' bold resolution was quickly squashed after he requested horses from the royal stables to accomplish it.

The women's march changed everything for the monarchy. The people demanded that the king be nearer them, and he and the queen were forced to return with the people to Paris. Among those accompanying them in this procession was Favras.

Marie did not mention her opinion about the royal family's relocation to Paris, which resulted in their being housed in the Tuileries Palace. The site was not far from Curtius' shop. The Tuileries had been neglected and empty for years and was a considerable come-down for the royals from their life at the Palace of Versailles. But, being in Paris nearer the people allowed the people to watch the king and queen, scrutinize their every move, and evaluate their decisions. The royal couple virtually became prisoners of the people.

Marie found herself as an observer to an ill-fated attempt to whisk the king and queen out of France. With Louis and Marie Antoinette at the Tuileries and essentially captives of the people, royalists were concerned about their safety and Marie noted that a plot to save the royal family was soon discovered – a plot allegedly led and planned by the same Favras who staunchly defended the royal couple in their last days at Versailles.

At the time, the Assembly was suspicious about Favras and orders were given to watch him. He was watched for some time, and although he remained in Paris, he was not found to be participating in any royalist schemes. However, he did attend some of the radical meetings held by revolutionaries in the Faubourg St. Antoine, and once attended a meeting where the orator provided a plan about attacking the Tuileries and assassinating the king. Favras was so worried that the orator had inflamed the passions of those listening and that Louis might be harmed, he reported the event to the captain of the king's disbanded body guards.

After his return to France, Favras must have also kept in touch with the Count of Provence. Supposedly because of Favras' relationship with the Count, he became drawn into a plot to save the royal family, restore the monarchy, and end the Revolution. Rumours claimed that the real mover and shaker behind the plot was the Count of Provence, called during the plot 'Monsieur,' supposedly to hide his true identity. Monsieur's goal was to acquire the throne for himself by getting Louis XVI out of the country.

To finance the plot, a great deal of money was needed. Monsieur was accused of using an intermediary, Claude-Louis-Raoul, Duke de La Châtre who in turned commissioned Favras to negotiate a loan and procure two million francs. Favras successfully acquired the loan, but his success was quickly undone because he had enlisted certain individuals who betrayed him.

Lafayette received word about the conspiracy on 21 September 1789 from a recruiting sergeant named Jean-Philippe Morel. According to Morel, there was a plot afoot in which Paris would be attacked and then Bailly, Lafayette, and Necker would be assassinated as the king was seized and delivered to Metz. When more information followed a few days later, Lafayette immediately commissioned Morel into the National Guard and gave him orders to find out more about the conspiracy. Unfortunately for Morel, everything he knew he had obtained from another recruiting sergeant, Tourcaty, who in turn had learned it from Favras.

Favras was arrested on 23 December 1789 and that same morning an anonymous pamphlet circulated. According to the pamphlet, there were to be two simultaneous events: The royal family would be rescued from the Tuileries and whisked out of France while Monsieur would be declared regent. Monsieur would then order 30,000 royalist soldiers to surround Paris, which would result in anarchy and allow for the assassination of Paris's main liberal leaders, Necker, Lafayette, and Bailly. Then to bring the city to its knees, food supplies would be cut off and starving Parisians would be forced to capitulate, thereby resulting in the reestablishment of the monarchy and the end of the revolution.

Favras was charged with heading this devious plot. Worried about the implications to himself, the Count of Provence did not waste time in standing before the Commune of Paris. He admitted that he signed the documents for the loan but disavowed any knowledge of any plot 'imputed to Favras'. To further dispel any connection to Favras or to the plot, the Count also declared his staunch and ever loyal attachment to the Revolution.

> 'From the day ... when in the Second Assembly of Notables I declared myself concerning the fundamental questions which divide men's minds. I have not ceased to believe that a great revolution is impending; that the King, by virtue of his intentions, his virtues, and his supreme rank, out to be at the head of it, since it cannot be advantageous to the nation without being equally so to the monarch; and, finally, that royal authority should be the rampart of the national liberty, and national liberty the basis of royal authority.'[6]

While the Count of Provence received applause for his speech, Favras' trial lasted about two months. During the trial, witnesses contradicted each other and the evidence against Favras was weak enough that even the anarchist editor of the republican newspaper, Révolutions de Paris, admitted the evidence against Favras was insufficient for a conviction.

Favras also denied that he had done anything wrong and regularly declared his innocence. Unfortunately, amid his declaration of innocence, a small band of Royalists attempted to free him from prison. They failed, but their attempt did not help Favras' claims of innocence, and, ultimately, the court found him guilty on 19 February 1790. Sentence was pronounced, and he was declared:

> 'Convicted of having formed a Project for a Counter-Revolution, by assembling the Malcontents of the Provinces – by introducing foreign troops into the Kingdom – by seducing a Part of the late French Guards – by spreading Division among the National Guards – by attempting the Life of three distinguished Guardians of the Public Liberty ... – by conveying the King and Royal Family to Peronne – by dissolving the National Assembly, and marching a Force against the City of Paris, which, by cutting off its Subsistence, should cause it to surrender.'[7]

Orders were given that Favras was to be taken from the prison of the Chatelet to the Cathedral of Notre Dame. There he was condemned on his knees and ordered to confess his sins. An immense crowd accompanied him to witness this humiliation. Afterwards, he was dressed in a linen frock covered with brimstone that also had an inscription on the back and front that read, 'Conspirator against the state'. He was taken by tumbril (essentially a dung cart, used to aggravate a convicted person's punishment) to the Place de Grève for his execution. His head and feet were naked, and he carried in his hands a two-pound lighted flambeau.

Marie remarked that the spectators attending the execution expressed a 'savage delight' to be present at the execution, and one historian wrote that the gallows for his execution were 'lighted up'. Marie says, 'It was to them a subject for cruel jests; and they parodied in various way the execution of this unfortunate man.'[8] At the gallows, the question of who Favras had conspired with still hung in the air. Marie wrote:

> 'What Fabvras [sic] himself stated on the night of the execution strengthened the belief that Monsieur was the person who

employed him. The unfortunate Marquis asked, if he made a declaration, naming his employer, would that save him? but as the reply gave him no assurance to that effect, he observed, "Then I will take my secret with me," and walked with the greatest firmness to the scaffold.'[9]

Controversy continued to surround Favras' execution long after. Not only was he the only counter-revolutionary conspirator executed before the fall of the monarchy, there was a great deal of belief that he was a martyr and that Monsieur was the mastermind behind the conspiracy. Later, Lafayette demonstrated this when he penned in his *Memoirs*, 'Favras died a hero of devotion and courage; but Monsieur, his accomplice, possesses neither of these qualities'.[10]

Chapter 6

Celebrations

Several months after Favras' execution and one year after the storming of the Bastille, Marie tells of attending a seminal celebratory festival, which was the first *Fête de la Fédération* (which is now called Bastille Day or French National Day) held on 14 July. Marie acknowledged that the enthusiasm for the fête by the public was 'beyond description'. It commemorated the revolution, the fall of the Bastille, and the events that had occurred in 1789. France was becoming a new country and there was great hope for freedom and prosperity. Thousands of people were anticipated to attend in Paris and similar scenes were to play out in communities throughout France. The projection for attendees and spectators in Paris was at least 100,000, although that number turned out to be much higher. In addition, dignitaries and delegates from foreign countries were also participating.

To accommodate the massive crowd, a monstrous amphitheatre, measuring two-thirds of a mile in length and one-third of mile wide, was built at the *Champ de Mars* (Field of Mars). The field was far outside Paris at the time, and, today, the Eiffel Tower marks the north end of it. In addition, huge earthen stands were constructed to accommodate up to 100,000 spectators and ran the length of the field on either side. Unfortunately, as the event drew near, it appeared as if the stands would not be ready. Of this Marie wrote:

> 'Twelve thousand workmen were at first employed in the requisite preparations; but soon, they not being found sufficient, the Parisians voluntarily lent their aid, and the spectacle became one of the most interesting and extraordinary kind; ecclesiastics, military, and persons of all classes, from the highest to the lowest, wielded the spade and the pick-axe, whilst even elegant females lent their aid, and consistent with

the feeling of the period, [I] assisted, and trundled a barrow in the Champ de Mars, and at last every section of the city sent forth its contingent, with colours and banners, proceeding, to the sound of drums, to the grand national work; and when arrived, they all united their labours, cheering each other throughout their toil; and, perhaps, never before or since was seen such a gay and animated assemblage of labourers.'[1]

Fortunately, the earthen stands were completed on time and everything was set for Wednesday 14 July. The only problem was that the weather chose not to cooperate with the celebration because wretchedly wet weather ensued, and some form of rain lasted all day. Marie attended the event and remembered Louis Legendre, a butcher turned politician, standing next to her at the celebration. Stout and strong, Legendre was known for his vulgar demeanour and addiction to swearing. Marie noted that 'when it began to rain, he looked up to the heavens, and poured forth his execrations against them for spoiling, as he termed it, the joys of the day'.[2]

Although Legendre's day may have been ruined, the rain did not dampen the spirits of those celebrating in Paris. The bad weather also affected other celebrations throughout France. In fact, the weather was so uncooperative everywhere, one newspaper reported, the rains caused some 'patriots to accuse the heavens of being aristocratic'.[3]

The night before the event, between ten and eleven o'clock, spectators began to arrive in small parties. The National Guard was already posted inside and outside the field to maintain order. As the parties arrived, they seated themselves in the stands. At day break, crowds continued to arrive, and by nine o'clock, people were pouring in from all the avenues, 'where parties of cavalry, composed of the Paris Guards Nationale, cautioned them as they entered, not to hurry, but take time, for there was room for all'.[4] When the event started, the surrounding hills of Chaillot and Passy were crowded with people.

In another part of the city, the grand procession got underway marching in the following order: a detachment of mounted Parisian National Guards with several musical bands; citizens of Paris elected in April 1789; Parisian National Guards on foot; 240 citizens chosen in August of 1789; city drums; 120 citizens of Paris chosen by districts to conduct the festival and each district's president; administrators of the city of Paris; the mayor of Paris; the guards and music of Paris, along with 160 deputies, 60 presidents, and other city attendants; the king with the president of the Assembly and the king's body guards; 100 infants in the arms of their mothers decorated with the national cockade; 400 children carrying banners with an inscription that read 'The hope of the people'. These groups were followed by an innumerable train of citizens and bands, and the procession closed with National Troops on horseback and two regiment of foot.

While everyone waited at the *Champs de Mars* for the procession to arrive, National Guardsmen and some of those not participating in the procession assembled in a great circle. To stave off boredom, they formed large dancing circles, marched to the beat of drums, or conducted sham fights, sometimes flourishing their swords. To these activities were added cries of 'Vive la Liberte!' 'Vive le Roi!' 'Vive le Confederation national!' 'Vive mon Frere!'

Other forms of entertainment also took place. At one point, there was a performance of what was called, a *Victim To Tyranny*. A man was carried to a spot and laid down with great solemnity inside a circle. A grenadier's cap was placed on his head and a musket stuck in his hand. An Abbé was also pulled into the circle, and then people marched around the men, amusing themselves and wasting time.

While the crowd patiently waited for the arrival of the procession, around seven in the morning a crucifix was placed on the altar. Then, at 10:30am, a grand procession of more than 100 priests took place. The procession included the Bishop of Autun, who was officiating the ceremony. The priests promenaded onto the field in a double line, carrying with them several sacred books. They then ascended the steps to the altar and consecrated it.

Just before noon, it was announced that the procession was nearing the triumphal arch that had been constructed for the occasion. The guards who had been entertaining themselves, suddenly snapped into formation to receive the procession. Fifteen or so minutes later, the procession appeared. The first of those in the procession who seated themselves consisted of citizens elected in April and August of 1789. Other dignitaries followed.

At one o'clock, Lafayette appeared, riding ahead of the cavalry. He was seated on a milky-white charger and was greeted by the enthusiastic crowd with cries of 'Vive LaFayette!' Lafayette then spent the remainder of his time overseeing arrivals, maintaining order, and directing procession participants to their proper seats.

Sometime after 3pm, the queen, her children, and her attendants arrived. They took their seats behind the king's chair. Newspapers reported that she 'looked divine'. She was absent of diamonds but decked out in pearls that appeared on her cap, neck, and ears. In addition, she may have a worn a size 6½ pair of white silk shoes featuring pleated tricolour ribbons that were auctioned off in 2012 and sold for £40,000.

CELEBRATIONS

After the queen was seated, the king arrived. Newspapers reported that he appeared to be in good spirits. He was seated next to the president of the Assembly in a state chair that had the crown removed to avoid any suggestion of the monarchy.

After the ceremony of consecrating the banners was completed, a heavy discharge of artillery occurred. At half past four, the real reason for the event began. It was a solemn oath that was read at the altar to which every deputy cried '*Je le jure*', ('I swear it') Lafayette took the oath, and the king followed:

> '[He] waiting till every thing was silent, read very audibly, and with infinite majesty of manner, the OATH assigned to him . . . "I, a citizen King of the French, swear to the nation to make use of all the power that is delegated to me by the constitutional law of the State, in maintaining the constitution, and causing the laws to be put in execution."'[5]

Louis then raised his right hand, extended his arm, looked steadfastly at the altar, and declared, '*Je le jure*'. Immediately, shouts of joy rent the air. They were accompanied by the clattering of fifty thousand swords and the booming discharge of artillery and cannons. One person noted that the effect of the king taking the oath was indescribable, and Frenchman were beyond joyous.

Later, that evening, Marie supposedly joined in the rejoicing and dancing because years later, in 1885, her three grandsons — Joseph, Francis, and Victor — gave an interview to a London newspaper reporting on what their grandmother told them of the event. They stated, 'Our grandmother assisted at the taking and demolition of the Bastile [*sic*], and joined in the Carmagnole danced upon the site of the destroyed State prison. Her partner was the famous [Prussian officer, adventurer, and author Friedrich von der] Trenck,'[6] who had been sent by orders of the Prussia king to be an observer of the revolution.

Trenck had written his biography in 1787. It was translated in 1788 and became popular reading in the late eighteenth century, thereby making him a celebrity. Trenck arrived in Paris in the middle of February 1790 and wrote about his visit to see Curtius' wax figures that occurred the day after he arrived. Apparently, Trenck had never met Curtius even though Curtius was exhibiting Trenck's likeness in wax. Trenck paid to see the exhibition, examined his wax likeness, and then approached Curtius:

> 'I went up to him and said, "Sir, I saw Baron Trenck himself a few years ago, and I perceive this figure no more resembles him

than it does the great Mogul." He looked at me with a mixture of surprise and contempt; and assured me, on his honour, that he was personally acquainted with Baron Trenck, and had modelled the face of his figure from the Baron himself at Francfort.'[7]

Trenck then took Curtius aside and revealed his identity. Whereupon the confounded Curtius begged Trenck to be allowed to copy his real features, but for various reasons Trenck refused. Trenck asserted that with his revelation, the wax figure in Paris was no longer a draw and Curtius was forced to send it to Madrid to draw on the purse-strings of spectators there.

The situation also resulted in Parisians being curious as to what Trenck looked like in real life. Trenck reported that thereafter, wherever he travelled, whether to sup or to dine, a stream of curiosity seekers gathered hoping to get a good look at him and that within six days, he was 'generally known'. Although Marie's claims to have danced and celebrated with Trenck at France's first *Fête de la Fédération*, knowing of Curtius' deceit, make it likely that Marie's story is as much a fabrication as Curtius' wax figure of Trenck.

After the *Fête de la Fédération*, Marie went back to making wax figures and politics continued as usual in France. Necker was again dismissed and Armand Marc, Count de Montmorin, installed in his place. The Assembly also decreed that France's white flag and the fleur-de-lys that had for so long been the emblem of the monarchy would be replaced by the tricolour. The new government also found itself attempting to put down a black slave uprising in the colony of Saint-Domingue led by Toussaint L'ouverture.

There were also other problems plaguing France. After the storming of the Bastille, riots became common. To avoid the violence, and because sometimes the violence was directed at nobility, nobles began to emigrate in a mass movement that lasted until 1815. Among those who decided to leave France were Louis's two old aunts, the daughters of Louis XV, Adélaïde and Victoire.

Their plan was to go to Rome but unfortunately, before the sisters reached their destination, they were stopped at Arnay-le-Duc, a commune in Burgundy. A debate among the Assembly then ensued as to whether the women should be allowed to leave. Fortunately, one wise deputy put an end to the debate when he remarked, 'All Europe … will be astonished to learn that a great assembly has spent several days in deciding whether two old ladies shall hear mass at Paris or at Rome'.[8]

With the women on their way to Rome, rumours that the king and queen would also soon flee were rampant, and, in fact, within a few days of the women's departure, a gathering of angry market women from Les Halles petitioned to see the king. They wanted him to recall his aunts, but Lafayette would not allow the women to see the king and ultimately, after a three-hour standoff, the women peacefully dispersed.

A few days after this, on 28 February 1791, another unsettling incident occurred. The Chateau of Vincennes had started out as hunting lodge for Louis VII. Over the years, it had been enlarged and converted into a fortress, but by the eighteenth century, it was functioning as a state prison. As it was old and rundown, the Assembly decided to restore it so that it could hold more prisoners. However, during the restoration of Vincennes a rumour circulated that an underground passageway existed, and that the Assembly's restoration was a means of concealing it so that it could be used at a later date to smuggle the king out of France.

On 28 February, a patriotic mob armed with axes, crowbars, and picks travelled to Vincennes to demolish it just like the Bastille had been demolished. Lafayette soon received word about the mob and their intentions. He gathered together most of his National Guardsmen guarding Tuileries and headed to Vincennes to stop its destruction. He arrived there just as they were demolishing some of the parapets.

Meanwhile, in Paris, nobles heard about the departure of Lafayette and the National Guard. They began to worry about the king's safety as most of the National Guard was now absent. The nobles then surmised that a conspiracy was afoot to assassinate the king and his family. They decided they must act to protect them, and three to four hundred young nobles carrying concealed weapons, primarily knives and daggers, headed to the Tuileries.

As nobles intermittently arrived at the Tuileries, the few remaining National Guardsmen began to suspect that some sort of counter-revolution might be occurring. About that time, Lafayette, who had restored order at Vincennes and arrested sixty men, arrived back at the Tuileries. He learned about the arriving nobles and went to disarm them, but they adamantly refused to cooperate, still fearing for the king's safety.

The situation remained critical and if it had not been for Louis' intervention, the situation might have devolved into a bloody fray. The king requested that the nobles surrender their arms and promised they would be returned the next day. Fortunately, the nobles did as he asked, but, unfortunately, after doing so, Lafayette had them jailed.

In the end, the event that became known as the 'Day of Daggers' (*Journée des Poignards*), proved to be unlucky for Louis. Lafayette posted a proclamation that men 'of a justly suspected zeal'[9] were no longer permitted inside the Tuileries walls. The radical press also did not help the situation. They presented the Day of Daggers as a pre-empted counter-revolution. As for the nobles, the weapons they had surrendered were sold off, and they were left feeling contempt for a king who they claimed betrayed them and forced them to surrender.

In early 1791, Mirabeau was elected President of the Assembly, and it was around this time that Marie created his portrait in wax. The presidency was a position he had long desired, but as fate would have it, Mirabeau's youthful excesses, strenuous schedule, and delicate political finagling took a toll on his health. He began to be racked with pain having contracted pericarditis.

Despite his pain, Mirabeau could not stay away from the Assembly. When he appeared, he was deemed more eloquent that ever, and this happened even if he appeared at the meetings 'with his head swathed in bandages, the blood trickling down his cheeks from leech-bites'.[10] Mirabeau's ability to continue working was attributed to the good medical care given him by his friend Cabanis. In fact, Cabanis' care allowed Mirabeau to continue to function almost up to the moment he died.

Mirabeau left the Assembly on 27 March never to return. He had spoken five times that day and was physically exhausted. He obtained some rest that night but the following morning, he remained exhausted and his suffering increased until he took a hot bath. Later, that same evening, he felt well enough to visit the Italian Opera but fell ill during it and had to be taken home before the performance concluded.

News about Mirabeau's deteriorating condition quickly spread throughout Paris. People who passed his house did so silently and rattling carriages turned off on preceding streets to avoid passing his house on the Chaussèe d'Antin. Everyone quietly waited until it was announced that Mirabeau was dead at the age of 42.

This sudden and seemingly mysterious death on Saturday, 2 April 1791 caused Marie and many others to suspect poisoning. To quell fears that Mirabeau had been poisoned or that his death was somehow unnatural, an autopsy was ordered to ascertain whether he had died of natural causes. Pursuant to that order at noon, the following day, on Sunday, an autopsy was performed under a tent in Mirabeau's garden with various judges, municipal officials, and surgeons present. The findings determined that he was not poisoned.

Mirabeau's death affected everyone. The Assembly adjourned so that members could attend his funeral, and the municipality ordered eight days of mourning. Jacobins passed various resolutions commending him, ordered a marble bust to his memory, and designated the second of April would thereafter be observed as the anniversary of his death. Marie mentions that on the day of his funeral, theatres were shut, amusements and festivities cancelled, and balls, parties, and receptions postponed. Preparations were also made to honour Mirabeau with a funeral worthy of the great deeds ascribed to him, as his loss was deemed a public calamity. Throughout Paris businesses were closed so that everyone could join in the universal grief that had gripped the nation:

> 'The very trees of the Boulevards, along which the body passed ... were full of people. The windows of the streets were full of spectators, and added to the interest and majesty of the doleful spectacle. The populace who, on such occasions, are very pressing, let the procession pass with a proper decorum, of their own accord, no guards being appointed to keep them off.'[11]

Numerous newspapers reported on the funeral detailing the event from the moment the procession left the Chaussée d'Antin, which was renamed Mirabeau Street in the president's honour. Marie witnessed this funeral cortege and was amazed. She described it as being like nothing she had ever witnessed and noted how the lighted flambeaus produced what she described as a 'very solemn effect'.

The cavalry led the funeral marching magnificently at the forefront. They were followed by various detachments, long lines of officers, and numerous clergy. Mirabeau's 'heart was carried a-part, surmounted with a cypress wreath'.[12] Mirabeau's family members and other officials followed, including Paris's mayor, important members of the Jacobin Club, and various leaders well-respected within society. Six divisions of the Parisian army closed the procession.

The funeral itself was filled with pomp and circumstance, solemn music, and 'astonishing silence'. Authorities had decided that the Pantheon would be designated as the place to hold all great Frenchmen, and Mirabeau was to be the first to be given this honour. However, as the Pantheon had not been converted from a church to a mausoleum, Mirabeau's body was placed in state in a vault of the cloister of St. Eustache until the new edifice was ready.

Chapter 7

Setting the Stage

'Whoever applauds the King shall be beaten – whoever
insults him shall be hanged!'

Placards throughout Paris in response
to the king's flight

A new invention was about to play an important role in Marie's life. In April 1792, this new machine was erected at the Place de Grève, and it would see heavy usage during the next few years, becoming emblematic of French Revolution. The machine was the guillotine, and the first time it was used was to efficiently lop off the head of condemned highway man Nicolas Jacques Pelletier. France's master executioner Charles Henri Sanson publicly executed Pelletier on 25 April 1792. At first, the public was unhappy with the results and demanded executions be carried out using the old reliable gallows rather than the new device.

The guillotine was not named for its inventor but for a doctor, Joseph-Ignace Guillotin, an impressive man who after being granted a Master of Arts so impressed the Jesuits with an essay that they persuaded him to enter their fraternity, where he was appointed a professor of literature. After a few years he decided Jesuit life was not for him and he left to study medicine, distinguished himself and gained a diploma from the faculty at Reims. He then entered a competition and won a prize given by the Paris faculty that entitled him to use the special title of Doctor-Regent. He afterwards worked with Benjamin Franklin to investigate the veracity of Franz Mesmer's claims of animal magnetism. Guillotin also drafted a pamphlet about the constitution that so intrigued the *Parlement* that they requested he present his viewpoints to them. Added to these accomplishments, Guillotin had been chosen on 2 May 1789 as one of ten Paris deputies to serve in the Estates General.

While serving, Guillotin focused on medical reform. At the time, beheading was preserved for nobility and accomplished with an axe or sword, which, of course, was not always immediately successful and sometimes caused the condemned person to suffer. Although most Assembly members favoured capital punishment, Guillotin was against it. However, after he was outvoted, he decided to make execution as painless as possible.

A presentation about methods of carrying out the death penalty took place in the Assembly on 10 October 1789. At that time, Guillotin proposed that criminals should be decapitated 'by the effect of a simple mechanism'.[1] This suggestion fulfilled several of Guillotin's goals. All criminals would be punished with the same type of punishment despite rank. All criminals would also be punished by the same humane means, decapitation. In addition, decapitation eliminated the use of barbaric and painful methods of killing that include hanging, quartering, burning someone alive, drowning, or ripping someone apart on the wheel.

Guillotin also recommended four other propositions: the punishment was not to inflict disgrace upon the criminal's family; anyone reproaching a criminal's relative would be reprimanded and punished; property of the condemned would not be confiscated; and finally, bodies of executed criminals would be delivered to their families, buried in the usual manner, and no registry would mention the criminal's means of death.

Many members of the Assembly greeted Guillotin's propositions contemptuously, and the Assembly adjourned without debating the subject. Nevertheless, Guillotin was not deterred. He brought his proposals up again on 1 December. This time he also read a long, detailed paper, and his earlier proposal that all criminals be punished by the same method was approved. However, members argued about adopting decapitation as the method, one member saying that decapitation 'might tend to deprave the people by familiarizing them with the sight of blood'.[2] Arguing for decapitation, one of Guillotin's next statements ended the debate, provoked laughter, and forever haunted him. Guillotin said: 'Now, with my machine, I strike ... off your head [*je vous fais sauter la tête*] in the twinkling of an eye, and you never feel it'.[3]

Guillotin's phrase was seized upon by the press. Levity and humour were quickly attached to it and a comedic song circulated. Three years before the actual machine existed, the name guillotine, given in derision, stuck, despite the inventor of the decapitation machine being a French surgeon and physiologist named Antoine Louis and despite the decapitating device initially being called a *louisette* or *louison*.

Already in existence were some guillotine-like devices that decapitated a person. One was the Halifax Gibbet which may have been used as early as the 1200s. It was mounted on a stone base, had an axe head fitted to a wooden block, and the axe was released by withdrawing a pin or cutting a rope. Another guillotine-like device was the Scottish Maiden that was built of oak. It had lead weights attached to a blade, and a peg kept the blade in place. When the peg was pulled, the blade fell. However, the disadvantages to these machines were that sometimes a person's neck was crushed rather than the head being decapitated.

To create the decapitation machine, a committee was formed with the French surgeon Louis heading it. According to Sanson's grandson, during the designing of the guillotine, Guillotin sought out his grandfather's advice, and the old man insisted 'on the urgent necessity of a machine which would keep the sufferer's body in a horizontal position, and ensure prompter and safer operation than could be expected of hand-work'.[4] That was precisely what Guillotin wanted to achieve, and the two men discussed how to achieve this but arrived at no satisfactory solution.

By chance, Sanson knew a man named Tobias Schmidt. Schmidt was a German harpsichord maker; Sanson played the violin and had purchased some musical instruments from Schmidt. The two men also frequently played duets together, Sanson on the violin and Schmidt on the clavichord. One night, Sanson casually mentioned the dilemma to Schmidt, who according to Sanson then drew a few lines on a piece of paper and handed it to him. Supposedly, the drawing was a rough sketch of the guillotine.

Although the Assembly approved a law on 3 June 1791 that anyone sentenced to the death penalty would have his or her head severed, the guillotine was not adopted as France's official means of execution until 23 March 1792. Schmidt had supposedly pressed Sanson to assist with the decapitation device and was hired to build it based on Louis' design. On 10 April 1792, Schmidt was paid 960 francs for the machine and the scaffold. The price also included a leather bag used to dispose of the severed heads, which was referred to as the 'family picnic basket'.

The guillotine was a tall, upright frame painted blood-red like the executioner's coat and the baskets that caught the severed heads. The blade slid up and down in grooves and was attached to a metal weight called a mouton. The condemned person was positioned face down under the blade with their body resting on a wooden bench. The person's arms, back, and legs were restrained with leather straps, and their neck was secured in place by an arched or moon-shaped piece of iron called a lunette. The blade was held in place with two ropes and when the ropes were released the blade fell quickly and forcefully.

The guillotine was initially set up in the Cour du Commerce, rue Saint-André-des-Arts, which was opposite the offices of Marat's radical newspaper, *The Friend of the People*. The guillotine's first victims were two sheep and two calves, followed by three human corpses obtained from Louis' medical peers at a prison hospital. The device did not work as perfectly as everyone hoped. Although the animals and the first corpse cleanly lost their heads, the second corpse had its head still partially attached to its torso, which was considered unacceptable.

A discussion ensued as to what to do. There were three possibilities: accelerate the motion of the blade; increase the sliding weight; or change the shape of the blade. Louis and Guillotin decided the blade must be changed from a convex shape to an oblique one, and the oblique one was installed. However, there is also another story that circulated about how the oblique blade came into use which is much more ironic as it involves Louis XVI, who was known to spend many a night blackening his hands as a locksmith. With such mechanical skills, he supposedly noticed the drawing of the crescent-shaped blade and remarked that such a blade was not practical for all necks. He then took a pen and changed the blade's crescent shape to an oblique one.

Several months after Mirabeau's grand funeral, in June 1791, the royal family was discovered trying to escape France in a customised berline de voyage that held six adults. They were returned in disgrace to their prison-like home at the Tuileries. Marie mentioned that she was uneasy about the ferocious tone of the people after the king's flight which had 'plunged Paris into the utmost consternation'.[5] She also noted that despite the placards ordering silence, some loud roars and disapproving cries erupted upon his return to the city. Marie also maintained that along the way, some patriots attempted to harm the *gardes-du-corps* (life guards), who were driving the berline. In fact, Marie stated that the queen became so fearful for their safety, she called to Lafayette and told him to protect them.

The ill-fated escape had begun a few days earlier when, under the cover of darkness, the royal family stole out of the Tuileries in disguise. They pretended to be servants of a wealthy Russian Baroness de Korff. Their plan was to escape to the royalist stronghold of Montemédy. After driving for 22 hours and within 31 miles of Montemédy, their escape came to a grinding halt in the town of Varennes.

Along the way, the restless king had peered out the berline's windows. Stiff from being locked up in the berline, he got out several times to stretch his legs. During these breaks, he talked with some villagers. 'His heavy, placid features were familiar to those who saw him, and among those was Jean-Baptiste Drouet, Sainte-Menehould's postmaster and a fiery republican'.[6]

Drouet's recognition of the king resulted in the royal family being taken into custody and arrested. They returned to Paris in their berline, accompanied by the National Guard. The closer the berline got to Paris, the larger the crowds that surrounded it, until a crowd of about 30,000 engulfed the carriage. Near Paris, Lafayette met them; he wanted to avoid trouble, and so he guided the royal family on a circuitous route back to the Tuileries Palace and into Paris.

Their entrance into the city was a solemn one and filled with no joy for Parisians. Prior to their arrival, placards had been posted throughout Paris warning spectators of what behaviour was expected. The placards read, 'Whoever applauds the King shall be beaten – whoever insults him shall be hanged!'[7] The National Guard lining the streets were also ordered to reverse their arms, representative of the action taken on public days of mourning. Thus, when the berline rolled in, for the most part, Parisians rolled out a deafening welcome mat of silent disgust.

The king's flight left a bitter taste in the mouths of all Frenchmen but particularly all Parisians. He had taken an oath at the *Fête de la Fédération* and made promises supporting the constitutional monarchy. Now Parisians knew the truth, and they were bitterly disappointed. Newspapers reported that the public's unhappiness resulted in a petition by Jacobins that in part stated:

> 'Never was any question of more importance than that which relates to the King's flight; … it is necessary to quickly decide the fate of that individual; that his own conduct ought to afford the basis of this decision; that Louis XVI after having accepted the royal functions, and sworn to defend the constitution, deserted the post entrusted to him; protested by a written declaration, signed with his own hand, against this very constitution; attempted by his flight and his direction to deprive of effect the executive power, and overturn the constitution; … that his perjury, his flight, his protest … amount to a formal abdication of the constitution Crown entrusted to him; that the National Assembly have so decided in possessing themselves of the executive power, suspending the power of the King, and detaining him in arrest; that fresh promises on the part of Louis XVI to observe the constitution cannot afford to the nation a sufficient security against a new perjury, and a new conspiracy.'[8]

As a result, and in response to his flight, the Assembly suspended the King's duties on 15 July.

Although France considered the King a disgrace, the country was honouring Voltaire, the subject of Marie's first wax bust. The Assembly had earlier announced that Voltaire was to be interred in the Pantheon with Mirabeau. Voltaire was a popular choice because as an atheist he could serve as the secular saint of the Enlightenment. Marie claimed that the announcement infused Parisians with untold joy.

Before Voltaire's body even reached Paris, it seemed as if his disinterment took on a life of its own. The National Guard of Romilly offered to convey his body to Paris, and their offer was accepted. They arrived at the monastery of Scellières on 9 May and found eager citizens willingly snatching up shovels, pick axes, and spades to remove the earth that covered the coffin of the great Voltaire. People crowded around hoping to be the first to see the coffin and the body, and when the coffin was reached, there were excited cries of 'There it is! There it is!'

The coffin was opened, and two surgeons and four witnesses attested to the presence and condition of the body. After their examination, vespers, absolution, and libera were chanted, and then the National Guard who were standing nearby, their arms encircled with mourning crepe, fired a volley over the grave. The ceremony ended with the body being displayed to the crowd.

Information about the disinterment was then forwarded in a letter from the mayor of Romilly to the Villette, Voltaire's protégé. Villette, though homosexual, had been convinced by Voltaire to marry his adopted daughter, Reine Philiberte de Varicour, a woman of letters. The marriage proved disastrous, but Voltaire treated Villette like a son even after the marriage ended, and they remained close enough that it was at Villette's residence that Voltaire died. Among the information forwarded to Villette was the following:

> 'A chaplet of oak was fixed upon the head of Voltaire, and, the corpse being placed in a triumphal car, the procession moved slowly forward along the road to Romilly. As we passed, the way was strewed with flowers; some were thrown upon the shroud; and the women, holding their infants within their arms, made them kiss the Sarcophagus, and cover it with garlands of roses.'[9]

Voltaire's body finally arrived in Paris in July. His coffin was placed in the ruins of Bastille on 10 July. The following day, the procession to the Pantheon turned into a major celebration throughout Paris as the procession stretched from one side of Paris to another. It has been estimated that a million people attended and watched the procession. Some people thought the procession was pompous and maintained that such a lavish funeral should not have been given to 'a man who had spent his life in ridiculing religion, and corrupting morals.[10] Yet, the ceremony lasted nearly twelve hours.

Curtius had received a commission from the Assembly to provide a new model of Voltaire for the occasion and the new figure that he and Marie would prepare was to be an integral part of the celebration. Jacques-Louis David, a preeminent artist of the era, who painted in Neoclassical style and was an active supporter of both the French Revolution and Robespierre, staged the scene. Voltaire's waxen effigy was reclining upon a sarcophagus and dressed in vermilion robes. One newspaper provided a further summary:

'The car which conveyed the body was drawn by twelve horses, of a light grey colour, harnessed four abreast, and led by men in antient dresses. Numerous detachments from all the battalions of the Parisian National Guard opened and closed the procession of the funeral, which set out at two o'clock in the afternoon, from the spot where the Bastille stood ... In the train were men in antique dresses, carrying the statue of Voltaire on a frame. It was surrounded by pyramids, crowded with medallions, on which the titles of his principal works appeared. Upon another frame was a gilt box, containing a copy of the last edition of his works published by Beaumarchais; round this box were the Literati. At certain distances were placed different Revolutionary trophies, such as the chains, balls, and cuirasses, found in the Bastille; the colours, and plan of that fort in relief, carried by the workmen who had been employed to demolish it, and by the inhabitants of the Fauxbourg St. Antoine. Several full bands of music, both vocal and instrumental, attended the funeral, and hymns were chanted in praise of the philosophic poet.'[11]

The long procession was headed and closed by the National Guard, and along the way, the procession stopped at various spots. One stop was the Opera House and another Villette's home where an inscription to Voltaire read, 'His genius is everywhere, and his heart is here'.[12] In addition, as the procession passed Villette's house, four tall poplars had been tied together at the top with garlands to form an arch. When Voltaire's body passed underneath, a crown of roses were arranged to fall from the arch onto the sarcophagus.

Similar to the Fête de la Federation of 1790, a continual downpour marred the occasion, causing the colours on Voltaire's wax effigy to run and streak, and by the time the procession reached the Pantheon, Voltaire's effigy was ghostly white. Curtius was later blamed for the fiasco by those who organized the procession.

Three days after this procession, the day that had been set aside the year before as the Fête de la Fédération and reserved to forever celebrate the taking of Bastille, passed flatly and hardly with notice. Reporters, journalists, and engravers were too busy condemning the king for fleeing, and lauding Voltaire. However, these subjects were soon replaced when honours were bestowed upon an incorruptible patriot by the Assembly. That incorruptible patriot was Robespierre, an Estates-General representative and frequent visitor of Curtius and Marie's.

Robespierre, the son of a lawyer, was from Arras. Like his father, after completing his studies Robespierre gained a law degree, going into private practice and serving the poor. He also wrote an essay titled *Report on Degrading Punishments* (*Mémoire sur les peines infamantes*), which won first prize at the Academy of Metz. However, his essay alarmed royalists and the privileged classes because it questioned arbitrary justice and whether a criminal's family should share in his or her disgrace.

When Louis XVI called the Estates General, Robespierre wrote *Address to the Nation of Artois* (*Addresse à la nation artésienne*). In the document, he argued that if elections were held as they always were, the new Estates General would not represent the people. New elections were held shortly after he published the paper, and Robespierre ran for a position as a deputy in the Third Estate and won. Having won the election, Robespierre arrived in Paris in 1789. He then became involved with the Jacobin Club, whose meetings soon became rousing oratory events. Jacobin members supported universal suffrage, embraced separation of church and state, and promoted republican values.

Debates in the Jacobin club also eventually pitted Mirabeau against Robespierre. The moment came after a decree stated only active citizens would be allowed to serve in the National Guard. Because an active citizen was defined as a person whose annual tax amounted to the equivalent of three days' work, the right to bear arms applied only to the middle and upper classes and that upset the lower classes.

The following evening at the Jacobin meeting Robespierre began a rousing speech against the decree. Mirabeau was a more moderate member, and he stopped Robespierre, hoping to quash the radical turn that certain extremists were promoting within the club. Mirabeau's interference caused an uproar among the Jacobins. The uproar lasted for an hour and half before Robespierre was allowed to finish.

That would not be the last uproar associated with Robespierre. In February of 1792, the Assembly debated about declaring war on Austria. Robespierre and Marat were against it claiming that war would weaken the revolution and might increase the power of counter-revolutionaries, the generals, or even the King.

About the same time as Lafayette was sending his letter to the Assembly, on a Tuesday morning, 20 June, Marie claims to have witnessed an armed and 'ferocious' mob pouring out of the Faubourg St. Antoine. The mob marched to the Assembly, which at first objected to their noisy entrance but when they were ordered to withdraw and did, the Assembly reconsidered and allowed the group to return.

The mob was upset. They carried a petition demanding that the assembly resist any form of oppression and wanting any Frenchman who opposed their views to be ordered to leave France. Moreover, they were upset about Louis vetoing two decrees:

> 'First, it was decreed that all priests who refused to swear to the new constitution would be deported, and second, an army of 20,000 was to be permanently installed in and around Paris to protect it from invasion'.[13]

Having expressed their outrage over the vetoes to the Assembly, they were somewhat satisfied and left but headed to the Tuileries Palace to denounce 'Monsieur Veto' (the king) and 'Madame Veto' (the queen).

There the mob flowed into the Tuileries garden by the thousands. As they marched they chanted 'Down with the veto!' and beneath the palace windows sometimes they yelled and demanded that Louis appear. Also, among the mob, were marchers who carried 'horrid trophies'. One horrid trophy was the heart of a calf, stuck on the end of pike with an inscription that read, 'The heart of an aristocrat'.

According to Marie, after a time the mob got tired of marching, wanted satisfaction, and grew bolder. Hatchets and axes were heard pounding on the doors of the king's apartment, and then, after breaking through the door, the mob poured in destroying furniture and cornering him. Louis was conciliatory. He listened to the mob, but at some point, he was forced to drink wine to their health. He was also forced to wear a red cap, the 'bonnet rouge' or the 'liberty cap,' a soft, conical, brimless cap from antiquity that came to symbolize the French Revolution and the new order. The mob insisted the king show his allegiance to the nation by placing it on his head, and, as he had no choice, he did.

The mob similarly found the queen. She was down the hall when the mob appeared, and if they were mad at the king, they were furious with the queen. She was a foreigner and they intensely disliked her. In fact, they blamed her for most of their woes. She was cornered too and for three hours she was forced to listen to the mob's epithets and vociferous threats with her little son seated on her lap.

By the time the mob left, after suffering such imminent danger, the royal family could hardly sleep and stayed on edge. Perhaps they were right because Marie wrote:

> 'The affair … excited the deepest regret in the minds of every respectable individual, who regarded it as a dreadful warning as to what might be expected from the future: in fact, many considered it was intended to have proceeded much further than it did, and to have had for its object the murder of the king, which was prevented by the people softening at the sight of him, and being won by his conciliatory manner of receiving them.'[14]

Chapter 8

War with Austria and the September Massacres

Vive la nation!

Marie observed that the French populace enthusiastically welcomed the Assembly's declaration of war on the King of Bohemia and Hungary in April 1792. Thus, French troops carried great hopes for military success when they invaded the Austrian Netherlands on 28 April.

As the army needed men, a call was issued for volunteers, and the two men who worked for Curtius quit and enlisted. In fact, so many men answered the call that Marie and Curtius had trouble finding help. Marie claimed that in the quarter where she resided, there were hardly any men left. This burning patriotism was also noted by newspapers who publicized the zeal of enlistees:

> 'Ten thousand seven hundred and fifteen volunteers have entered themselves in eight days, and actually set out yesterday for the camp. These were provoked by no bounty, no enlisting money whatever was given to them – it was the working of the constitution on their hearts, and similar ardour burns in every department.'[1]

Besides joining the French Revolutionary Army, many other patriots supported the war effort in other ways. Marie described machines installed on the banks of the Seine to cast cannons, and when it was realized that there were an inadequate number of gunsmiths to aid in making firelocks, watchmakers and other workmen were procured to fabricate or aid in their creation.

Other elements also benefitted the war effort. Houses were searched for useful things, church bells melted down to make cannons, and some public buildings converted to barracks for soldiers. Foundries also created arms, and tanneries supplied harnesses, reins, and saddles. Saltpetre, a necessary element for explosives, was also required, and it was obtained in the most imaginative way, being retrieved from the mouldy substances that were commonly found in cellar walls.

Marie also found that the popularity of the war increased the popularity of the Girondins. The Girondins were composed of businessmen, financiers, industrialists, and other such men. Unlike the Montagnards, who were a radical left-wing faction within the Jacobins and whose support came from the *sans-culottes*, Girondin support came from local governments and provincial cities.

The Girondin were also opposed by the Cordeliers, a club founded by Georges Danton. Danton was born into a respectable family in north-eastern France. His father was Jacques Danton and his doting mother was Mary Camus. His childhood was somewhat traumatic because he was attacked by bulls not once but twice, when a baby and then again when he was seven. The resulting disfigurement, along with the scarring of his face from smallpox, contributed to the making of man who was a mixture of resoluteness, vehement passions, and political zeal. He was also capable of committing crimes, fond of pleasure, and a man of lax principles.

Danton founded the Cordeliers in late 1789 or early 1790 because he had worried about abuses of power. It was also under Danton and Marat's leadership that the Cordeliers became a political force. Danton was provocative and witty; the compelling speeches that he presented in a thundering manner to the Cordeliers and Jacobin Clubs were unmissable.

The Cordeliers, Jacobins, and Montagnards all opposed the more moderate Girondins, sometimes called Brissotins because of their prominent speaker, Jacques-Pierre Brissot. The Girondins reached their pinnacle of power and popularity in the spring of 1792. They had supported the war against Austria and had harshly criticized the court, but they had also opposed the momentum of the Revolution. This opposition between the Girondins and the radical elements of the revolution over political and social interests created intense hostility.

The war also gave the king a boost in popularity for a time. However, Marie noted that Marat's paper, *The Friend of the People*, continued to churn out 'calumnious' and inflammatory articles against the king, his family, and the monarchy. Perhaps that was why, on 20 June, a mob broke into the Tuileries Palace and cornered the king, ordering him to acquiesce to their demands.

Around this time, Lafayette, newly promoted to Lieutenant General, was in charge of a French army in the field fighting against Austria and Prussia. Concerned about the violence, he wrote a letter of condemnation to the Assembly against all the radical elements in Paris, which included the Jacobins. At the end of July, he showed up in person at the National Assembly to reproach the Jacobins and other radical elements. But this did little good, and instead resulted in Robespierre declaring him a traitor; Lafayette was compelled to leave Paris quickly while a mob burned him in effigy.

Tensions were further intensified by the sense that the war was turning against the French. In July, the Austrian commander, William Ferdinand, Duke of Brunswick-Wolfenbüttel assembled an invading force of combined Austrian and Prussian armies and quickly captured the French towns of Longwy and Verdun. On the momentum of those victories, he seemed to be rapidly advancing on Paris, which created terror among the population. Marie noted that Brunswick, who sympathized with the French monarchy, had also issued a proclamation threatening to burn down Paris if any harm came to the royal family. This proclamation, known as the Brunswick Manifesto, was intended to keep the king and his family safe and calm things down. However, Marie says it had the opposite effect. She described it as 'dictated in a haughty tone, befitting that of an imperious master to his abject vassals'.[2]

For some time, there had been talk of dethroning the king, but the Assembly had been dragging its feet. Robespierre now became more insistent that the king had to be dethroned to protect France. The belief that Paris would soon be invaded by the Austrian and Prussian Army, the Brunswick Manifesto, and Robespierre's vociferous demands scared the people and they revolted.

On 9 August, Danton and his allies met at City Hall and took possession. They then formed a new Paris Commune and increased the deputies to 288. The following day, on 10 August, the Assembly recognized this new body as the legal government of Paris. That same day, the Paris Commune decided to storm the Tuileries Palace and the National Guard of the insurrectional Paris Commune and revolutionaries, known as *fédérés* who had marched from Marseille and Brittany, quickly breached the palace. Although the king gave orders for his guards to leave, many of them did not receive the message until it was too late. 'They were shot, stabbed, stoned and clubbed to death, stripped and mutilated. Genitals were cut off, stuffed in gaping mouths, fed to the dogs, or along with other body parts, burned on bonfires'.[3]

Details of the attack on the Tuileries were also provided on 13 August to a Scottish newspaper who then published their report on 20 August stating:

> 'To procure arms, the populace broke open the gates of the Arsenal, and several of the buildings near the Tuilleries were set on fire. The mirrors and part of the furniture in the palace, were destroyed; but those who attempted to carry away any thing privately, were punished with instant death. The mattrasses of the beds were torn to pieces, and the Court of the Palace was covered with blocks of wood. Many of the citizens, by way of the triumph, carried the bloody clothes of the Swiss on the point of their lances. ... Towards 8 o'clock the light of the flames, the approach of night, and the sight of the dead bodies, particularly those of the Swiss, exposed quite naked, exhibited a spectacle awful and horrid beyond description.[4]

Marie claimed that the following morning at daybreak she accompanied a woman whose husband was in the National Guard. The woman wanted to search for her husband. Along the way, they saw others and feared that they too were on a similar mission to discover the fate of their loved ones. It was an intensely hot day, filled with complete silence, not even a leaf rustled. When they reached the gardens that had so often been a spot of joy, they were overcome:

> Wherever the eye turned, it fell upon many a mangled corpse, and in some places heaps of the slain were thrown indiscriminately together; the beautiful gravel walks were stained with gore; the statues, although somewhat spotted with blood, were uninjured; for such as the extraordinary respect manifested for works of art ... that when their victims sought refuge by climbing up the statues, the people would not fire at them lest they should damage the beautiful specimens of sculpture; they therefore kept pricking those who clung to them with their pikes; till the unfortunate wretches were forced to descend and were dispatched.[5]

Their search through the mangled corpses turned up nothing and they returned home unnoticed. As to the fate of the royal family, because of the imminent danger, they sought safety from the Assembly moments before the attack occurred. The Assembly suspended the king's authority, and, then, supposedly for their safety, the king, his family, his sister and Marie's former wax-student Madame Élisabeth, the queen's close friend and Superintendent of her Household the Princess de Lamballe, and some servants were taken a short distance away to the dismal Temple, a damp, cheerless medieval temple built by the Knights Templar in the twelfth century.

On 15 August, when Lafayette learned what had happened to the royal family, he assembled his army. He then unsuccessfully attempted to persuade them to march on Paris and save them. Two days later, the Assembly ordered Lafayette to relinquish his command and issued a warrant for his arrest. He escaped over the border on 19 August with seventeen companions, but unfortunately, he was captured by the Austrians near Rochefort, Belgium, and eventually imprisoned in Olmütz. In the meantime, on 10 September, his wife, who had remained behind in Paris, was placed under arrest. When she was released on 22 January 1795, she obtained permission to join Lafayette in captivity, with her two daughters. So, when guards opened Lafayette's cell door on 15 October 1795 and ushered his wife and daughters inside, he was surely speechless. The family then spent the next two years imprisoned together.

While Lafayette was fleeing to safety, preparations to replace the Assembly with the National Convention began. Danton, Robespierre, and the Paris Commune also soon demanded that a Revolutionary Tribunal be created to try political offenders and sentence them. Danton decreed the Tribunal was needed, saying, 'Let us be terrible to prevent the people from becoming so'.[6]

When the Tribunal was established, it consisted of a jury, a prosecutor, and two substitutes. It was also decided that there would be no appeals from any judgement made by this Tribunal, resulting in some rather extraordinary and god-like powers to determine the future fate of individuals.

Several other important decisions and decrees also occurred around this same time. One decree by the Assembly hammered in a final nail for religion. All remaining religious orders were banished from France. That decree was followed by another made on 22 August by the Paris Commune. They decided that citizens would no longer be addressed as Monsieur and Madame but rather *Citoyen* and *Citoyenne*, respectively. The Revolutionary Tribunal also gave a decree on 21 August that issued the first summary judgement ordering the guillotining of Louis Collenot d'Angremont, a royalist defender who had attempted to thwart the attack at the Tuileries on 10 August.

In the ensuing months, Marie would be asked to make the death masks of several royal household members. The first was the Princess de Lamballe.

Her death need not have happened as she had been given every opportunity to avoid her fate. When the king and queen had made their failed attempt to escape, they notified others including the Count of Provence, his family, and the Princess de Lamballe. They all escaped, and the princess ultimately settled in Aix-la-Chappelle, where she remained faithful to the queen and corresponded regularly with her.

Many of the Princess de Lamballe's letters to the queen expressed her wish to reunite with her. The queen welcomed her company, but she also feared what might happen if the princess did return to France. The Queen once wrote to the Princess de Lamballe after she requested that she be allowed to return, 'Do not return – do not throw yourself into the tiger's jaw; the present is too terrible'.[7]

Things changed for the princess in November of 1791 when the Assembly ordered émigrés to return or lose their property and face death. Most émigrés refused to obey, but the Princess de Lamballe was not one of them. She decided to obey, arrived back in France on 4 November 1791, and appeared at court six days later with a little white and red spaniel puppy that she named Thisbée, which signifies faithfulness to death and comes from Ovid's *Metamorphoses*.

In response to the Brunswick Manifesto and the advancing enemy troops, between 2 and 7 September, the September Massacres occurred. These massacres were a series of brutal murders that happened because Parisians feared they would be wiped out by the invaders. Rumours had been swirling for some time that if the Austrian and Prussian forces reached Paris, they would free all the prisoners. Parisians believed that these prisoners, along with non-juring priests and others who opposed the revolution, would attack and kill those supporting the revolution. Moreover, the Brunswick Manifesto had assured revolutionaries the goal was to re-establish the monarchy and mete out terrible punishment to anyone who resisted or harmed the king.

Marie described the situation as 'breathless terror'. She further claimed that Marat was one of the greatest supporters of these brutal attacks and that he suggested to Danton that the prisons be set on fire. Moreover, Marat's support and radical articles caused fear to grip Paris and panic ensued. An attempt was made to raise an army to protect the city as people believed the enemy was practically at their doors.

The people were most worried about those they termed their 'worst foes'. These foes were those accused of supporting the king and his royal cause. In consequence, the first of the attacks occurred against these foes on

2 September, when twenty-four priests were being transferred to the Abbey of Saint-Germain-des-Prés and this was followed by attacks on hundreds more people. At the Place Dauphin, several *'aristocrates'*, including children, were reputedly roasted alive. Another horrific incident involved a Swiss soldier who was forced to dress the hair of a Swiss officer. The soldier was then ordered to take off the officer's head. When he refused, the solider was 'cut to pieces and two women sawed the officer's head from his body'.[8] A mob also found a countess and her two daughters, reputedly stripped them, washed them in oil, and roasted them alive.

The same devilish mob was not content after killing the countess and her two daughters. Reportedly, they also brought six priests to the site. There they ordered the priests to eat the roasted flesh of the earlier victims and threw one of the priests into the fire. Supposedly, the other five priests, embracing one another, then jumped in on their own. By this time, the crowd was said to be bloodthirsty enough they would have removed the priests if they could, just to prolong the priest's suffering.

Between 2 and 7 September, the Revolutionary Tribunal held summary trials and almost 1,400 prisoners were condemned and executed by guillotine. Among those sentenced to die was the Princess de Lamballe. She died on 3 September after refusing to renounce the king and queen. Her death sentence was carried out by a mob and although stories about her death are highly contradictory there are some that are blatantly false. They include accusations that she was gang-raped, her breasts were cut off, and her body hacked into fragments. However, it is true that her head was severed and placed atop a pike, after which a parade ensued with her headless body being dragged behind.

This parading spectacle arrived at Curtius' shop. One rumour mentioned that Marie was then forced to make the Princess de Lamballe's face beautiful by applying makeup, but if true, Marie never mentioned it. However, she *did* mention that she was forced to create a cast of her face. Marie's great-grandson, John Theodore Tussaud, also mentioned the incident in his book:

> 'Perhaps the most horrifying experience undergone by Madame Tussaud during this terrible period was when the mangled head of the greatly beloved Princess de Lamballe was brought to her that a cast might be made. In vain did she protest that she could not endure the ordeal. The brutal murderers compelled her to comply.'[9]

Despite the Princesse de Lamballe's murder being categorized as a traumatic ordeal for Marie, years later she recounted the gruesome details. It was printed in an exhibition catalogue in 1819, where she once again reiterated her part:

> 'The murderers carried the bleeding head to Madame Tussaud, and ordered her to take a model of it which dreadful order more dead than alive she dared not refuse to obey'.[10]

The same day that the princess was murdered, one eye witness to the massacre, French writer Nicolas-Edme Retif de la Bretonne, described in gruesome detail what he saw when he went outside.

> 'I arose, distressed by the horror. The night had not refreshed me at all, rather it had caused my blood to boil ... I go out and listen. I follow groups of people running to see the "disasters" — their word for it. Passing in front of the Conciergerie, I see a killer who I'm told is a sailor from Marseilles. His wrist is swollen from use. I pass by. Dead bodies are piled high in front of the Châtelet. I start to flee, but I follow the people instead. I come to the rue St.-Antoine, at the end of the rue des Ballets, just as a poor wretch came through the gate. He had seen how they killed his predecessor, but instead of stopping in amazement, he took to his heels to escape. A man who was not one of the killers, just one of those unthinking machines who are so common, stopped him with a pike in the stomach. The poor soul was caught by his pursuers and slaughtered. The man with the pike coldly said to us, "Well, I didn't know they wanted to kill him. ..."
>
> 'There had been a pause in the murders. ... I told myself that it was over at last. Finally, I saw a woman appear, as white as a sheet, being helped by a turnkey. They said to her harshly: "Shout 'Vive la nation!'" "No! No!" she said. They made her climb up on a pile of corpses. One of the killers grabbed the turnkey and pushed him away. "Oh!" exclaimed the ill-fated woman, "do not harm him!" They repeated that she must shout "Vive la nation!" With disdain, she refused. Then one of the killers grabbed her, tore away her dress, and ripped open her stomach. She fell, and was finished off by the others.'[11]

Bloodshed and violence was everywhere. Several thousand people were killed, including many aristocrats. After the massacre stopped, one newspaper provided a report on Monday, 10 September:

> 'The streets of Paris, strewed with the carcases of the mangled victims, are become so familiar to the sight, that they are passed by and trod on without any particular notice. The mob think no more of killing a fellow-creature, who is not even an object of suspicion, than wanton boys would of killing a cat or a dog. We have it from a Gentleman who has been but too often an eye witness to the fact. In the massacre last week, every person who had the appearance of a gentleman, whether stranger or not, was run through the body with a pike. He was of course an Aristocrate, and that was a sufficient crime. A ring, a watch chain, a handsome pair of buckles, a new coat, or a good pair of boots in a word, every thing which marked the appearance of a gentleman, and which the mob fancied, was sure to cost the owner his life. EQUALITY was the pistol and PLUNDER the object.'[12]

The September Massacres in Paris resulted in somewhere between 1,200 to 1,400 prisoners being executed. There were also smaller scale executions that occurred in other cities and provinces throughout France. As the Girondins were at their peak in power, it was no wonder the Cordeliers, Jacobins, and Montagnards blamed them for the bloodshed.

Although Parisians may have been fearful of the Duke of Brunswick, his march on Paris ended on 19 September when the French Generals François Kellermann and Charles Dumouriez joined together at Vlamy. Up to this point, the French Revolutionary Army had been woefully unprepared to fight and initially suffered several debacles. They also had retreated with little resistance as most of the soldiers were inexperienced and feared fire.

The same day that the National Convention held their first session was the same day that the Duke of Brunswick and French forces met at Vlamy. The Duke of Brunswick expected the French to retreat and fired within 2,500 yards of the French army. This time, instead of retreating, the French returned fire. Neither side inflicted any serious damage because both armies were at maximum range. However, for the Duke of Brunswick to advance, he knew he would have to cross 'an artillery-killing field,' and he chose to retreat and save his men.

There was also another version of the battle that praised the Frenchman's patriotism. It was claimed that at a critical moment Kellermann cried out, 'Vive la Nation!' The cry then rang repeatedly up and down the French line, thereby startling Prussian troops and shaking the Duke of Brunswick's resolve and his men's determination. Thus, having crushed Prussian confidence and morale, it was alleged the Duke of Brunswick knew his troops were doomed, and so he turned tail and retreated.

During these years, Marie maintained that Curtius continued a friendship with Robespierre and that she saw Robespierre regularly because he was one of the most frequent guests at Curtius' dinner table. In addition, according to her, he was usually seated next to her, and so they conversed regularly. Of these times she wrote:

> 'He was always extremely polite and attentive, never omitting those little acts of courtesy which are expected from a gentleman when sitting at [a] table next to a lady, anticipating her wishes, and taking care that she should never have to ask for anything. ... Robespierre's conversation was generally animated, sensible, and agreeable; but his enunciation was not good; ... There was not anything particularly remarkable in Robespierre's conduct, manners, or appearance, when in society; if noticed at all, it could only be as a pleasant, gentlemanly man, of moderate abilities.'[13]

Over the years, Robespierre had continued to represent the common patriot. It was because of this commitment and his strong principles of honesty that he acquired the nickname of 'Incorruptible'. He had also been steadily stepping closer to the pinnacle of political power even while possessing what people consider to be an enigmatic personality. On one hand, he wept when his pet bird died, but on the other hand, he seemed to have no compunction about imposing a death sentence, and he reportedly sent both friend and foe to the guillotine. A more in-depth description of Robespierre was given by Charles Franklin Warwick, an American author who also served as Philadelphia's mayor from 1895 to 1899. Warwick said of Robespierre:

> 'He was timid, secretive, reticent, and reserved. He had those qualities that reveal themselves in deeds, not in words. He was vain, conceited, and ambitious. He was neither sordid nor avaricious. He could be neither cajoled, bribed, nor driven. He

neither fawned upon his friends nor flattered his enemies. He asked no favors from the mighty. He was absolutely wanting in that magnetism that attracts men, and that open candor that wins friends; and yet he developed, in time, a wonderful power of impressing and influencing men. ... One by one his enemies fell before him, and, at last, he became the dictator of the Revolution.'[14]

Robespierre's step to becoming a dictator began the same month as the September Massacres. That was the month when he was elected the first deputy of Paris in the National Convention. After his election, he and his allies seated themselves in the highest benches located at the back of the hall where they acquired the name the 'Montagnards' and he sat with such men as Marat, Desmoulins, and Danton.

Chapter 9

The End of the Monarchy

Liberté, égalité, fraternité.

Despite the tumult and executions, Curtius' wax exhibitions continued to attract visitors and draw crowds. However, the popularity of the exhibits had less to do with quality and more to do with the patriotic fervour that Curtius himself displayed for the Revolution. Illustrative of this was the fact that he kept abreast of the revolution and as quickly as the revolution brought change, Curtius recorded it by having Marie chop off a wax head and replace it with a new one.

Marie and Curtius also obtained something that most itinerant wax modelers did not possess – a fixed location. Instead of moving from place to place with his show, Marie and Curtius strove to create a permanent exhibition that would draw the public to them. Thus, by swapping out the wax figures regularly, they enabled patrons to constantly enjoy something new and also kept the wax figures accessible and in the public view.

They also distinguished themselves from other wax modelers by creating wax figures from contemporary individuals, which were cast from live subjects. They relied on personal relationships with those whose figures were cast. The wax figures were also enhanced by having real hair and teeth thereby making them look as life-like as possible. Curtius had made a name for himself by sometimes dressing his figures in clothing that was obtained from the actual person and he occasionally used personal knick-knacks. Marie watched and learned from Curtius. She learned about staging a scene and the personal touches and she would ultimately take these fundamentals to a whole new level.

Like Curtius and other good French citizens, the friend of the people, the widely disparaged Duke d'Orléans was also busy adapting to changes wrought by the revolution. One change the Duke embraced was calling himself Citoyen Philippe Égalité. Perhaps he got the idea from Robespierre who was the first to express the motto '*liberté, égalité, fraternité*' (liberty, equality, fraternity) in a speech in December of 1790. The new name was not the only thing that Philippe Égalité adopted. By 1792, like others, he was seen wearing the dress of the *sans-culottes*, which Marie described:

> 'It consisted of a short jacket, pantaloons, and a round hat, with a handkerchief worn sailor-fashion, loose round the neck, with the ends long and hanging down, the shirt collar seen above, … the hair cut short, without powder, a la Titus, and shoes tied with strings. This dress, at that period, was in every respect remarkable, as it consisted of all that was the reverse of what was the fashion of the day; cocked hats being universal, a round hat never till then having been seen; the hair being worn very long, and powered; and buckles being in use for the shoes.'[1]

The king never embraced the *sans-culottes* dress, and it is almost certain that if he had been given a choice he would never have become *citoyen*. However, he had no choice. The day after the Duke of Brunswick retreated, the Assembly abolished the monarchy. They also stripped Louis of all titles and honours, and from that date forward he was an ordinary citizen called Citoyen Louis Capet.

The next event proved even worse for the king. It became known as the *armoire de fer* (iron chest) incident. Marie mentions this discovery in her *Memoirs*. It occurred at the Tuileries Palace in late November when an iron chest holding secret documents was discovered hidden behind wood panelling in Louis's apartment. It was revealed because rewards were offered to patriots for any valuable information about the king or queen.

François Gamain had been a locksmith at Versailles, and after the royal family moved to the Tuileries, Gamain had been instructed to install an iron chest in the king's bedchamber behind the wainscoting. Gamin claimed that no one else knew about it, and when he learned a reward could be obtained for information, he approached the Girondin Minister of the Interior, a man known as Citoyen Roland (Jean-Marie Roland, de la Platière). Interestingly, a slipshod search of the royal family's apartments had been previously conducted, but nothing was discovered. This time, Gamain led Roland to the exact spot where the chest was hidden:

> 'Gaiman released the secret spring, removed some bricks, and revealed the iron door. Trembling with excitement, Roland seized the papers and kept them for several days without anyone's knowledge'.[2]

Roland was delighted with the discovery because inside were documents and correspondence involving the king's ministers. When Jacobins learned of the discovery, they were understandably livid and accused Roland of both destroying and planting evidence. Newspapers supported the Jacobins and reported on suspicious circumstances surrounding Roland's discovery as he had failed to inform anyone else about the documents for several days.

The discovery also implicated Mirabeau. It showed that he had been supporting and aiding the king and that he hoped he would escape. In fact, the revelations about Mirabeau were so damaging, his body was removed from the Pantheon one dark night and reburied anonymously without ceremony in the Clamart graveyard where executed criminals were laid to rest.

Marie referred harshly to the king's deception, noted his lies, and added that it just added to his other 'derelictions of duty'. The discovery showed everyone the extent of his duplicity and that he had been conspiring with enemies of the revolution. It was also obvious that the king disliked the idea of a constitutional monarchy and that he believed in the Divine Right of Kings. Thus, the *armoire de fer* incident ultimately sealed his fate.

On 11 December, he was brought before the National Convention and accused of high treason and crimes against the state. The trial dragged on until the National Convention declared him guilty of conspiracy against public liberty. On 19 January, in a vote that lasted twenty-one hours, his fate was determined. It was immediate execution. Beside the 'la mort' votes given by Robespierre, Danton, Desmoulins, David, and Marat, there was also the king's own cousin, Philippe Égalité the former Duke d'Orléans, who voted for his death.

The execution was scheduled two days later. On a drizzly 21 January 1793, he mounted the scaffold with dignity as trumpets blared and drums beat. He spoke a few words: 'I die innocent; I pardon my enemies; I only sanctioned upon compulsion the Civil Constitution of the Clergy ...'[3] and he would have said more, but the remainder of his words were drowned out by beating drums. The guillotine fell at 10:15am. 'Thus, perished Louis XVI. King of France, aged thirty-nine years, five months, and three days, having reigned eighteen years'.[4]

After the execution, despite a drizzling rain, mobs gleefully cheered. They also likely danced the carmagnole round the guillotine. As these celebrations ensued, the king's corpse and severed head were transported to the cemetery of the Madeleine on rue Anjou Saint-Honore. Before his body was interred in Ditch No. 4, Curtius was ordered to obtain his death mask. At the time, Curtius was busy with other duties, so it was Marie who obtained the mould. She never revealed how the event came about, only that the mould occurred within five hours of his death. It would have been an easy task for her. All that she needed to accomplish it was a few necessities that she could have easily carried in a drawstring bag. When a person was alive, quills would have been inserted into the nostrils to help the person breath, but a dead person needed no such precaution. Therefore, the first action would have been to oil the King's face to allow for the mould to be easily removed. A thick coating of plaster would have then been applied and smoothed over his face.

When the mould hardened and was removed, a reproduction could be made from the mask, either in plaster or wax. The mould and any replicas made from it would accurately represent the modelled person's skin, along with any personal characteristics, such as the person's pores, scars, or wrinkles. Moreover, although there were no strict rules involving wax modelling, one nineteenth-century person talked about how a mould was created from wax rather than plaster.

> 'A band of cloth is placed around the head of the person whose face is to be copied. This band encircles the head about where the ears are, and leaves exposed all the chin and forehead – in fact, the entire face … Soft wax is now poured over the face, and is kept by the band from running too far. It quickly hardens, and is easily removed. The eyebrows, eyelashes, moustache, and beard have been previously greased or covered with soap and water to prevent the wax from adhering to the hairs. In spite of this precaution, however, some few of the hairs will adhere to the wax mould, and are pulled out of the skin when the wax is removed. This mould is now an exact copy of the face, from which it has been taken, but, of course, it is the opposite of a human face, for where the protuberances of the latter are, they are represented in the mould by corresponding indentations. Among sculptors the result of this process is known as a "flying mould".'[5]

Another interesting fact is that there was a difference between a cast removed from a plaster mould versus a wax mould. The plaster mould had to be moistened with water and was achieved by allowing the mould to stand in a dish of water so that it would absorb a sufficient amount to enable the cast's removal. Oil was sometimes used too, but not when the item was delicate, because oil tended to dissolve the wax surface of the cast.

Madame Tussaud at age 42.

Madame Élisabeth, Louis XVI's
younger sister.

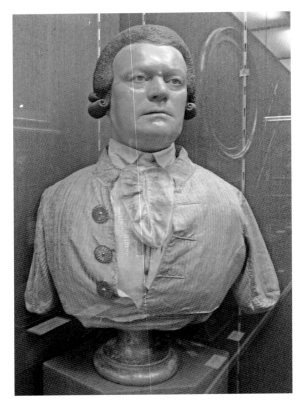

Left: Wax bust of Dr. Philippe Mathé Curtius by Madame Tussaud.

Below: Princess de Lamballe by Louis-Édouard Rioult (left) and Louis Philippe d'Orléans with a Freemasonry insignia of the governing body of French freemasonry (right).

Honoré Gabriel Riqueti, Count of Mirabeau in 1789 by Joseph Boze.

Wax figure of Voltaire from 2018 at Madame Tussauds. © C.L. Weber.

Maximilien de Robespierre in 1790 by unknown artist.

Joseph-François Foulon of Doué and Foulon's son-in-law Louis-Jean Bertier of Sauvigny.

Picture of Dr. Philippe Mathé
Curtius created by Madame
Tussaud. © C.L. Weber.

Conspirateur
contre l'État

T. M. FAVRAS.

Exécuté le 19. Fev.r 1790. Place de Grève, accusé d'avoir
projetté l'enlèvement du Roi et de sa Famille.

Thomas de Mahy, Marquis de
Favras. Author's collection.

Joseph-Ignace Guillotin by unknown artist.

Georges Danton speaking to the National Convention.

Right: Self portrait of Jacques-Louis David in 1794.

Below: Jean-Marie Roland and Madame Roland.

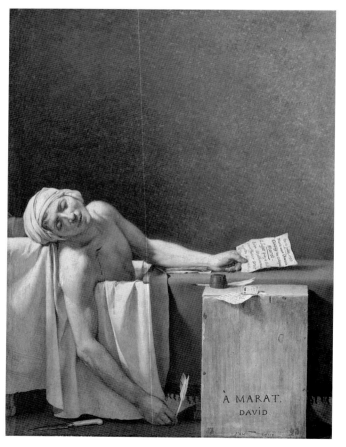

Above: Jean-Paul
Marat and
Charlotte Corday.

Left: "The Death
of Marat" by
artist Jacques-
Louis David
in 1793.

Josephine de Beauharnais and Napoleon Bonaparte.

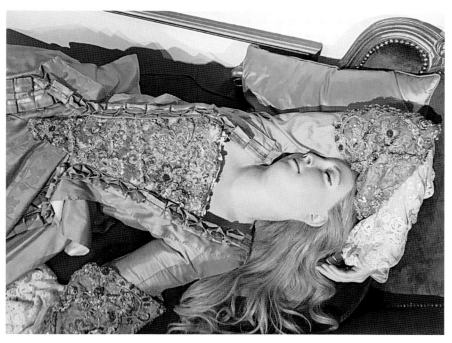

Madame du Barry, the Sleeping Beauty. © C.L. Weber.

Jean-Lambert Tallien.
Author's collection.

Antoine-Quentin
Fouquier-Tinville.
Author's collection.

Wax figure of Madame Tussaud in her austere dress and quaint bonnet. © C.L. Weber.

Colonel Edward Marcus Despard.

As seen in 2018 at Madame Tussauds, a wax figure of Madame Tussaud at work. © C.L. Weber.

Wax figures of Marie Antoinette and Louis XVI as shown in 2018 at Madame Tussauds. © C.L. Weber.

Above: 1849 caricature of the "Chamber of Horrors" by "Punch." Author's collection.

Right: Maria Malibran.

William Corder and Maria Marten. Author's collection.

William Burke (left) and William Hare (right).

Wax figure of Queen Victoria
as seen today at Madame
Tussauds. © C.L. Weber.

Death mask of Madame
Tussaud © C.L. Weber.

Plaque at St. Mary's Catholic Church in honor of Madame Tussaud. © C.L. Weber.

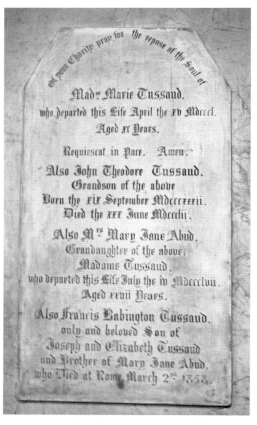

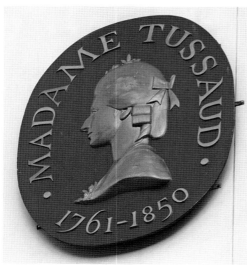

Logo in 2018 as seen on Madame Tussauds building on Baker's Street in London. © C.L. Weber.

After the cast's removal was accomplished the painting began. Waxes of proper colours were added, and hair-pencils or other tools were used to colour the wax. Powder colours moistened with turpentine and tempered with wax might also be used to achieve proper colouring. Sometimes, after the colouring, the wax piece was then covered with mastic varnish to help preserve it.

While Marie was busy with Curtius' waxworks, in April of 1793, the National Convention established the Committee of Public Safety. The committee was tasked with protecting the republic against both foreign and internal enemies and overseeing the executive government. It was also composed of nine members including Danton, who dominated the committee.

In the meantime, although factional disputes caused problems, the *sans-culottes* were also upset about increased grain prices, inflation, and military defeats, and they began to question the Girondins' political strategies. The Girondins' unpopularity increased further when they hesitated to adopt defensive measures to protect France and failed to fulfil the economic demands of Parisian workers.

On 2 June 1793, 80,000 armed insurgents surrounded the National Convention's meeting hall. The insurgents demanded the immediate arrest of the Girondins, and Convention members yielded to their demands. Twenty-nine Girondins were arrested, but many escaped to the provinces, fearing the worst. Roland, the man involved in the *armoire de fer incident*, was also denounced as a traitor. Fearing he would be arrested at any moment, he fled Paris and was sentenced to death in absentia. In the meantime, as Roland found safety with some spinster sisters in Rouen, his wife was arrested in Paris.

In July, with the defeat of the Girondins, the Committee of Public Safety was restructured. The Revolution also entered a more radical phase with the new committee now consisting of twelve members with only one member being original. Among the new members was Robespierre. Although the committee made decisions in common, three members soon formed a Triumvirate. They were Robespierre, Georges Auguste Couthon, and Louis de Saint-Just.

The new committee, spearheaded by Robespierre, was much more powerful and soon became a *de facto* dictatorship. It meted out harsh punishments to anyone deemed to be an enemy of the Revolution. Through the committee, a police force was established and directed by them. They were also responsible for maintaining public order, appointing judges and juries, supervising state bureaucracies, appointing generals, and provisioning the army and the people. Additionally, the committee was given the important responsibility of interpreting and applying laws decreed by the National Convention.

As this was occurring, Madame Roland was convicted of harbouring royalist sympathies and was executed on 8 November 1793. On the platform, when the executioner let the guillotine blade drop and cut off her head, it was business as usual. When her head fell, an official checked her name off his list. Sometimes the severed head went with the body to the cemetery, and other times the head went to Curtius or Marie to create a death mask. Madame Roland's head must have escaped notice because it did not become a wax one. However, some relics belonging to Madame Roland did eventually end up in Curtius' museum and Marie described her physical features in her *Memoirs*. Madame Roland's head was buried with her body at the cemetery pit at a convent of Benedictines situated in the rue de la Madeleine called Ville l'Evêque.

When Roland learned of his wife's death, he was distraught. On 14 November, he bid the spinster sisters farewell and left Rouen. The following morning, he was found leaning comfortably against a tree. His discoverer at first thought he was asleep but then noticed he had committed suicide with a small cane-sword through his heart, and he had these words pinned to his chest:

> 'Whoever thou art that findest me lying here, respect my remains. They are those of a man who devoted his life to being useful, and who has died as he lived, virtuous and honest … Not fear, but indignation, made me quit my retreat on learning that my wife had been murdered. I did not choose to remain longer in a land polluted with crimes.'[6]

According to Marie, in 1793, Charlotte Corday was busy reading the Caen papers and sympathizing with the Girondins there. Corday was sceptical about the turn the revolution had taken, and she had heard some of the Girondins speak while living in Caen and had a good impression of them. She also identified with their political principles and values. Moreover, she believed the Girondins would save France.

At the time, the ideological leader of the Montagnards was Marat and his journalistic pieces were filled with uncompromising stances and harsh tones. Corday believed Louis XVI should never have been executed, and as the Revolution became more radicalized, Charlotte became more convinced that Marat needed to be eliminated. She primarily blamed him for the radical turn in the revolution and believed that his death was the only way that France could be saved.

Charles Jean Marie Barbaroux also inspired Corday. Barbaroux was a unique individual who spoke of himself in the third person. He had been elected to the National Convention in 1791 and joined the Jacobin Club. From the first day of the Convention session, he despised Robespierre and accused him of trying to establish a dictatorship. Barbaroux also opposed Marat's radical values and fought against the Montagnards. After the fall of the Girondins, he found refuge in Caen. He then organized a Girondist rebellion by calling meetings to recruit soldiers to march on Paris. Corday and her friends regularly attended these fiery meetings.

Corday also garnered the attention of a young man named Monsieur de Franquelin, who perhaps to impress the fair Corday, armed himself and enlisted in the battalion of Caen. From a balcony, she watched as his battalion passed by, and she was so impressed that it confirmed her resolve to do whatever it took to support the Girondins. That is supposedly the point when she finally decided that she needed to do something.

Corday said her farewells to her family by falsely telling them she was going to England to escape the horror occurring in France. Then she set out for Paris arriving there on 11 July. Her plan to support the Girondins was to assassinate Marat publicly. The assassination was to happen either in front of the National Convention or perhaps at the Bastille Day parade on 14 July. Unfortunately for Corday, Marat was stuck at home conducting business because he was suffering from a chronic blistering of the skin. One contemporary dermatological journal article described his condition as 'incapacitating, itching, and burning ... with open sores ... [that] began in the anogenital area, later spreading over his whole body'.[7] The authors of the article also catalogued Marat's disease as a proliferative histiocytic disorder.

The day after her arrival in Paris, Corday went out and bought a stout six-inch kitchen knife with a dark wooden handle and silver ferrule which she hid in her dress. She realized that the only way she would see Marat was if she went to his home, and, so, one day prior to the fourth anniversary of the Bastille falling, on 13 July 1793, Corday climbed into a carriage. She arrived at Marat's home around 11:00am.

Corday's attempt to see Marat failed and she was turned away. She tried again later that same evening and arrived around 7pm. This time Marat's wife, Simonne, was suspicious of Corday and refused her entry. Corday became argumentative, and Marat overheard the argument. He remembered receiving a pleading letter from a woman earlier in the day, and so he had Corday ushered into, of all places, the room where he was taking a warm sulphur salted bath.

The room was humid, small, and dimly lit. Marat's shoe-shaped bath dominated the scene. He was sitting in his watery throne in the centre of the room. Across the top of the bath was a board that served as a makeshift desk, and next to the tub stood a small table that held his inkwell and medicine glass.

A sallow and sickly Marat peered out from the bath. Clothed in a squalid sleeveless gown, his head was wrapped in a vinegar-saturated kerchief to control the itching. He was busy at work. His next book was soon to be published and he was performing his final edits with his quill, although Corday probably imagined that he was creating proscription lists or planning new bloodshed.

Corday approached. She told Marat that she was there with important news about a group of dissidents. These dissidents, she claimed, were planning to march on Paris to deliver it from the anarchists. Marat was intrigued and immediately demanded the names of those involved. As she provided each name, he wrote it down declaring coldly after each one, 'For the scaffold'. Then, as if having satisfied himself with a great feast, he supposedly concluded their meeting by stating that all the dissidents would be guillotined in a few days.

His words, his callousness, his satisfaction, was too much for Corday. She pulled the kitchen knife from its hiding place and sprang forward with disgust. Then with all the strength that she could muster, she plunged the knife with both hands into Marat's right side.

Marat let out an anguished cry and fell backwards in the bath. Her attack was on target. The doctor's autopsy later reported that the knife had penetrated beneath Marat's collarbone so deeply that the doctor's index finger could easily penetrate through the lung and that the 'carotids had been opened'.[8]

Marat's cry brought immediate help. A servant, a messenger, and Simonne rushed into the room. They tried to staunch the bleeding, but blood was gushing from the wound. A dentist living above heard the commotion and rushed downstairs. As he helped carry the mortally wounded Marat to his bed, Corday was secured to await the arrival of the police, and that is where Marie found her when she arrived having been ordered to the gruesome scene to create an on-site death mask of Marat.

Years later, Marie wrote in her *Memoirs* that she visited Corday in prison and conversed freely with her. Marie noted that Corday was engaging and that she was a tall young woman, with noble features, fine manners, and extreme grace. Another more objective physical description of Corday described her as 'twenty-four years old, height five feet one inch (*cinq pieds un pouce*), hair a brown chestnut (*châtains*), eyes grey, forehead high, nose long, mouth medium, chin round, cleft (*fourchu*), face oval'.[9]

In her *Memoirs*, Marie also recalled a time when Marat got into trouble and was forced to go into hiding. She said that he arrived at Curtius' house with nothing more than a few necessities. When he left a week later, he told her she was a good child and thanked Curtius for the asylum. Marie claimed she did not see him again until she was summoned to create the death mask of his still warm head.

Marat's death made him an immediate martyr for the Jacobins. He was glorified in death and his death became the greatest piece of propaganda promoted during the Reign of Terror. Jacques-Louis David was asked to paint Marat's death scene days after the event. It became one of his most famous masterpieces and is likely based on a display at Curtius' salon as the figure David painted looks more like wax than a corpse.

Called *La Mort de Marat*, this idealistic painting immortalized Marat but contained numerous inaccuracies. One inaccuracy is that Marat's skin is shown as being unblemished instead of scabbed and rotting. The knife that remained stuck in Marat's chest, David shows lying on the floor near the bath. Moreover, the shoe shaped bath was altered, Marat was not nude, and he did not die holding Corday's letter.

Marat's funeral was also propaganda for the Jacobins. All but his face and wounded breast were embalmed. Moreover, prior to the burial, on 16 July, he was displayed for all to see at the Church of the Grey Friars. One Parisian citizen provided a description:

> 'On the right was the bath in which he received the fatal blow, on the left his shirt all stained with blood. The body, lying on a bed of state ... was uncovered as far as the waist, in order that the wound might be fully exposed; it had a greenish hue, like the corpse of a drowned man.'
>
> 'The head was crowned with a laurel wreath. By the side of the bed stood two men constantly besprinkling the body, and the sheet ... with aromatic vinegar, whilst throughout the church perfumes were continually kept burning. In spite of these precautions, the odour was insupportable, and Marat's devotees themselves were obliged to make their visits as short as possible.'[10]

In the meantime, as Marat was being glorified, Corday went on trial. Newspapers reported that she appeared calm and behaved with 'firmness and decorum'. She wore a white dress to symbolize the purity of her motives, and when one artist attempted to draw her portrait, 'she changed her situation to accommodate him, and requested a copy of the drawing might be sent to her family'.[11]

Despite her cooperativeness, she was ultimately convicted, and in preparation for her execution, her hair was cut off and she was dressed in a scarlet gown that some say caused a 'strange radiance' to spring from the condemned woman. Her hands were tied, and she was led to the tumbril where a sudden summer thunderstorm drowned out the yells and howling that arose from the crowd. It took the tumbril two hours to reach the execution spot. By that time, her scarlet gown was soaked and clinging to her. She left the tumbril without assistance, passed through the crowd, and mounted the steps.

As the executioner busied himself with preparations, his assistant tore away Corday's fichu to reveal her neck. She then turned to address the crowd, but just as Louis' voice had been drowned out by the beating of drums, so too was hers. It was then that the executioner indicated the spot where she was to lay her head and a serene Corday complied. The guillotine fell. Her head was severed. A man named Legros (who may have been assistant to Sanson as he used as many as six assistants at a beheading) forced his way up the scaffold and immediately picked up her severed head, held it aloft for the crowd, and then slapped her face several times with his open hand. 'A sudden blush was then observed to overspread her skin'.[12] This cowardly act against a woman was disapproved of by the crowd, and Legros was later sentenced to three months in prison. However, Corday's blush created much controversy.

People soon inquired about the blush. They asked of the famous Dr Guillotin, 'Do you know that it is not at all certain when a head is severed from the body by the guillotine that the feelings, personality and ego are instantaneously abolished?'[13] Although he could not answer that question, others began to investigate whether a severed head might be alive or still have feelings.

After her execution, Corday's body was immediately autopsied. Jacobin leaders could not believe that she had devised such a plot on her own and insisted that a man must somehow be involved in the conspiracy with her. They also thought that she could not be a virgin. Thus, they were sorely disappointed and extremely surprised to learn that she was indeed still *virgo intacta*.

The body was conveyed to the cemetery of the Madeleine on rue Anjou Saint-Honore in Paris, where Marie dutifully obtained a mask from the dead woman. Marie also mentioned that Corday met her death as stoically and bravely as Madame Roland, and like Madame Roland, Corday left behind a 'reputation for courage'. Historians generally agree Corday was buried in Ditch No. 5. Ditch No. 4 held the body of the king, and Ditch No. 6 would be readied shortly for Marie Antoinette and Philippe Égalité.

Marie Antoinette soon followed the fate of her husband and Corday. She was accused of a variety of wrong doings in mid-October of 1793, and opinions remained strong that she had also violated her marriage bed and that she was a sexual deviant, something the radical press had long been fostering. It also came as no surprise when she was declared guilty of treason.

The Queen's hair was hacked off and she was dressed in a white waistcoat that left her neck and shoulders bare. She was transported from her cell in a tumbril to the same spot where her husband had met his fate. Marie did not witness the disgraced queen's execution, but she did report seeing the tumbril and remembered hearing the jeering crowds. She left no record of the emotions that she might have felt as the tumbril passed.

The day of the queen's execution was slightly misty. Along the route to the scaffold, all of Paris was there. Streets were lined two rows deep with many clapping, jeering, and hooting citizens; some spat on her, and some in the crowd cried out *autrichienne* (Austrian bitch) or hurled similar epithets. During this nearly two-hour journey to the scaffold, the queen reportedly remained composed.

She was just as composed when she reached the scaffold, springing from the cart and striding forward, perhaps eager to greet death. As she walked to the scaffold she accidentally stepped on the executioner's foot, and her last words were, 'Pardon me sir, I did not mean it'.[14]

A few weeks later, Philippe Égalité, who had been arrested on 7 April, met a similar fate. One historian wrote about Philippe Égalité's reaction learning that his arrest was imminent. At the time, he was dining with a friend:

'As the fish course was being served Merlin de Douai rushed in and told the host that the Convention were about to destroy him. Philippe appeared shocked, and putting his hand to his head demanded to know what he had done to deserve this. [His guest] who was carefully squeezing the juice of a lemon over his sole, shook his head sadly and said, "Frightful business, Monseigneur, but what do you expect? They have taken everything they wanted from you and now that you are no more use to them they will do with you what I am about to do with this lemon," and with that he threw it into the fireplace … and without another word resumed his meal.'[15]

Philippe Égalité was declared guilty on 6 November. He told his judges that he wanted the sentence carried out quickly. He did not have to wait long as his execution was accomplished within hours. Marie wrote that his last meal contained the most 'delicious luxuries,' and another historian noted:

'He dined quietly in his cell on eight oysters and lamb cutlets accompanied by a bottle of Bordeaux. At three o'clock in the afternoon one of the judges entered and asked if he had anything more to say to the court; he smiled but said nothing. At five o'clock, with his hair carefully powdered in the manner of the old regime and wearing a green frock coat carefully buttoned, he walked confidently from the prison and climbed into the tumbril.'[16]

Three men were executed before Philippe Égalité. He watched them die without emotion. When his turn came, he handed his coat to his valet and unwaveringly stepped forward. Spectators claimed that he went to his death with exemplary courage.

Chapter 10

The Beginning of Terror

'Terror is nothing more than speedy, severe and
inflexible justice.'

Robespierre

Marie's world was subjected to an even bloodier turn when, on 5 February
1794, her regular house guest Robespierre lectured the Convention on
terror and the necessity for it. He believed that terror had a moral purpose
and wanted to create a 'republic of virtue'. He concluded that to establish
such a republic, high morals (virtue) were required and that terror was
mandatory to eliminate any opponents. He demonstrated this by once
declaring:

> 'If the mainspring of popular government in peacetime
> is virtue, the mainspring of popular government during a
> revolution is both virtue and terror; virtue, without which terror
> is baneful; terror, without which virtue is powerless. Terror is
> nothing more than speedy, severe and inflexible justice; it is
> thus an emanation of virtue; it is less a principle in itself, than
> a consequence of the general principle of democracy, applied
> to the most pressing needs of the patrie.'[1]

Robespierre's words gave life to the idea that there could be a moral reason
for violence. His words also provided a lofty picture of what he imagined
society could achieve and what society could be after the Revolution:

> 'The peaceful enjoyment of liberty and equality; the reign of
> that eternal justice whose laws are written, not on marble or
> stone, but in the hearts of all men, even in that of the slave who
> forgets them and of the tyrant who denies them.'[2]

To reach this lofty goal, France would have to go through the terror, and in a sense, the terror had begun even before Robespierre's speech. Jacobin Bertrand Barère de Vieuzac, who was one of the most prominent members of the National Convention, proclaimed on 5 September 1793, 'Let us make terror the order of the day!'[3] Rather than have the people initiate another September Massacre, Vieuzac believed the government should control the violence.

September 1793 was also the same month that the Committee of Public Safety decreed the 'Law of Suspects' (*'loi des suspects'*). The decree abolished individual freedom, eliminated redress, and made it possible to arrest, convict, and punish anyone based on suspicion of 'bad citizenship'. Before long, neighbours were turning in neighbours, denouncing them for economic reasons, or just making accusations to get even. For many Frenchmen, this was the beginning of the 'Reign of Terror'. The result of the decree was that France's prisons were soon overflowing. To alleviate the overcrowding, people were placed under house arrest.

After the 'Law of Suspects' went into effect, over a four-month period, between November 1793 and February 1794, a series of mass executions also occurred in Nantes. According to Marie, the usual process for dispatching criminals there was determined to be 'far too slow,' and so other quicker strategies were designed to eliminate anyone accused of being against the revolution or anyone thought to be a royalist sympathizer.

Overseeing the operation in Nantes was Jean-Baptiste Carrier, whom Marie described as tall, good-looking with gentlemanly appearance and manners. Carrier had helped set up the Revolutionary Tribunal and had originally been sent to Nantes to suppress a revolt by anti-revolutionaries. Later, in his capacity as the people's representative (*représentant-en-mission*), Carrier set up what was called the 'Legion of Marat'. It was composed of soldiers whose mission was to watch the inhabitants of Nantes and give mandates of arrest against persons they suspected of being disloyal to the revolution. Moreover, the soldiers could search any suspect's house and request doors be broken down if inhabitants did not willingly open them.

In addition to the Legion of Marat, Carrier was responsible for setting up a tribunal and conducting 'fair' trials for the accused. Once prisoners were found guilty, the Legion of Marat was responsible to quickly dispose of the guilty party, but because so many prisoners were found guilty, Carrier invented a variety of disposal methods. Among the disposal methods was a firing squad where the condemned were lined up and shot one by one. However, he also invented more torturous ways to execute people.

One of Carrier's most unpleasant and sadistic execution methods was mass drownings (*noyades*). Carrier and his minions nicknamed these mass drownings 'immersions', 'bathing parties', or 'national baptisms'. Moreover, the first of the mass drownings involved Catholic priests, called the 'refractory clergy'. They had been arrested and held at Saint-Clément Convent before being transferred to Nantes. On the evening of 16 November 1793, a special customized barge was taken to the docks and ninety condemned priests were ordered to be drowned at once. The barges were railed off so that they could not jump overboard. When the barge was 'at a certain distance, valves in the sides of the vessel were opened, and ... [the barge] sunk,'[4] thereby drowning the priests en masse.

If the drownings were not dramatic enough, 'boats with guards followed in the wake of the ship, and whenever a priest appeared struggling with the waves, he became a target for ball practice'.[5] Despite the guard's best efforts to ensure all the priests were killed, three escaped. They were rescued by sailors, but the sailors were forced to return the priests to Carrier, who took them the following night with more priests and drowned them. Afterwards, a great feast was held on the same barge used to drown the priests, and someone reported that Carrier celebrated by toasting to the drowned victims.

It was not just priests that Carrier executed in Nantes: old men, pregnant women, and young children were killed. No one was safe as every age, every sex, and every class of people were executed without distinction. Moreover, it was said of Carrier that he did his work so well, fish became unwholesome feeding upon the bodies and 'the Loire was poisoned by corpses, [to the point] that its use for drinking and cooking was prohibited'.[6]

Marie also mentioned that sometimes Carrier's drownings had a sexual component. For instance, at first, people were drowned in their clothes until Carrier announced something new called 'Republican marriages'. Republican marriages were achieved in the following way:

> '[It involved] stripping boys and girls, then lashing them together face to face, and ... turning them round in a most ingenious sort of waltz to national music, until they reached the river or field of execution, where they were either cast into the Loire, or massacred by a detachment of the *armée Revolutionnaire.*'[7]

A gunner named Wailly was aboard a ship named *La Samaritain* and he and his friends witnessed some of the drownings at Nantes. Wailly left a first-person account. He claimed he witnessed 'horrible carnage' and heard the most 'horrible cries'. He also noted that after the people perished, their executioners stripped them of their belongings – clothes, jewellery, and their paper money (*assignat*) – and sold everything to the highest bidder.

Accounts of the number of victims that died at Nantes varies. However, according to French journalist and historian, Louis-Marie Prudhomme, victims by Carrier amounted to 32,000. He provided a partial breakdown, which is shown in the table below, and lists how 10,244 victims were executed:

	Method of Execution	Number	Method of Execution	Number	Total by Group
Children	Shot	500	Drowned	1,500	2,000
Women	Shot	264	Drowned	500	764
Priests	Shot	300	Drowned	460	760
Nobles			Drowned	1,400	1,400
Artisans			Drowned	5,300	5,300
Total		**1,064**		**9,160**	**10,224**

Residents of Nantes watched as their friends, neighbours, and relatives were caught up in Carrier's net. It took some time, but residents of Nantes finally began to turn against Carrier, which was about the same time that he was recalled to Paris. However, it still took several more months before a critical look at Carrier's conduct was ordered.

Besides affecting the citizens of Nantes, the Law of Suspects decree also affected the members of the National Convention, who were the supporters of the terror. Perhaps, they had not expected it to infiltrate and increase the fear and paranoia of their own members in the Convention, but that is exactly what happened. The fear resulted in Danton, Desmoulins, and their supporters called Dantonists, being arrested on the night of 29-30 March 1794. It all began months earlier, when Danton collaborated with Desmoulins in hopes that they could shift the direction of the revolution and stabilize the government. They had done this through *The Old Cordelier* (*Le Vieux Cordelier*), a newspaper that opposed extremism, challenged the terror, and defied Robespierre. Robespierre and his supporters saw this as an affront to the revolution, and, thus, the revolutionary allegiance of Danton and the Dantonists was called into question.

Danton had also become wealthy during the French Revolution. His wealth looked suspicious, his financial success was questioned, and he was accused of shady dealings. Danton's defence was that he acquired his wealth from his salaried position, but accusers alleged he acquired it from corruption. One twenty-first century historian wrote:

> 'It is now generally accepted that Danton was an informer for the royal court in return for payments from the funds of the Civil Lists. It is nevertheless difficult to prove how such payments influenced his conduct, since his actions demonstrate that his devotion to the nation and the revolutionary cause was beyond doubt.'[8]

When Danton was condemned, it was Louis Antoine Léon de Saint-Just who stood before the National Convention. Saint-Just was ambitious but only to serve the poor and the peasants. He also wanted to achieve a new society, and after being elected to the National Convention in 1792, he became one of the most radical of the Montagnards. Saint-Just also quickly became a major leader in the National Convention. He developed a close friendship with Robespierre and became a zealous supporter of terror. Like Robespierre, he had wanted Louis XVI executed and, had, in fact, argued in his first speech that he should be executed without a trial. Saint-Just then spearheaded the movement to make sure it happened.

As Saint-Just stood before the Convention, he charged Danton, Desmoulins, and the other Dantonists with conspiring to restore the monarchy and lacking patriotism. He proclaimed:

> 'The revolution ... depends upon the people, not on the renown of particular men. In the sacred love of our country, there is something terrible which sacrifices even our affections. Your committees have charged me to demand justice on men ... whose object was to confound the republican government.'[9]

Political in nature as opposed to criminal, the trial was set for Danton, Desmoulins, and the Dantonists supporters. They were brought before the Revolutionary Tribunal on 2 April and their trial lasted four days. Great precautions were taken to assure that they would all be convicted. Proof rested largely on the accusations made by Robespierre as there were no witnesses called to support any of the charges.

Danton had a somewhat formidable appearance, but it was not just because of his facial disfigurement. He was gigantic in height, stout and muscular in build. He also had an 'immense' head. He was generally seen with a frown on his face and thundered when he spoke. During the trial Danton's loud and resounding voice roared through the hall and enabled the crowd that stretched out along the quays and across the Pont Neuf, to hear him. Marie wrote of the trial:

> 'Danton lost not his courage nor his gaiety; and … even beguiled the hours by rolling up little bits of paper and throwing them at the judges. But when the time came for his defence, he vociferated his anathema against his accusers and the court in so abusive a strain, that the president rang his bell as the signal for silence; but its puny tinkling was drowned in the stentorian roar of Danton, who heeded neither the president nor his bell, but hurled upon his judges every epithet that could express the sovereign contempt in which he held them. He bid them to take his life, if it was that they craved, declaring he was tired of it, and the sooner he was rid of it the better. He, however, recapitulated some portions of his life, and the services he had rendered the public, whilst the people displayed much sympathy for him, which somewhat intimidated the tribunal. Fearing a movement of the popular in favour of Danton, they brought the affair to a close as soon as possible.'[10]

Robespierre probably had no doubt that Danton would be convicted. Sentence was passed at 2pm. Danton, Desmoulins, and thirteen others were found guilty. They were taken from the Conciergerie to the Place de la Revolution in three tumbrils on 5 April 1794, Danton and Desmoulins riding in the first one. They were executed at 5pm. Desmoulins was guillotined third and Danton was last. Newspapers reported that Danton showed the 'utmost contempt' for death.

As the Convention had compelled Curtius and Marie to make death masks, a contemporary eyewitness places Curtius at the graveside of Madame Emilie de Sainte Amaranthe shortly after Danton's execution. She was executed on 17 June 1794 and the eyewitness stated that before Curtius pressed her head into wax, 'he made up the face with a posthumous smile, rendered her beautiful and charming'.[11]

Soon after Curtius made this death mask, Robespierre sent him with the army to the Rhine because he could speak German. He had been absent before in a similar capacity, and during such absences, Marie was left in charge of the waxworks. However, this time his absence resulted in a terrible fright for the household.

Midnight was the common time for dreaded visits and arrests to occur and this came to the Curtius household sometime before the end of the Terror on 9 Thermidor (27 July) when Marie, her mother, and her aunt were arrested. Marie later blamed a jealous neighbour for encouraging their arrests and condemning them as royalists. The neighbour's name was Jacques Dutroy, and he held two jobs. One job was working as a clown or *grimaçier*, meaning he grimaced and pulled funny faces for audiences. His other job was assisting the executioner Sanson, a position that makes it likely Dutroy was indeed the informer.

Marie maintains that Dutroy purposely informed authorities while Curtius was absent because he knew Curtius would be unable to intervene. It must have been a frightening experience for Marie and her relatives to be arrested, and they must have feared they would face the guillotine. Marie stated that they 'were carried off in the middle of the night by the gens d'armes and placed in a fiacre [hackney coach]'.[12]

Marie was first imprisoned at La Force, where the Princess de Lamballe had been held, and then transferred to a former Carmelite monastery called Carmes, where Marie met Josephine, Napoleon Bonaparte's future wife. At the time, Josephine was the wife of Alexandre de Beauharnais, whom she had met through her aunt. Her aunt was the mistress of Alexandre's father, François. François became ill and wanted to ensure that if he died, his money stayed in the hands of the Beauharnais, so, he arranged a marriage for Alexandre that also happened to be financially beneficial to Josephine's family.

Josephine was the eldest daughter of a wealthy Creole sugar-plantation owner. François heard about her, but 19-year-old Alexandre considered her at 15 to be too close to his own age. He wanted to marry her 12-year-old sister, Catherine-Désirée instead.

A deal was struck, but, unfortunately, Catherine-Désirée died from yellow fever before the marriage occurred. To replace Catherine-Désirée, Josephine's youngest sister, 11-year-old Manette, was then suggested. She also became ill and could not travel, and that left Josephine as Alexandre's only option. So, on 13 December 1779, they married, but, unfortunately, their marriage proved unhappy and eventually resulted in a legal separation.

During the Revolution, Alexandre's patriotism became suspect, partly because he poorly defended Mainz. He was then imprisoned. Josephine tried to obtain his release, but that action and the fact that she was friendly with counter-revolutionaries, resulted in the Committee of Public Safety ordering her arrest on 21 April 1794. Marie claimed that while imprisoned she came to know Josephine. Marie described Josephine in lofty terms and maintained that she was the 'most amiable' person in prison. Marie also stated:

'She did all in her power to infuse life and spirit into her suffering companions, exhorting them to patience, and endeavouring to cheer them. When the great bolts were undrawn, a general shuddering was excited amongst all the prisoners; but Josephine would rally them, by bidding them have courage; ... Madame Beauharnais did not give way to despondency.'[13]

There was little to keep anyone's spirits up while imprisoned. The food was horrid. There were no beds or warm bedding. Everyone slept on the cold floor upon straw piles. Marie also noted that their hair was closely shorn each week in case they were condemned. Moreover, when cell bolts were withdrawn everyone shuddered for fear it was their turn to face the guillotine.

While imprisoned at Carmes, Josephine later shared a narrow and gloomy cell with one of the most beautiful women in France, Delphine de Custine. Delphine became suspect because of her treasonous relatives. First, her father-in-law, Adam Philippe, Count de Custine affectionately known by his troops as 'Général Moustache,' had been executed in August of 1793 for treason. Delphine's husband was also convicted of treason and executed a few months later in January of 1794. Delphine was then unexpectedly arrested and initially confined to her rooms, but when she plotted to escape, and the plot was discovered, she was imprisoned at Carmes.

Delphine and others imprisoned with Josephine give a strikingly different account of Josephine's behaviour than that related by Marie. They claim that Josephine was anything but courageous or supportive and maintain she 'wept copiously'. Moreover, according to one historian, '[Josephine] showed as much fear and despondency as Delphine showed energy and courage; she spent her life foretelling the future from cards and lamenting her fate'.[14]

No official records indicate that Marie was imprisoned at La Force or Carmes. However, bribes were regularly taken to keep people's names off prison records, so, it may be that either Curtius or one of his friends had the name Marie Grosholtz expunged from the records. In addition, Marie claims that they were freed thanks to the painter David and that he intervened because Marie's wax models were valuable to him in creating his paintings.

While Marie was imprisoned, the revolution claimed its next victim. This time it was Louis's sister and Marie's former wax-making student, Élisabeth, who had been imprisoned with the royal family at the Temple in August of 1792. A year later, she had seen her brother executed in January and then her sister-in-law in October.

Élisabeth had always supported her brother and was known for her courage and fidelity to him and to the monarchy. After the royal family's failed flight to Varennes, for instance, Élisabeth was joined in her carriage by two commissaries who had been appointed to return the royal family to Paris, one of whom was the politician Antoine Barnave.

Barnave was well known to Marie as she claims he regularly visited Curtius' home. Élisabeth spoke to Barnave about her brother's reason for having attempted to flee. This discussion was later mentioned by Madame Tourzel, who had played the part of the Russian Baroness de Korff when the royal family attempted to escape France. According to Madame Tourzel, Élisabeth stated in part:

> 'You are too clever, M. Barnave, not to have recognised at once the King's love for the French and his desire to make them happy. ... The King ... profoundly afflicted by the crimes committed throughout France and seeing a general disorganization in all departments of Government, with the evils which result; determined to quit Paris ... to go to another town in the kingdom, where, free in his own actions, he could persuade the Assembly to revise its decrees and where he could in concert with it make a new Constitution ... for the happiness of France.'[15]

After the royal family's return to Paris, Élisabeth was free to leave, but she stayed with her brother. Later, when her aunts fled, she could have left but again chose to stay. When the insurrection of 10 August happened, she was still there, and Rochefoucauld described her reaction to that traumatic event in his unpublished memoirs:

> 'I was in the garden, near enough to offer my arm to Madame de Lamballe, who was the most dejected and frightened of the

party; she took it. ... Madame Élisabeth was calm, resigned to all; it was religion that inspired her. She said to me, looking at the ferocious populace: "All those people are misguided; I wish their conversion, but not their punishment."'[16]

Robespierre had not necessarily considered Élisabeth a threat to the revolution, and, in fact, an order was issued to exile her after Marie Antoinette's trial. However, on 9 May 1794, she was transferred to the Conciergerie and brought before the Revolutionary Tribunal on charges of treason. They accused her of assisting in the king's flight, supplying émigrés with funds, and encouraging the resistance of the royal troops during the events of 10 August 1792.

The executioner Sanson reported that his son, Henri, saw Élisabeth on the day she was taken to the Conciergerie. Henri claimed she was 'wan and pale'. During the trial, she was given the luxury of sitting in an armchair. She answered all the questions calmly and denied firmly all the charges brought against her. Her denials did not matter to the Tribunal. She was found guilty and sentenced to be executed the following day.

One English paper gave 'fresh particulars' relating to Élisabeth's execution. They reported that she was preceded by 25 other prisoners suffering the same fate. The paper also noted that she suffered for no crimes of her own but rather because of crimes 'falsely imputed' to her and that the Revolutionary Tribunal sentenced her to execution out of 'political necessity'. The events surrounding her execution were then provided:

'Having ascended the scaffold, she immediately cast up her eyes to heaven, and prostrate on her knees, and wringing her hands, demanded of the King of Kings that fortitude which the horrors of her situation had rendered so necessary. Having continued in prayer till the moment when she was to submit her head to the ensanguined instrument, she advanced with perfect resignation, with a kind of heroism inspired by religion, and perfectly resigned to the decree of Providence – Though she bled the last amongst her 25 fellow-sufferers, she displayed a courage, a fortitude superior to them all. ... All the other ladies who suffered with the Princess were either so very old, so dishevelled, so disfigured by rouge, or so very filthy and ragged in their dress, that the sight of them almost smothered the rising sentiment of compassion. The Princess and her 25 fellow-sufferers were dispatched in less than 18 minutes. – The people, accustomed to such spectacles, saw this scene of horror with great tranquillity, and at the conclusion shouted, *Long live the Republic!* – Thus, died the virtuous Elizabeth Phillippina Maria of France, after having lived, in a most sainted and spotless reputation, 30 years and seven days.'[17]

If Marie mourned the death of her dear Élisabeth whom she claimed to have lived with for eight years, she showed no obvious signs in her *Memoirs*. Instead, she remarked on how differently Élisabeth behaved at her execution compared to that of Louis's mistress, Madame du Barry. According to Marie:

'[Madame du Barry] uttered the most piercing shrieks, and gave herself up to violent paroxysms of despair, struggling even to the last with such force, the executioner had much difficulty in strapping her to the board to which the victims were attached.'[18]

After Madame du Barry was executed, Curtius got busy modelling her head. Palloy, the man who had turned the destruction of the Bastille into a commercial success, stopped by the shop soon after Curtius had completed Madame du Barry's likeness:

'He marveled at the likeness, and Curtius told him in a businesslike sort of way that yes, he thought it especially good since he had been able to go to the cemetery of the Girondins and inspect the freshly severed real thing. Despite, the cold, he had sat down then and there to achieve the best wax image he could to convey her expression at the coup de grâce.'[19]

Chapter 11

Peak and Fall of Robespierre

'To the bar! To the bar!'

In her *Memoirs*, Marie recounted her experience at a national celebration of Robespierre's newly proposed religion called the 'Cult of the Supreme Being' (*Culte de l'Être suprême*). The new religion was the next step in France's repudiation of Christianity and Catholicism, which were blamed for perpetuating the injustices of the monarchy. The new religion was also a reaction by Robespierre to France's first state-sponsored atheistic religion, the 'Cult of Reason' (*Culte de la Raison*), which had first appeared around the time of the queen's trial.

The Cult of Reason was spearheaded by radical revolutionaries like Jacques Hébert, Antoine-François Momoro, Pierre-Gaspard Chaumette, and Joseph Fouché. The religion was based on the principles of Enlightenment and anticlericalism. Its goal was the perfection of mankind through the attainment of Truth and Liberty, and its guiding principle was to be devoted to reason. To bring this civic religion to fruition, a celebration known as the 'Festival of Reason' (*Fête de la Raison*) was scheduled for 10 November 1793. Other fetes were also to be held in Bordeaux and Lyons, but the largest ceremony was scheduled at the Paris cathedral of Notre Dame, renamed the 'Temple of Reason' and turned into a theatre.

During the celebration, the Christian altar was dismantled and an altar to 'Liberty' was raised. A 'Goddess of Reason' was also worshiped. However, to avoid idolatry and statuary, the Goddess was played by a live woman. There are conflicting reports about who played the role, but whoever served as the goddess was described as possessing 'unparalleled beauty' and 'was borne in triumph over the heads of the people to receive their worship, with all the pomp and display the promoters could invent'.[1]

Some people thought the Festival of Reason was 'lurid', 'licentious', or 'scandalous'. Robespierre was among those who was against this anti-Christian religion, and he vehemently denounced it. Armed with almost dictatorial power, Robespierre then proposed formation of the Cult of the Supreme Being.

Robespierre believed that reason led to virtue and that virtue was the goal, so the Cult of the Supreme Being was not solely based on reason. The Cult of the Supreme Being supported the idea of a supreme being and immortality of the soul. However, it was not consistent with Christian doctrine as the only way virtue could be attained in the Cult of the Supreme Being was through fidelity and devotion to liberty and democracy.

To inaugurate this new religion, a national celebration, known as the 'Festival of the Supreme Being', was decreed by Robespierre after he gave a long panegyric on the republic's mortality, democratic government, and the French nation. The celebration included a man-made mountain on the Champ de Mars. Robespierre also decreed that the main festival, which was to be massive, was to be celebrated in Paris with smaller celebrations mandated throughout France. Moreover, although Robespierre assumed leadership for the event, the festival was organized and choreographed by David, the same man who had staged the scene for Voltaire's procession to the Pantheon and had painted *The Death of Marat*.

Marie maintained that it got underway at 5am on 8 June 1794 when a general summons was issued throughout Paris, inviting all male and female citizens to decorate their houses with the colours of liberty, 'either by displaying new flags, or embellishing their old ones with garlands of flowers and greens'.[2] Afterwards, throngs of citizens went to their respective sections to await a signal to march to the Tuileries.

Youth formed a square battalion and in the centre of the square flew the streamers and flags of the armed force of each section. Men held oak branches and women flowers. At the mountain, each of the 48 sections selected '10 old men; 10 matrons, 10 young girls, their age being between 15 and 20 years; 10 youths, their age between 15 and 18 years; and 10 male infants, their age below eight years'.[3]

At 8am artillery was discharged from Pont Neuf. The artillery announced the moment when everyone was to march to the Tuileries. In addition, adjacent to the Tuileries was an amphitheatre that had been constructed for use by the Convention members.

At noon, the National Convention preceded by Robespierre, promenaded to the amphitheatre. The deputies were wearing matching blue coats with red facings, short culottes, and hats with tricolored feathers. They carried a bouquet of flowers, fruit, and ears of corn. Music greeted them upon their arrival, and Robespierre gave a signal that resulted in silence. Robespierre then opened the festival with a ringing speech.

'The day forever fortunate has arrived, which the French people have consecrated to the Supreme Being. Never has the world which He created offered to Him a spectacle so worthy of His notice. ... Liberty and virtue together came from the breast of Divinity. Neither can abide with mankind without the other.'[4]

After this portion of his speech, a hymn was sung. In front of Robespierre's chair were three emblematic figures – atheism, discord, and selfishness – which had been created by David from combustible materials. The idea was to set fire to them so that they would be reduced to ashes. Robespierre took a torch and lit the emblems and from the ashes emerged a statue of Wisdom. Unfortunately, according to Marie, the dramatic effect was lost as the statue was obscured by a lot of smoke. Robespierre then continued with his speech:

'The monster which the genius of kings had vomited over France has gone back into nothingness. ... kings have always conspired to assassinate humanity. ... O People, fear no more their sacrilegious plots! ... Frenchmen, you war against kings; you are therefore worthy to honor Divinity. ... Our blood flows for the cause of humanity. Behold our prayer. Behold our sacrifices. Behold the worship we offer Thee.'[5]

Another hymn was sung. A procession then formed to march to the symbolic mountain that had been erected at the Champ de Mars. There the second portion of the festival would occur. French historian Albert Mathiez, known for his Marxist interpretation of the French Revolution, described the scene:

'The first twenty-four sections at the head, the last twenty-four in the rear; between them the Convention, preceded by the National Institute of Music; and in the midst of the deputies, an immense car on the antique model, draped in red and drawn by eight oxen with gilt horns; on the car was a plough with a wheatsheaf and a printing press, both shaded by a tree of liberty.'[6]

At the Champ de Mars, Robespierre and the deputies climbed to the summit of the mountain where the tree of liberty shaded them. The musicians who had preceded them sat on either side (men on the right, women on the left) and battalions of adolescents from the 48 sections surrounded the mountain's base, with the remainder of people covering the field. More hymns were sung, but this time the chorus was accompanied by the voices of thousands sharing in the celebration. Finally, the young girls tossed their flowers into the air and the young men drew their sabres. A grand symphony also played, and another volley of discharges occurred amidst patriotic cries of 'Vive la Republique!'

To remove Christian associations related to the *ancien régime*, the Convention changed the Gregorian calendar to a more rational and scientific system. The new revolutionary (or republican calendar) would be used by the French government for about 12 years. The new calendar also started on 22 September 1792. Years were written in roman numerals, and there was a ten-day week, called a decade, that consisted of *primidi* (first day) *duodi* (second day) *tridi* (third day) *quartidi* (fourth day), *quintidi* (fifth day), *sextidi* (sixth day), *septidi* (seventh day), *octidi* (eighth day), *nonidi* (ninth day), and *décadi* (tenth day). Three decades made up a thirty-day month and twelve months formed a year, with the extra five or six days placed at the end of each year.

The name of each day was changed too. Instead of Monday through Sunday, a different name was assigned to each of the 365 days. These names were the creation of politician and poet Fabre d'Églantine. Days were named for such things as a flower, seed, animal, tree, plant, or thing, and they replaced Christian festival names or days named for saints. For instance, 4 September was called *nerprun* (buckthorn), 25 October *betterave* (beet root), 23 January *perce-neige* (snowdrop), 14 February *guède* (woad), 2 March *orme* (elm), 13 April *roquette* (rocket), and 4 June *oeillet* (carnation).

Months also acquired new names. Each month's name was also based on a special meaning. For instance, the autumn months were *Vendémiaire* (grape harvest), *Brumaire* (mist), and *Frimaire* (frost). Winter consisted of *Nivôse* (snowy), *Pluviôse* (rainy), and *Ventôse* (windy). Spring was *Germinal* (germination), *Floréal* (flower), and *Prairial* (meadow). Finally, the summer seasons included the months of *Messidor* (harvest), *Thermidor* (summer heat), and *Fructidor* (fruit).

As far as Robespierre was concerned, his festival held in the month of *Prairial*, on the day called *fourche* (pitchfork), was a huge success. Throughout the celebration, Robespierre beamed with joy, allowing nothing to dampen his enthusiasm or delight. He had been elected four days earlier as President of the Convention, and he saw the festival as his moment to shine and be lauded and appreciated by the masses who could also view him as their leader.

Unfortunately for Robespierre, although he was pleased with the festival, others were unhappy and felt that he had taken things too far. When he

111

descended the mountain, some deputies denounced him as being too prideful and critics mentioned his 'pretended superiority'. One fellow statesman, Jacques-Alexis Thuriot, was overheard remarking, 'Look at the bugger; it's not enough for him to be master, he has to be God'.[7]

Laws had been enacted to increase arrest rates and to centralize the Terror. This was accomplished by ordering all political prisoners transferred to Paris for final judgment. Thus, with many revolutionary courts in the provinces suspended (there were a few exceptions) and most prisoners transferred to Paris, Parisian prisons were overflowing with prisoners by April.

To help solve the overflow situation and the problem of unreliable deputies who did not support the Terror, the triumvirate of Robespierre, Couthon, and Saint-Just decided a new law was necessary. Couthon, who had been confined for about a year to a wheelchair because of paralysis in his legs, proposed the new law. He presented it to the Convention in the name of the Committee of Public Safety. However, they had never reviewed it, and the Committee of General Security (a police agency that with the Committee of Public Safety oversaw the Terror) did not even know it was being drafted. The new law concentrated power in a few hands. It also extended the reach of the Revolutionary Tribunal, did away with all conflicting legislation, freed the Tribunal from the Convention, and streamlined the Terror. The law broadened the definition of 'enemy' and obligated citizens to bring to justice anyone thought suspect. Trials were limited to three days and the accused could present no defence as judgement was based solely on accusations with the verdict being one of two outcomes: acquittal or death.

When the deputies learned of the proposed law, they were immediately worried. Up to this point, the deputies could not be arrested without their fellow deputies ordering a trial. If the new law passed, deputies would lose their immunity, and they feared that adversaries would expose one another to the Terror. In fact, Robespierre was planning to purge the Convention of certain deputies. The deputies wanted to adjourn and examine the proposal. Robespierre refused and insisted a vote be taken. Under duress, it passed.

Two days after the festival, on 10 June, the law of 22 *Prairial* was enacted. The law increased the dangers at home at the same moment that danger from foreign invaders was decreasing. Marie wrote about the new law:

> '... no sooner was it in force, than the inhabitants of Paris became paralysed by the iniquity of its operations, stripping, as

it were, the courts even of the slightest semblance of justice, and the victims, ... descending from the highest ranks even to the lowest'.[8]

This new law also had the effect of speeding up the judicial process, thereby making it impossible for the Revolutionary Tribunal to keep dispensing justice effectively. It also made an immediate impact as 'an average of five executions a day rose in Germinal, the rate then went to seventeen in Prairial and twenty-six in Messidor'.[9]

The day after the law's enactment, Robespierre was absent, and an amendment was added that allowed members of the Convention to be impeached. When Robespierre learned about the amendment he was furious. On 12 June, he demanded that the deputies revoke the amendment and then he issued veiled threats. He particularly clashed with a colleague named Jean-Lambert Tallien.

Tall and imposing in appearance, Tallien was only 24 years old when he was elected to the National Convention in 1792. Soon after his election, he took a seat on the high benches with the radical members of the Montagnards and was in the thick of everything. He promoted the insurrection on 10 August, supported the September Massacres, spearheaded the opposition to the king, voted for the king's death, and helped to overthrow the Girondins. After the Committee of Public Safety and the Committee of General Security were established, he and a colleague, Claude-Alexandre Ysabeau, were sent to squash resistance and establish Terror in the province of Bordeaux in September 1793. They arrived in Bordeaux in October. Tallien was the more conspicuous of the two, and, with his sweeping power, he was willing to forcefully put down the resistance and subjugate Bordeaux. One nineteenth-century historian from the University of California, Berkeley wrote of Tallien:

> 'He made an immense bluster over his ferocity; he took a lodging from which he could see the guillotine work, and was always talking in his speeches at the club at Bordeaux of the terror, and of the necessity to feed "la sainte guillotine."'[10]

What happened next involved an aristocrat Marie described as having a noble appearance and remarkable grace. She was Theresa Cabarrus and was the former wife of an émigré, Marquis de Fontenay. Fontenay had fled at the outbreak of the Revolution in 1790, and Theresa divorced him in 1791. She then began using her maiden name Cabarrus. In Bordeaux, Theresa's stunning beauty captured Tallien's attention and there are several stories about how it happened.

The first story is that Theresa had plans to go to Madrid, but to do so, travellers had to produce a signed passport, a certificate of *non-émigration*, and a *carte de sûrete*. She neglected to have these documents and was arrested as *suspecte* and thrown into prison. Although she did not know Tallien personally, she wrote him and protested against her imprisonment. She also informed him that she was the 'worthiest of citizenesses' and beseeched him to grant her a hearing.

The blonde and curly-headed Tallien was purportedly curious about Theresa as he had heard about her extraordinary beauty. Intrigued, he went to the prison and interviewed her. Their interview went well, and he left the prison captivated and desperately in love. Hence, a few hours later, she was granted her freedom, which caused some people to allege that Theresa became involved with Tallien to save herself from the guillotine.

A second version, often claimed to be the truth and purportedly told by Theresa to her daughter, is that Theresa was staying with an uncle and heard of about 300 Bordelaise aristocrats who were anxious to escape Bordeaux with their lives. To do so, they had paid passage on an English vessel that was sitting in the harbour, but because not all the aristocrats had paid their full passage, at the last moment the captain refused to sail.

Theresa heard about this and was indignant. She took 3,000 francs to the captain so that the ship would set sail, and instead of getting a receipt she asked for a passenger list, which she then took home. As the captain was readying the ship to sail, he told several people on shore about the beautiful Theresa who had given him a hefty sum of money for the safe passage of the aristocrats. The day the ship sailed, those on shore repeated the story about Theresa to those searching for the aristocrats. The searchers decided to get revenge against Theresa for paying the aristocrats' passage and began searching for her. They found her the next evening attending the theatre. The searchers accosted her, claimed she had freed counter-revolutionaries, and demanded the passenger list. She refused to provide it, and so they jostled and rudely handled her.

Tallien witnessed the event, stepped through the crowd, and calmed the searchers. As he was doing so, his colleague ordered Theresa arrested. As the order was being executed, Tallien recognized Theresa. It seems that he had encountered her several times in Paris, once when she was getting a portrait painted, once at the home of a mutual friend, and once at the Convention. She was extraordinarily beautiful, and her beauty caused him to hurry to visit her in prison where he was further disarmed:

'Theresa was the loveliest woman of her time, fully aware of her charms, and knowing how to use them; and now that she must either conquer this stern citizen of twenty-four or die, she plead for life and liberty till he, in his turn, sued for love.'[11]

Although exactly how their relationship began may be in question, there is no question they had a relationship and that Tallien afterwards notably softened in his stance in Bordeaux. This was demonstrated by a decline in the number of people executed, which some people attribute to Theresa's influence and kindness. In fact, many people were supposedly saved because of her, which resulted in her nickname 'Our Lady of Thermidor' ('*Notre-Dame de Thermidor*') or 'Our Lady of Salvation' ('*Notre-Dame des Bonsecours*').

Theresa's sudden release from prison, Tallien's unexpected moderate tendencies, and a report that Tallien was having a relationship with Theresa characterized as '*liaison intimes*', garnered Robespierre's attention. Concerned, Robespierre had Tallien recalled and he left Bordeaux in February to return to Paris to explain his actions, while Theresa stayed behind.

A few months later, during the first week of May, Theresa left Bordeaux for Orléans. From there, she travelled to Paris. It was a risky move for her, because the Convention had earlier decreed that nobles and foreign-born persons of countries fighting against France must leave Paris. So, when Theresa was spotted in Paris a warrant was issued, and she was arrested on the night of 30-31 May in Versailles.

Theresa was first imprisoned at La Force and then later at Carmes with Josephine and Delphine. Theresa knew the ultimate result of her imprisonment would be execution, and so, on 7 Thermidor (25 July), she sent Tallien a dagger and a taunting, accusatory letter about his inability to save her. She wrote, 'To-morrow I go to the tribunal; I am dying of despair that I ever belonged to such a coward as you!'[12]

Robespierre's clash with Tallien and his veiled threats caused the Convention to finally accede to his wishes. As Robespierre wanted, they restored the original text that had been drafted by Couthon. However, the enactment of the law of 22 *Prairial* multiplied Robespierre's enemies.

As the Terror accelerated, plots formed, and Robespierre's enemies began to coalesce. These enemies would be galvanized by Tallien who, with others, hoped to get rid of Robespierre because he had made 'virtue the order of the day and ... they prepared to overthrow the statesman, who was not satisfied with being a politician but wished to be pontiff as well'.[13]

As Theresa sat in prison, she was being promised her freedom if she would testify against Tallien. In the meantime, Tallien and about a dozen Montagnards were plotting against Robespierre. They were now fearful that he would attack them and have them guillotined, the same way he had guillotined Danton, Desmoulins, and the Dantonists.

On 8 *Thermidor* (26 July), Robespierre gave a two-hour speech to the Convention. He had been absent for about a month, partly because of his health and partly because he was aware of the danger he had caused himself with the law of 22 *Prairial*. In his speech, Robespierre declared himself a true defender of virtue, defended his policies, and alleged that conspirators existed within the very bosom of the Convention, which he declared must be purged to protect the republic.

Shouts from the floor rose asking him to name these conspirators, but he refused. Refusing to name the conspirators was a major miscalculation on his part as it created intense fear among members of the Convention. The deputies conspiring against him were particularly fearful and worried that he might name them. Hence, they decided to act and that same night they banded together and developed a plan to permanently remove Robespierre from power.

The next morning as Saint-Just began to speak, Tallien interrupted him. A stunned Saint-Just stood silent as Tallien accused Robespierre of abusing his power, being a tyrant, and creating a dictatorship of terror. Cries of support for Tallien issued forth from the floor. Robespierre tried to speak, but Tallien's accusations reached fear pitch when he dramatically withdrew the dagger Theresa had given him and declared that he would kill Robespierre if the Convention refused to act.

Robespierre turned for support to the Montagnards. He got none and was further repulsed by deputies in the Convention. Saint-Just was then shoved from the lectern and someone demanded Robespierre and his supporters be indicted. A faint applause was heard at first, increasingly amplified; it soon resounded throughout the Convention. The walls shook. 'To the bar! To the bar!' was the cry, and then someone cried for the arrests of Robespierre, his brother Augustin, Couthon, Saint-Just, and two other supporters, François Hanriot and Philippe-François-Joseph Le Bas.

When the Paris Commune heard the news that Robespierre and his supporters were under siege, they ordered troops to march to the Convention to free them. The Convention responded by ordering their own troops under the command of Paul Barras. Although Robespierre, Augustin, Couthon, Saint-Just, Hanriot, and Le Bas were arrested, they all obtained their freedom within hours. The men then gathered and confined themselves inside City Hall while outside the troops of the Paris Commune surrounded and protected them.

In the meantime, the Convention declared those confined at City Hall outlaws. This meant that they could be executed within twenty-four hours without a trial. Because Robespierre refused to head an insurrection, eventually, the troops of the Paris Commune dispersed. After they dispersed, around two in the morning, Barras and his troops arrived at City Hall to re-arrest Robespierre and his supporters.

To avoid capture, Augustin jumped out of a window and broke both his legs; Hanriot also jumped from a window and landed in a sewer very much alive; Couthon was discovered injured at the bottom of a staircase having thrown himself from his wheelchair; Saint-Just stood motionless beside Le Bas as he shot himself in the head; and Robespierre discharged a pistol into his own mouth to commit suicide. Unfortunately for Robespierre, instead of instant death, the shot 'fractured his lower left jaw, and left it hanging down by the flesh and ligaments'.[14] A field officer named Charles-André Méda, subsequently claimed he fired the shot that injured Robespierre. However, the fact that Robespierre shot himself was later distinctly stated in an official report, and, in addition, the surgeon who dressed Robespierre's wound, declared his wound was self-inflicted.

The mangled and wounded Robespierre spent a miserable night lying on a table with his bleeding jaw supported by his left hand holding a woollen pistol-bag that absorbed the blood. After twenty-four hours of misery, without a trial, he was conveyed in a tumbril along the same route that thousands of his victims had taken. On the way to the Place de la Revolution, the streets were lined with people. Marie alleged that a multitude of relations of those executed by Robespierre surrounded him as he travelled to the guillotine, and she reported one woman exclaimed, 'Murderer of all my kindred! descend to hell with the curses of every mother in France!'[15] A nineteenth-century writer later provided details of his execution:

> '[At the Place de la Revolution] the brutal executioner tearing the bandages from his shattered head, and twisting the fracture jaw, that it might not interfere with the action of the 'sacred machine' – and finally, of his emerging slowly to the surface of the scaffold, more dead than alive, and exhibiting, stained and torn, the same fantastical coat of sky-blue silk in which only six weeks before he had figured, … in a power surpassing that of monarchs.'[16]

Robespierre was not the only one guillotined on that day. His brother Augustin, Couthon, Saint-Just, and twelve others were also executed. They were buried in a common grave at the Errancis Cemetery. Later, probably in 1848, their remains were moved to the Catacombs of Paris.

Chapter 12

The End of Terror

'Does one punish an axe?'
Antoine-Quentin Fouquier Tinville

Marie received Robespierre's head shortly after it was removed from his body. On orders of the National Assembly, she took a mould of it, and the death mask was soon displayed at Curtius' salon. While she would continue to get severed heads for some time, the death of Robespierre marked a shift in who were candidates for the guillotine, because a day after Robespierre's execution, immediate changes were made to the Committee of Public Safety. New members were appointed and term limits were also established that required one quarter of the committee members to retire every three months. In addition, many unpopular laws that had been enacted by the committee were repealed.

These changes and others eroded the power of the committee, and between this period and the establishment of a new governing body, known as the Directory, the Thermidor reaction occurred. The Thermidor reaction also refers to the French Republican calendar date when Robespierre and his radical supporters were attacked in the National Convention, 9 Thermidor Year II (27 July 1794). In addition, from out of the Thermidor reaction came the Thermidor regime.

The Thermidor regime consisted of those who had revolted against Robespierre, and they now treated those who supported the revolution and the Terror the same way counter-revolutionaries had been treated. They hunted down Jacobins and supporters of Robespierre and executed them. This included seventy of Robespierre's allies from within the Paris Commune who were guillotined on 5 August. The Jacobin club was also purged, so that three months later, on 11 November, the Jacobin Club closed.

For those who supported the Thermidor regime, there were other bright spots. More than five hundred suspected counter-revolutionaries who were awaiting trial and expecting to be executed were suddenly released.

Josephine was among those freed. Her release occurred on the day of Robespierre's execution, but, unfortunately, her husband and his cousin had been executed five days earlier. Theresa also gained her freedom a few days after Josephine. Moreover, by 5 August, the Thermidor regime decreed that all inmates arrested under the Law of Suspects were to be released.

The Thermidor regime demanded that those involved in the Terror give an accounting of their activities. Thus, people like Tallien and Carrier found themselves defending their actions. Tallien's accounting cleared him of any wrong doing, and he re-joined the leadership, but Carrier was not so lucky.

The recounting of Carrier's many killings and diabolical tortures enabled all sorts of accusations of inhumanity to be levelled against him. He was thus arrested on 3 September, and, at trial, Carrier behaved as unemotionally as he had when conducting the drownings in Nantes. He was also quick to distance himself from any wrong doing by claiming:

> 'I took but little share in the policing of Nantes; I was only there in passing, being first at Rennes and later with the army. My principal task was to watch over and see to the victualling of our troops, and for six months I supplied 200,000 men there without its costing the State a halfpenny. Hence I have little information to offer in the matter. I know little or nothing of the accused.'[1]

According to Marie, when the vote was taken as to Carrier's fate, of the 500 members, 489 voted for his death. After the verdict, although Carrier declared he was an innocent man, he was executed that same day, on 16 December 1794. On the way to the guillotine, he was quiet and composed, and when his head fell into the blood-red basket, a loud applause from spectators marked the moment.

Like Robespierre, the National Assembly ordered Marie to create a model of Carrier's head, which she did immediately after his execution. Robespierre and Carrier's busts were soon on display at Curtius' salon. The head of Robespierre was interesting, but Carrier's head completely enthralled the public because everyone knew of his nefarious deeds.

Despite the trials against those who supported the terror and despite the release of those affected by the Law of Suspects, the Thermidor regime was highly unpopular. Part of the reason for the regime's unpopularity had to do with the fact that there were still many people who supported Robespierre, and they blamed the Thermidor regime for his death. There was also great unhappiness about the new changes and rebellions against the regime. Thus, France remained in a fragile state with warring factions.

In the war against Austria and Prussia, France had made progress by recapturing lost territory. By June of 1794, the Vendean Insurrection was checked, Lyons and Toulon recaptured, and the victory at Fleurus was a strategic win resulting in France's enemies withdrawing from Belgium. These wins made France safer from foreigners, but the law of 22 *Prairial* still made it more dangerous for the French public as the number of executions increased.

The executioner Sanson had argued persuasively for the guillotine, exclaiming that the old methods were too demanding and that with the new guillotine, he would be able to keep up with increased demand. In fact, Sanson and his guillotine were so efficient that in 13 minutes he could behead 12 victims, and at the height of the Terror, it was claimed, he decapitated some 300 victims in three days.

Although the beheadings might have solved some problems for revolutionaries, they created others. Constant and frequent beheadings meant a lot of blood from its victims, and one problem with all the blood was that it congealed between cobblestones, formed small pools around the guillotine, and discoloured the streets. Marie wrote that at one point there was so much blood in the suburb of Fauxbourg St. Antoine (renamed Faubourg-de-Gloire during the revolution), a channel was established so that the blood could flow more easily into a common drain.

Imprisonments and beheadings also resulted in victims abandoning their dogs. Hungry, abandoned dogs began roaming Parisian streets, and because they were starving, they lapped up the blood when they found it. For those who escaped the guillotine, they soon found themselves being threatened by hungry packs of ferocious dogs. To avoid being torn apart, an armed force was established to protect pedestrians.

Dogs were not the only problem. The guillotine was so busy lopping off heads that those living next to the Place de la Revolution constantly heard it in action. The noises increased their sense of horror. Moreover, neighbours next to the guillotine complained about the nauseating stench of blood that permeated the area. It became so strong that homeowners could not stomach it, and some were forced to abandon their homes. To solve the problem, the guillotine was moved to the Place de la Bastille, near the homes of *sans-culottes*, thinking that they would accept it. They complained too, and so, finally, it was relocated to the outskirts of Paris.

The tide of public opinion had also begun to turn against Curtius and his wax figures. The Terror had left people fearful of having fun and enjoying themselves. France also remained in a fragile financial state. The rich nobles had fled, and many of the ordinary people did not have money to spend on such things as visiting a wax exhibition. Thus, Curtius' exhibitions were not as profitable as they had once been, and moreover, as early as 1792, an almanac gave his exhibition a less than stellar review.

By 1794, Curtius was facing worse news. There was still the problem of whether a person was loyal to the French Revolution and these worries would be ongoing until 1799. At a meeting of the Societe republicaine des arts, Athanas Detournelle proclaimed Curtius a charlatan promoting false stories that might hurt the Convention. Detournelle also declared the dangers the public might face if they continued to patronize Curtius' wax exhibition:

> 'Curtius's salon must be empty. ... It is time to open people's eyes to charlatanism; ... he [must] not publicly display these ridiculous busts whose false illusion easily fools those without acquired knowledge. ... I will cite more than one example of the danger of displaying these cold copies; I have seen volunteers preferring Le Peltier and Marat in these stories to the beautiful paintings of the Convention.'[2]

As Curtius was struggling financially, worse news came for Marie when on 26 September, Curtius died. It happened around the same time Carrier was arrested and while preparations were being made to disinter Mirabeau from the Pantheon and replace his remains with Marat's. Curtius had suffered a short illness, and although Marie visited him regularly, she was not there when he died as she was busy running the business for him in Paris.

Since 1793, Curtius had been living over three miles away in a house that he purchased in Ivry-sur-Seine. He died there at 4 o'clock in the afternoon while Marie was attending to business at the Salon. At the time of his death, Curtius was with servants, Guérin and his wife.

His death certainly must have been difficult for Marie because she loved and respected him. However, she never mentioned the difficulties in her *Memoirs* nor did she say how she felt about his passing. Curtius' death also put Marie on the history map because from this point forward, she was easier to track in having replaced Curtius as the wax modeler.

Marie probably did not learn that Curtius had died until later that evening because she did not appear at his home until the following morning. When she arrived, two friends accompanied her. Marie requested a post mortem be done and later alleged that an autopsy found he had been poisoned. Marie also blamed his death on his association with Général Moustache because shortly before General Custine was guillotined, Curtius had sung the general's praises as a patriot.

The attending doctor at the deathbed did not mention poison, and, in fact, he reported, Curtius died of natural causes. Moreover, Curtius must have known that he was ill prior to his death because a month before his death on 31 August 1794 (14 *Fructidor* Year II), he visited his lawyer and dictated his will. The will was notarized by Sieur Hubert Gibé and attested to by two witnesses. It read:

> 'I declare I do not have, or know of, any female heir either in France or in a foreign country. I give and bequeath to the poor of the Section du Temple in Paris, all my silver ware and all my jewellery. ...
>
> 'I appoint and institute as my residuary legatee the Citizeness Anne Marie Grosholtz, spinster, of full age, my pupil in my art who has lived with me under my roof for more than twenty years.
>
> 'I desire that she should have from my estate, immediately after my death, everything that the law allows me to give, in view of my not having an heir. I make her executrix of my Will.'[3]

Despite Curtius being ill, the last few months of his life showed he had been concentrating on business. As Robespierre was meeting his maker, Curtius packed up and sent an exhibition to India that consisted of twenty life-size figures:

> 'It was well advertised in the *Calcutta Gazette* and *Madras Courier*. The whole exhibition travelled in the charge of an Italian named Dominick Laurency ... The exhibition was completed by a model of the Bastille and the decapitated head of Foulon.'[4]

For all practical purposes, it seemed as if Marie would inherit everything. After his death Curtius' assets had to be noted and his estate had to be inventoried. He had three properties: the house at Ivry-sur-Seine, a rental property in the Rue des Fosses du Temple, and his home and workshop on the Boulevard du Temple.

All the sites were packed with treasures as Curtius loved to purchase things. Yet, despite the properties and treasures, what was likely of most interest to Marie was the objects associated with Curtius' exhibitions. The exhibitions and their contents made up her livelihood. One twenty-first century author provided a list of the contents:

> 'Thirty-six life size figures, seven half-length and three reclining figures, including those of madame du Barry and the Princesse de Lamballe. There were also cases of miniatures, relics and assorted *objets d'art*, including a significant collection of paintings, both framed and unframed. A large portion of the fixtures and fittings was mirrors, sconces, and candelabras.'[5]

Curtius did not just leave assets behind either. He also left a pile of unpaid bills and taxes. There were doctor's bills, bills for locksmiths, and bills for masons. His finances were complicated, and they got more complicated when Marie found herself facing a financial predicament. Curtius' house at Ivry-sur-Seine had a partial mortgage. If she wanted to keep it, she had to mortgage it and the house in the Rue des Fosses du Temple. She decided on taking out a mortgage and did so with a Madame Salomé Reiss on 17 May 1795.

As Marie was navigating the complications of Curtius' finances, France was attempting to stabilize itself. Among the important happenings between February and March of 1795 were three events: Jacobin leaders of Lyons were assassinated; Jacobins in Tulon were arrested; and food riots happened in Paris. There was also a trial held for one of the most important people during the Reign of Terror, Antoine-Quentin Fouquier-Tinville, a relative and friend of Desmoulins. He headed the Revolutionary Tribunal and served as the public prosecutor during the time of the Terror. For his role in the French Revolution, Fouquier-Tinville acquired a sinister reputation of ruthlessness. He also became infamous for ringing a tiny bell to silence arguments and terminate appeals of the accused.

In his role as prosecutor, Fouquier-Tinville was passionless and steadfast. Marie described him as the accuser and condemner of the queen. Moreover, he was remembered for assisting in the arrest of Robespierre, Couthon, and Saint-Just, before he himself was denounced and imprisoned on 1 August. Contemporaries alleged that neither money nor pity could touch Fouquier-Tinville's heart or change his purpose. Despite having prosecuted what is estimated to be over 2,400 counterrevolutionaries, he did not see himself as culpable in his role as prosecutor.

Word that he was to be arrested arrived while he was at work at half past two in the afternoon. At the time, he was drinking his usual daily refreshment of brandy. He then went to his office, sent a note of warning to his wife, and walked through the August heat to the Convention and afterwards surrendered himself at the Conciergerie.

Fouquier-Tinville claimed to be innocent. He was amazed that Thermidorians were willing to sacrifice him, despite the fact he had just been carrying out his job. While imprisoned, he kept his wits about him, worked on his defence, and remained tenacious and shrewd. He continually believed that at any moment he would be set free. He thought of himself as victim, nothing more than the Convention's axe, depicted by his question, 'Does one punish an axe?' He claimed at trial that he had merely followed orders, 'that he had acted only according to the decrees of the Convention, in conformity with the laws "of justice and humanity."'[6]

Despite his defence, Fouquier-Tinville was seen as odious. People believed he had created a slaughter house that had nothing to do with law or justice. Thus, while it might have come as a surprise to him, it was probably no surprise to most people that a verdict of guilty was delivered against him for the following crimes:

> '[T]o promote the dissolution of the National Convention, and to arm the Citizens against each other; of having caused an innumerable quantity of citizens to perish under the forms of law; of having drawn out lists of proscription; of having ordered women with child to be executed; of having tried and condemned 30, 40, and even 60 persons at a time within three hours; of drawing out indictments in such a confused manner, that the father has often been executed for the son, and the son for the father; of having refused to persons accused a copy of the act of accusation against them; of having packed juries, instead of chusing them by lot &c.'[7]

A stoic Fouquier-Tinville responded to the verdict of guilty:

> 'Since it has been decreed that I should lose my head on the scaffold, posterity, to whom all things must be known, will discover who the real conspirators are. I desire to be led to immediate execution. I am ready'.[8]

On the day of his execution, he was taken through an immense crowd to the Place de Greve. Marie did not say if she personally witnessed his execution on 7 May 1795, although she did mention that he supposedly trembled as he ascended the scaffolding steps. She also remembered his first appearance at Curtius' house, which was etched in her mind. He had come to dine, and she described his countenance as repulsive. Tall, with a sallow complexion, narrow forehead, dark hair, and a complexion pitted with small pox, Fouquier-Tinville was dressed in deathly black.

As France's fragile state continued, surprising news came about the death of the 10-year-old son of Louis XVI and Marie Antoinette, whom Marie had modelled. The Dauphin, Louis-Charles, called by royalists Louis XVII, died at the Temple on 8 June 1795 under what most people considered suspicious circumstances. Thus, almost immediately a rumour arose that he had not died but escaped.

Louis-Charles' sad story begins after his father was executed and he was removed from his mother's care on 3 July 1793. The Committee of Public Safety ordered a cobbler named Antoine Simon and his wife to care for the boy and turn him into a patriotic citizen. Many stories exist that alleged Simon and his wife mistreated and abused Louis-Charles. However, the stories are not necessarily supported by fact or by the testimony of those who saw Louis-Charles during this time, which includes his own sister, Marie-Thérèse-Charlotte (known as Madame Royale but later the Duchess of Angoulême).

When Simon's care of Louis-Charles ended on 19 January 1794, the Dauphin was alleged to be in good health. However, from that point forward his care and what happened to him appears murky. Records related to this period disappeared. Additionally, no one saw him for six months until Paul Barras (the same Barras that had sent Convention troops to arrest Robespierre) visited him on 27 July 1794 (9 *Thermidor* Year II).

According to Barras' report, Louis-Charles was being held in harsh conditions and suffering from severe neglect. Barras appointed a new guardian, ordered him and his room cleaned, and assigned new caretakers. Louis-Charles' care then improved as he was fed properly, taken outside for walks, and inspected frequently, along with his surroundings. However, he remained mute, and no one could extract a word from him, no matter who visited, including three commissioners from the Committee of Public Safety.

On 31 March 1795, a new guardian was appointed for Louis-Charles, but in May, doctors discovered he was seriously ill. It was too late, as he died two and half months later on 8 June.

An autopsy was performed the following day by Dr Philippe-Jean Pelletan, who confirmed that Louis-Charles had died of scrofula, which is known today as a form of tuberculosis. In addition, during the autopsy, Pelletan noted numerous scars that were claimed to have been inflicted upon him while he was imprisoned at the Temple.

After the autopsy, Pelletan smuggled Louis-Charles' heart out in his coat pocket and preserved it in alcohol. Thus, when Louis-Charles was buried on 10 June in the Sainte-Marguerite Cemetery, he was minus his heart, and to make his death more troublesome, he was buried without a headstone marking the spot. Pelletan left the stolen heart sitting on a shelf for fifteen years, and after the alcohol evaporated, the heart dried out and became desiccated.

After the autopsy and Louis-Charles' burial, rumours sprouted up that he had not died but rather had been spirited out of the Temple and escaped. Part of the reason for these rumours had to do with the fact that a positive identification of the body was not made by his sister after his death, irregularities also existed with his death, autopsy, and funeral, and many members of the Convention obstinately refused to believe he was dead. Thus, the legend of the 'lost Dauphin' was born and for years, rumours circulated that he had survived.

These stories were reinforced by numerous claimants. In fact, when the Bourbon Restoration occurred in 1814, some one hundred claimants alleged they were Louis-Charles. Claimants declared they were smuggled out of the Temple and there were also stories about another boy being substituted, thus explaining the dead child at the Temple. One of the most persistent of the claimants was a German, Karl Wilhelm Naudorff. When he died, he had inscribed on his tomb '*Louis XVII, roi de France et de Navarre*' and the Dutch government allowed his son to bear the name Bourbon.

While claimants were maintaining they were the real Louis-Charles, Pelletan gave the heart to the Archbishop of Paris in 1830. He passed it on to Henri, Count of Chambord, the grandson of Charles X. It then fell into the hands of Italian aristocracy after the Count died in 1883. They returned it to France in 1975 claiming that it was the heart of Louis-Charles. French authorities did not necessarily believe the story, but they did place the heart in a crystal urn at the Basilica Saint-Denis.

In 2000, an historian, Philippe Delorme, pressed to have a DNA test conducted on the heart. A couple of samples of DNA were extracted by two researchers (Jean-Jacques Cassiman of the University of Louvain in

Belgium and Ernst Brinckmann of the University of Muenster in Germany). They compared the DNA samples with locks of hair from Marie Antoinette, two of her sisters, and two living maternal relatives.

DNA tests showed beyond a doubt that the heart belonged to a child of the Hapsburg family, and as Louis-Charles was the only child held at the Temple, they determined it was his heart. The French initially were unconvinced. They called together their own historians and scientists, and, eventually, the 'French ministry of culture conceded that "mounting evidence" had persuaded it to approve the heart's transfer from urn to [royal] crypt'.[9] Thus, the mystery of Louis-Charles and the 'lost Dauphin' story were permanently put to rest.

Chapter 13

Becoming Madame Tussaud

'Curious Busts from Nature as Large as Life'
Advertisement by Madame Tussaud

On 19 October 1795 (28 *Vendémiaire* Year IV), Marie wed François Tussaud and became Madame Tussaud. François was twenty-eight and Marie thirty-three. They married at the Préfecture du Département de la Seine, in the city of Paris. Although there were witnesses to the marriage, neither party had any relatives present:

> 'The witnesses … were, for François, a painter Girard, aged fifty-five, and Inspector of Buildings. The witnesses for the bride were Louis Sallé, who had accompanied her to Ivry-sur-Seine and helped her at the time of Curtius' death.'[1]

François had been born in 1767 in the commune of Mâcon, in the department of Saône-et-Loire, where residents of Mâcon were referred to as Macconais. François was born to Claude Tussaud and his wife Marguerite Robin. However, according to a great-grandson of Madame Tussaud's, the Tussaud family used variant spellings of their last name. These spellings included 'Tussot, Tusseau, Tuissiaud, Tussiaut, Tusseaut, Tussiau, or Thusseaud'.[2] Of further interest, the great-grandson claimed it was François who was the first in his family to adopt the spelling Tussaud.

Exactly how Madame Tussaud and François met is unclear. It seems likely they met in Paris as there were plenty of reasons for François to have travelled to Paris and leave his widowed mother before the Revolution occurred. For instance, the first restaurant, the Taverne Anglaise, opened in 1786 in the shopping arcade known as the Galerie de Bois, located in the Palais-Royal. Construction was approved for a new bridge, the Pont Louis XVI, a year later, and Louis XVI agreed in 1788 to convene the Estates General on the suggestion of Necker. Moreover, 1788, was also the year when many people suddenly took up an interest in French politics. Any of these reasons might have been the catalyst that caused François to travel to Paris.

After the revolution began, there were plenty of reasons for François to have stayed in Paris. For instance, the Fête de la Federation was held in 1790, Mirabeau was entombed at the Pantheon in 1791, and, in 1792, the government called for volunteers for the army declaring that France was in danger of foreign attack. The year 1793 was not only the guillotining of Louis XVI and Marie Antoinette but also the same year that the Museum Central des Arts (later called the Louvre Museum) opened. That opening was followed the next year by Robespierre's famous celebration, the Cult of the Supreme Being.

François claimed to be a civil engineer, and, so, perhaps, school might have been another draw. Paris had the most prestigious school for training engineering officials and civil engineers. It was founded in 1747 by Daniel-Charles Trudaine, one of the primary developers of France's road system. The school was the École Nationale des Ponts et Chaussées, nicknamed Ponts. It was located on the Champs-sur-Marne, about 11 miles east from the centre of Paris, and its curriculum included such subjects as geometry, algebra, and hydraulics with visits to building sites and drawing maps. However, there is no indication that François attended this school or any other engineering school while living in Paris.

About a month before Madame Tussaud's marriage, on 22 August 1795, the Convention had adopted a new Constitution. It was approved by national referendum about a month later. A governing body that was to go into effect in October had also been established. Known as the Directory, it was to consist of five directors who were to be elected by the Council of Ancients, the upper house of the French legislature under the Constitution of the Year III. The Council of the Ancients had received the names of possible candidates from the Council of Five Hundred, who were the lower house of the French legislature. However, by September, no directors had been chosen, and Parisians remained unhappy with the state of France.

Despite the establishment of the Directory and the approval of a new Constitution, unemployment remained high and critical bread shortages still existed. So, when Parisians learned that two-thirds of the deputies of the Convention would remain in place in the new Directory, they were livid and planned a march against the Convention.

Rumours of an armed royalist uprising also began to circulate. To ensure that deputies of the Convention sitting at the Tuileries were kept safe, Barras was now tasked with defending the Tuileries and the Convention. He was familiar with the achievements of a young general and decided to appoint him to defend the Tuileries. This general was Napoleon Bonaparte.

Napoleon was Corsican by birth. He had been born into an Italian family of minor nobility and of moderate means, which gave him some advantages over many Corsicans. One advantage was that he was admitted into a military academy and then into Paris' elite École Militaire, where he trained to become an artillery officer. Thus, by the time the Revolution broke out in 1789, he was already serving as an artillery officer in the French army.

The Revolution also provided him with numerous opportunities to advance, and he took advantage of those opportunities becoming a general by age 24. It seemed as if nothing could stop him until Robespierre fell. That was when Napoleon found himself under house arrest. According to his contemporaries, he was arrested because of his association with Robespierre, although his secretary claimed the arrest occurred because associates were jealous of him rather than that he had any special association with Robespierre.

Whatever the reason, Napoleon's arrest did not last long, and in April of 1795, he was assigned to command an infantry in one of the French Revolutionary Armies, known as the Army of the West. The Army of the West was being sent to quell the revolt happening in the Vendée that had begun in 1793. The revolt involved counter-revolutionaries loyal to the royalist cause, and ultimately resulted in the death of thousands of people.

Napoleon saw the appointment in the Army of the West as a demotion. He wanted to avoid it at all costs and declared himself in poor health to avoid being sent there. Unfortunately, his refusal affected his career prospects, and it looked like he might be sidelined as he was transferred to the Topographical Bureau.

When Barras called on him, Napoleon was already familiar with what happened on 10 August when insurgents stormed the Tuileries Palace and massacred the Swiss guards. So, to prevent a reoccurrence, he knew he needed artillery. To obtain it, Napoleon ordered a daring dark curly haired cavalry officer, Joachim Murat, to acquire large cannons. When royalist rebels attacked on 5 October (13 *Vendémiaire*), Napoleon's strategy worked splendidly. Using the cannons Murat seized from the sandy plains of Sablons, streets were cleared with what the famous nineteenth-century historian Thomas Carlyle called a 'whiff of grapeshot'.

Soon after, five directors were elected to the Directory on 31 October 1795. They were Barras; Louis Marie de La Révellière-Lépeaux, a staunch republican who proposed Louis XVI be executed after his flight to Varennes; Jean-François Rewbell, an ally to Barras; Lazare Nicolas Marguerite Carnot, a man who went from an army captain at the beginning of the French Revolution to an elected Convention member and vocal opponent of Robespierre; and finally, Étienne-François Le Tourneur, a former captain of engineers, specialist in military and naval affairs, and ally to Carnot.

The day after their election, these five men – Barras, La Révellière-Lépeaux, Rewbell, Carnot, and Le Tourneur – moved into the Luxembourg Palace. The Committee of Public Safety had previously occupied the palace, but when the five directors arrived, nothing was prepared for them. There was no furniture or heat. As to the Council of Five Hundred, they continued to meet in the same spot were the Convention met, a cold, damp, rectangular and foul-smelling riding school that had accommodated horses before people.

Of the five directors, Madame Tussaud claimed to know Rewbell. She thought him about 'middle height, rather stout, and strongly made; he was not very good-looking, but extremely agreeable in manners; he possessed much vigour of character, and singular aptitude in the transaction of business'.[3] The director's unusual costumes also caught her eye, resulting in her description of them, 'A cherry-coloured cloak, white silk pantaloons, turned down boots, waistcoat of silk, à l'Espagnol, the whole richly embroidered with gold, Spanish hat and feathers'.[4]

Soon after the election of the directors, a deal was struck to exchange Madame Royale, Louis and Marie Antoinette's only surviving child, for several prominent republic prisoners. She had been imprisoned in the Temple since August of 1792. After the death of her brother in June 1795, a woman was placed with her to serve as her companion. That woman was Madame Chauterenne, and it was at that time that Madame Royale was told that her brother had died.

She must have expected to die in prison also, but she learned the day before her release that she was to be exchanged for several prominent republican prisoners being held in Austria. An agreement had been reached that she would be exchanged at the Swiss frontier. To accompany her on her journey, Madame Royale could select a companion. She selected Madame de Sérent, who had served Madame Élisabeth as her *dame d'atour*. However, the government refused Madame Royale's selection. They instead assigned Renée Suzanne de Soucy, the daughter of her former governess, Madame de Mackau, to accompany her.

On 18 December 1795, at 11pm, the evening before her seventeenth birthday, Madame Royale left the Temple. She was placed under the guardianship of a captain of the gendarmes whose last name was

Méchin. After a six-day journey, she arrived at Huningue, a little town near Basel, Switzerland, that was besieged by Austrians in 1796 and 1797. There she settled into a room in the Corbeau Inn and penned a letter to Madame Chauterenne:

'I was recognized the first day at Provins. You have no idea how people ran to see me. Some called me my dear lady, others my dear Princess. Some wept with joy, and I also was near weeping. … What a change from Paris to the departments. At Charenton people were already refusing to take the assignats. They murmur loudly against the Government. … They all seemed grieved at my departure. I am known everywhere, notwithstanding the care of those who surround me. … if you knew how I feel! What a pity that such a change should not have taken place earlier! I should not have seen my family perish with so many thousands of innocent people. … My companions are very worthy people. Our M. Méchin is a good man, but very timid; he is in constant fear lest the émigrés come and seize me, or the Terrorists kill me.'[5]

The following day, 25 December, a second carriage arrived. It carried Madame Royale's dog, Coco. This joyous reunion was captured in detail:

'Coco, who was not restrained by any considerations of etiquette, scrambled through the half-open door and rushed towards his mistress, displaying such joy at being restored to her that they thought he would die for want of breath. Someone having remarked that the dog was very ugly, Madame's eyes filled with tears and she murmured, "I love him. He is all I have now to remind me of my brother."'[6]

The following day, the official exchange took place. Madame Royale was exchanged for six prisoners at the country home of a man named Reber. The spot was less than ten minutes away from the Corbeau Inn. She arrived at 6pm and the exchange occurred an hour later. When she was placed into the hands of the Austrian envoy, he attested to the following:

The undersigned, in virtue of the orders of his Majesty the Emperor, declares having received from M. Bacher, French ambassador delegated to this end, Madame the Princess Marie-Thérèse-Charlotte, daughter of his majesty the King Louis XVI.'[7]

Those at the exchange reported that it 'passed calmly'. Afterwards, Madame Royale took refreshments and left with Imperial agents a little after 9pm heading to Lauffenbourg. Her final destination was Vienna. She had never been to Vienna despite it being the birthplace of her mother and the capital of her cousin, the Holy Roman Emperor Francis II.

Of the six prisoners that Madame Royale was exchanged for, one prisoner is worth mentioning. He was the fiery republican and postmaster at Sainte-Menehould who had recognized the heavy placid features of the king when the royal family was fleeing to Montemédy. His name was Jean-Baptiste Drouet and if he had not taken immediate steps to warn citizens about the king's flight, France's history might have been different.

Although Madame Tussaud gave a cursory mention to Madame Royale's release, she had much more to say about Napoleon and his wife, Josephine. Napoleon and the widow Josephine (whose real name was Marie-Joseph-Rose Detascher) married a few months after Madame Royale's exchange occurred. Their wedding happened in Paris on a Wednesday, on 9 March 1796 (19 *Ventôse* Year V) at 3 Rue d'Atin, which was the address of the Hôtel de Mondragon that had been converted into the town hall of Paris's second district.

The civil ceremony was slated to occur at 8pm but as Napoleon arrived two hours late, it didn't happen until 10pm. Witnesses to the marriage included not only Josephine's ex-lover Barras but also Tallien, Citoyen Etienne Calmelet, and Aide de Camp Jean-Léonor-François Le Marois. The ceremony between Napoleon and Josephine was officially registered by Citoyen Charles Leclerq.

The wedding certificate showed many irregularities. For instance, Napoleon was described as 'Chef de l'Armée de l'Intérieur' (Head of the Home Army) when in fact he had just been appointed Head of the Army of Italy. His birth was also stated to be 5 February 1768, making him 18 months older than his true age, and his address was listed as that of a town hall. Josephine's birth date was also entered incorrectly such that 1767 was written instead of the correct year, 1763.

The newlyweds hardly had a honeymoon because two days after the ceremony, Napoleon took command of the Army of Italy and arrived at the front on 27 March where he began almost immediately to launch attacks. His victories during the Italian campaign quickly placed a bright shining star over him and from April to the end of October wherever he turned his eye, victory was his. Madame Tussaud commented that his 'extraordinary success' dazzled not only France but Europe.

As Napoleon was achieving military success, Madame Tussaud was left alone to struggle and make ends meet as her husband travelled to England during 1796 with a show billed as 'Curtius's Grand Cabinet of Curiosities'. Times were tough. The financial state of France remained so poor that the country was practically on the verge of declaring bankruptcy, as was Madame Tussaud.

To prevent the Parisian wax business from failing, François took an exhibition on the road and visited Cheshire, Cambridge, Norwich, Birmingham, and London. Visitors could enter the exhibition for a shilling and see Curtius' curiosities from nine in the morning until ten at night. The curiosities included paintings, sculptures, engravings, and inked drawings of battles, sieges, and bombardments, a 26-gun glass frigate and figures created from rice paste. Yet, at the real heart of the show were the items related to the French Revolution. These included profiles of the king and queen made from hair, a model of the guillotine, and the following:

> 'Curious Busts from Nature as Large as Life, Of the King, Queen, Dauphin of France, &c. ... A MODEL of the TEMPLE at PARIS, Where the ROYAL FAMILY were confined – Reduced to a Scale of 1 inch to 10 feet. ... The HEAD of M. DELAUNEY, Governor of the Bastile [sic].'[8]

One English visitor to Curtius' curiosities was so impressed by what he saw, he wrote a poem prefaced by the following:

> 'Your curiosities have impressed upon my mind so deep a sense of their inestimable worth that out of the justice to yourself and my own feelings, I cannot let them pass unnoticed. I have been an admirer of many curious cabinets, but never yet found any equal to your's. Accept them, with my sincere wishes for your welfare, the following petit piece of poetry, written on seeing them.'[9]

Around the time that François returned from England, one disturbance that Madame Tussaud mentioned involved Napoleon's older brother, Joseph. On 7 May 1797, the Directory appointed Joseph as ambassador to Rome. They hoped that he would undermine the Papal government. However, Napoleon was unhappy with the French Directory and had lost confidence in their abilities partly because he disapproved of their plan to undermine the Pope and partly because he considered such an idea premature. He saw the Republican party in Rome as weak and too ill prepared to support a government.

Joseph Bonaparte knew how his brother felt and so was hoping to establish good relations in Rome. It looked initially as if he might succeed because he was well received and obtained a cordial response from the 80-year-old Pope Pius VI. However, soon after Joseph's arrival, an Austrian officer named General Johann Provera was appointed commander of all the Papal forces. Napoleon disliked Provera because he had been fighting the French in Italy. So, when Joseph communicated Provera's appointment, Napoleon threatened the Pope, and his threats worked because the Pope dismissed Provera.

Provera's dismissal occurred despite Rome being home to many competing and discontent forces. For instance, although the Papal government was in power, they were busy putting down insurrections. The Austrians and other Europeans were also trying to influence the Pope to align with them against the French. In addition, there were other revolutionary parties, both native and foreign, struggling to rouse the populace of Rome to their sides and overthrow Papal power.

On 27 December, members of one of the discontent parties informed Joseph that a revolt was about to occur. They hoped that he would support them, but he supposedly refused, citing his impartial status. The movements of this revolutionary party were also known to the Papal government and the next day members of the Papal government also called and told Joseph again that a revolt was about to occur. They also wanted French support, but although Joseph appeared to sympathize with the Pope, he did nothing and did not offer them his support.

The next morning, around 4am, Joseph was awakened by a messenger with news that 100 insurgents had assembled at the Villa Medici and were surrounded by Papal troops. Joseph did not respond but went back to sleep. Later, when he awoke, he heard that a conflict had occurred and that some of the insurgents who had been wearing French cockades had been arrested.

Joseph went to investigate. He learned that none of the men wearing the cockade were with the French foreign service, which he told the Secretary of State. He also informed the Secretary that he thought the men should be arrested and then he supposedly named six other individuals who had taken sanctuary illegally within his jurisdiction.

When Joseph left the Secretary, he returned to his residence, the Palazzo Corsini, which also served as the French embassy. There he found

Adjutant-general Sherlock and General Léonard Mathurin Duphot, who was to be married the next day to the sister of Joseph's wife. The three men and others gathered, discussed the events of the day, and then sat down to dinner.

As they did so, a porter informed Joseph that about twenty insurgents were attempting to enter the palace. Apparently, the insurgents had attacked the barracks of the Papal troops and the troops had chased them to the embassy. The porter also reported that some of the insurgents had been distributing French cockades to passers-by and shouting '*Vive, la Republique*'.

As Joseph was hearing this, the commotion outside increased. Soon the insurgents were using the palace as the centre for their activities, apparently believing that Joseph would provide them sanctuary. He went to address the insurgents and Duphot, Sherlock, and his other guests accompanied him. As they left the dining room, they heard a volley of discharges from firearms.

When they reached the commotion, they discovered that soldiers had entered the embassy. Their entrance was a violation of established courtesy, for as long as the French flag was flying over it, the embassy was regarded as French soil and protected from attack. Still, Papal troops were firing through three vast arches of the palace. They had killed many insurgents and others were bleeding and wounded. To escape the fire and preserve themselves, the insurgents had fled even farther into the courts of the embassy.

Joseph pushed through the fleeing insurgents. When the pursuing troops saw him, they immediately stopped shooting. He then demanded to know who had given them orders that allowed them to enter the embassy and order the soldiers out. However, for some reason, confusion erupted and some of the soldiers retired while others advanced.

> '[Joseph] drew his sword, and Generals Duphot and Sherlock and two other officers of his escort armed with swords or pistols and poniards, ranged themselves at his side to resist their advance. The musketeers retired just beyond pistol-shot, and then deliberately fired a general discharge in the direction of Joseph and his friends.[10]

None of the discharges hit Joseph or those immediately surrounding him. However, a few men at the rear were killed. Joseph and Duphot then advanced as the soldiers were reloading. Joseph again ordered the soldiers out and informed them they would be severely punished if they did not obey. The soldiers ignored him and continued loading their muskets.

Suddenly, Duphot, who was extraordinarily brave, leaped into the midst of the soldiers and began fighting. He prevented one soldier from reloading and he struck another. Joseph and Sherlock joined the melee, but as they did, some of the soldiers grabbed Duphot and dragged him out of the embassy and with extreme malice, shot him in the chest.

> 'The heroic general fell, and immediately painfully rose, leaning upon his sabre. Joseph … in the midst of … indescribable confusion called out to his friend … to return. General Duphot attempted it, when a second shot prostrated him upon the pavement. More than fifty shots were then discharged into his lifeless body.'[11]

In the meantime, as Joseph and Sherlock escaped, the mangled body of Duphot was retrieved. Despite Joseph sending several dispatches to the Pope requesting help, no one came to their assistance. The following day, he fled Rome for Florence. From there, he accused the grey-haired Pope of having assassinated Duphot, and thereafter, nothing could induce him to return to Rome.

Madame Tussaud was having her own problems in France. For all the hopes that she put into her marriage, it did not turn out to be a happy one. The poor French economy likely contributed to her woes. Between 1790 and 1796, people refused to pay taxes, the deficit grew, and inflation was rampant and did not end until 1803. Bad harvests in 1794 did not help France's financial outlook and although food was available, it cost consumers dearly. Another blow fell in 1795. During the winter months of January and February, the Seine froze so solidly goods could not be transported up and down the river, and that forced many businesses to close and created high unemployment.

François had the possibility to earn a good living as a civil engineer, but he did not and may have even worked for Curtius for a time, which may have been how François and Marie met. If France's inflation was not enough to undermine the Tussaud's marriage, François' gambling did. He frittered away their money and left all financial concerns to his wife. Nonetheless, their marriage did result in children. Marie Marguerite Pauline was born in Paris on 1 September 1797. Unfortunately, she died about six months later. All Madame Tussaud had to remember her by was a wax sculpture that she made before the child's death. The couple then had a son, born on 14 April 1798; he was named Joseph but affectionately called 'Nini'.

Chapter 14

New Directions

'I have no wish to deceive you; but I know how
to astonish you.'
Paul Philidor (Philipstal)

Napoleon Bonaparte went off to Egypt, and despite his defeat there returned to Paris on 16 October 1799 as a hero. Madame Tussaud recalled his appearance:

> '[H]e was dressed in the costume of a Mamaluke, in large white trowsers, red boots, waistcoat richly embroidered, as also the jacket, which was of crimson velvet. He arrived about eight in the evening, the cannons of the invalids fired a salute. His first visit was to his mother.'[1]

Napoleon had been successful in a previous Italian campaign, and shortly after returning from Egypt he put in motion the Coup of 18-19 *Brumaire* (9-10 November) that ushered in the period of the French Consulate. The coup involved Napoleon's brother Lucien, whom Madame Tussaud described as being the 'finest looking' of all the Bonaparte siblings. Besides Lucien, Napoleon was also aided by four others in the coup. First, the French Catholic Abbé Emmanuel Joseph Sieyès who had been elected to replace Rewbell; second, the director Joseph Fouché; third, speaker of the Council of Five Hundred, Roger Ducos; and, lastly, Charles Maurice de Talleyrand-Périgord, better known as Talleyrand, who was a bishop, politician, and diplomat.

The coup began after three of the five directors were induced to resign, which meant no quorum was possible, and, thus, the Directory was practically abolished anyway. Lucien Bonaparte then falsely claimed a Jacobin plot was afoot to overthrow the Directory. For their supposed safety, Sieyès arranged for the Council of Ancients and the Council of Five

Hundred to meet at the Palace of Saint-Cloud. In addition, the councils were told that Napoleon and his troops would protect them.

At Saint Cloud, Lucien, who had been elected President of the Council of the Five Hundred, was chairing the meeting. A state of emergency needed to be declared for the coup to succeed and for the Directory to be dissolved. Lucien put forth the suggestion, but it was not well received. In fact, the Council howled him down, suspicious of his motives. Instead of dissolving the Directory, the idea was then generated that every deputy should swear allegiance to the constitution.

While that slow and laborious process was taking place, Napoleon was growing anxious and impatient. He marched to Council of Ancients, who were meeting in a long gallery, called the Gallery of Apollo, and intruded. When he spoke, a heated exchange began as a few deputies thought something was fishy. Those deputies protested, and others challenged him, which put Napoleon on the defensive and had him declaring that he was no 'Caesar'.

He left and marched to the orangerie where the Council of the Five Hundred were meeting. An orangerie is a large conservatory, greenhouse, or hothouse, in this case a long narrow building, and its entrance allowed for only two deputies to pass through its doors at a time. The organerie had been hastily converted to hold the Council of Five Hundred and had a podium erected in the centre of the building. It also had long narrow windows, under which the deputies stood and milled about listening to the discussions.

When Napoleon entered, he headed for the podium, but his intrusion was not well received. He faced a tempest of criticism and was jeered, denounced, and physically attacked before he could reach the podium. In fact, he and his brother were howled down and forced to retreat. It was then that Lucien made a stupendous move. He approached the guards of the Council and flat out lied with exceptional persuasion.

Lucien claimed that some of the deputies were conspiring with the English and that they had just tried to assassinate his brother. In addition, Lucien also maintained that most of the deputies were being held hostage. With all the drama that he could employ, Lucien then theatrically drew his sword from its scabbard, pointed it in a threatening manner at his brother's chest, and swore that he would kill anyone, including his own brother, if he ever betrayed the Republic.

It was an inspiring moment. What Napoleon had been unable to achieve by force, Lucien did with dramatics. The guards cleared the chamber, which effectively ended the reign of the Directory and ushered in the era of the French Consulate. Exactly how the chamber was cleared has been debated.

Some people claim it was a chaotic situation with deputies diving out of windows and hiding in bushes. Another version maintains that the event was much more orderly. In the end, however, the coup d'état of 18 *Brumaire* resulted in Napoleon serving as First Consul with two other consuls (initially Roger Ducos and Sieyès who were soon succeeded by Jean-Jacques Régis de Cambacérès and Charles-François Lebrun). Napoleon's role was initially intended to be minor, which was confirmed by the new 'Constitution of the Year VIII'. However, he rewrote the constitution so that although he appeared to preserve the Republic, he in fact created a dictatorship.

Shortly after the coup, Madame Tussaud had another son, named François like his father. The dark-haired baby boy was born on 2 August 1800, and that was the year that a fed-up Madame Tussaud separated from her husband.

The year 1801 was the same year that Madame Tussaud created a likeness of Marie Antoinette's daughter, who was Madame Royale but now married and known as the Duchess of Angoulême. In addition, Madame Tussaud also made a likeness of Josephine the same year she married Napoleon. The likeness so impressed Josephine she then commissioned a likeness of her husband as a gift to the First Consul sometime in 1801.

At 6am on the appointed day that Madame Tussaud arrived to model Napoleon's face, Josephine supposedly greeted her with kindness. Napoleon said little during the sitting, and, according to Madame Tussaud, when he did speak, he did so in short, abrupt sentences. However, he supposedly appreciated Madame Tussaud's likeness so much that he later returned with two gentlemen, André Massena and an aide-de-camp. Massena was already familiar to Madame Tussaud whom she described as 'striking' in appearance, stout, and about medium height.

There were also two other men hinted to have patronized Madame Tussaud because of her relationship with Napoleon. They were consul Cambacérès, whom Madame Tussaud described as imposing with large features, a good complexion, and a prominent nose. The other man was the consul Le Brun. Le Brun, in contrast to Cambacérès, was described as extremely handsome with light hair and a fair complexion.

Madame Tussaud was not the only person who captured Napoleon's attention when it came to wax. When he was in Italy, he visited the workshop of Felice Fontana, a natural philosopher whose wax skills interested the Grand Duke Leopold (later Leopold III). Leopold then invited Fontana to Florence. Under Fontana's direction an immense number of anatomical wax preparations were created that showed in the minutest detail all parts of the human anatomy.

Marie Antoinette's older brother, Joseph II, also heard of Fontana's wax creations. He then procured a large collection of anatomical wax figures for Vienna's surgical school. Like Joseph II, Napoleon was interested in wax models for medical purposes. He ordered some models from Fontana, but an argument erupted over the price and resulted in none being delivered. However, the benefits of wax modelling to surgeons still interested him and so, on 28 May 1806, he established a school in Rouen to train students on how to create wax figures.

The next mention Madame Tussaud makes of Napoleon involves a plot that occurred on 24 December 1800, when a '*machine infernale*' was created to destroy the First Consul. The plot became known as the 'plot of the rue Saint-Nicaise' or the '*machine infernale*' plot. It was an assassination attempt using a bomb concocted by a Pierre Saint-Régeant that indirectly involved a Breton politician named Georges Cadoudal.

A Chouan officer named Pierre Robinault de Saint-Régeant orchestrated the plot. Involved indirectly in the plot was Cadoudal, who had served as leader of Chouans during the French Revolution and who was also involved in several rebellions thereafter. In addition, Cadoudal also supported Louis XVIII by fighting against revolutionaries, but, ultimately found it impossible to continue fighting and thus became involved in conspiracies that supported Louis XVIII, including the *machine infernale* plot.

The bomb was to be placed north of the Tuileries Palace in the rue Saint-Nicaise. The idea was that when Napoleon left the Tuileries and approached rue Saint-Nicaise, a signal would be given, the bomb's fuse would be lit, and the explosion would kill him.

On Christmas Eve, the plotters readied the *machine infernale* and took it to the rue Saint-Nicaise in a cart with a big wine cask pulled by a mare. There Saint-Régeant paid 12 sous to a 14-year-old girl, Marianne Peusol, to hold the mare. The person who was to give the signal to light the fuse took his place, as did Saint-Régeant who was supposed to light the fuse. However, when Napoleon's carriage reached the spot for the signal to be given, the signal person panicked and delayed the signal a few minutes.

This resulted in Saint-Régeant lighting the fuse late. Afterwards, Saint-Régeant fled and the bomb exploded, but rather than killing Bonaparte, who had by then passed by, it killed three women, a grocer, and, of course, 14-year-old Peusol. At least fifteen people were also wounded,

and there was damage to at least fifteen houses. *Le Publiciste* reported on
26 December:

> 'All Paris has been curious to see the ruins produced by
> this terrible explosion. They are terrible. The houses which
> surround the ground and the little Carousel, are shivered to
> pieces; the entire streets of St. Nicaise, St. Thomas, Echelle,
> and Chartres, have been shaken, as by a violent earthquake. So
> great a shock, in this populous quarter, might have been fatal
> to a great many people. However, the number of victims is not
> so great as was at first supposed.'[2]

That same day, another paper, the *Journal des Defenseurs*, gave details
about the blast.

> 'The cask of powder which was blown up was hooped with
> iron, and contained a quantity of balls in such a manner,
> that the discharge must be a real discharge of cannister shot.
> The carriage on which it was placed blocked up the street at
> the time when the first guards of Bonaparte passed. – They
> made it draw off a second time, and thus there were two very
> remarkable movements. At that moment it was conjectured
> that the explosion, which was made by pulling the trigger
> of the gun with a string, these different movements altering
> the position of the carriage, prevented the cord from being
> sufficiently stretched in order to pull the trigger, and it was
> at that moment the coach of the First Consul, which drove
> rapidly, happily avoided the fatal blow.'[3]

Napoleon believed that extreme-left Jacobins had plotted his assassination.
Police initially arrested several Jacobins, who they accused of plotting his
demise. Fouché, the same man who had been involved in the coup d'état of
18 *Brumaire* and was now serving as Minister of Police, attempted to focus
on the Chouans. Napoleon refused to listen, believing that it had to be the
Jacobins who attempted to kill him, and he exiled 130 Jacobins.

In the meantime, positive proof against the Chouans was discovered by
Fouché. Napoleon still would not listen, insisting that it was the Jacobins
who tried to kill him. Despite these doubts, the Chouan bomb maker was
soon arrested. He gave up the names of his six fellow conspirators that

included Saint-Régeant and Cadoudal. Saint-Régeant was arrested and executed on 20 April 1801. However, Cadoudal avoided capture and fled to England.

Madame Tussaud had also been thinking about going to England. One reason she cited was the volatile state of France and the country's declining economy. Her business was also slowly failing. Later, however, she maintained that her real reason for going to England was to escape a husband she considered unsupportive and worthless. An opportunity to go to England presented itself after the Treaty of Amiens was signed on 27 March 1802. It temporarily ended the hostilities between Great Britain and France, which allowed her to leave. However, to visit England, she needed a passport. She claimed that Fouché initially refused to give her one and claimed that his reason was that her talents were of immense value to France.

Another reason that she wanted to head to England was financial. It had to do with a business offer she received from one of Curtius' old friends, Paul de Philipstal (sometimes spelled Phillipstal, Philipsthal, or Phillipsthall). However, Philipstal's real name appears to have been Paul Philidor, based on a booklet from 1805 that mentions Philidor's alias as 'Philipsthal'.

Philidor (also spelled Phylidor or Phyllidor) claimed to be a distant cousin of an eighteenth-century composer and famous French chess player, François-André Danican Philidor. Despite this supposed familial connection, it is unclear if Philidor was French, German, Flemish, British, or Swiss. What is known is that he did speak French fluently.

Philidor began presenting his roadshow in Berlin in early 1789. It was a prototype phantasmagoria show, which was a dream-like spectral show performed in darkness. Philidor's shows also involved seances and raising the dead. However, near the end of March 1789, after having conducted numerous shows, he was accused of being a fraud, prohibited from performing his shows again, and ordered to leave Berlin.

Philidor's roadshow then travelled to Leipzig, Dresden, Vienna, Regensburg, and München before ending up in Paris. In Paris, Philidor advertised one of his first shows in December of 1792 as a 'phantasmagorie' show, which he later changed to 'phantasmagoria'. An 1885 dictionary of the theatre claimed 'Filidort' performed at the Hotel Chartres on rue Richelieu twice a day, the first show at 5:30pm and a second one ending precisely at 9pm.

Although Philidor got into trouble in Berlin for raising the dead, he supposedly once said, 'I pretend to be neither priest nor magician; I have no wish to deceive you; but I know how to astonish you'.[4] In addition, at some point the astonishing Philidor began using the name Philipstal, which is the name he met Curtius under.

Philipstal soon owed Curtius a debt of gratitude because a show he produced in March of 1794 got him arrested in Paris. Apparently, Philipstal accidentally used a slide that made it appear as if Louis XVI was ascending to heaven. His republican patrons became upset, accused him of supporting the monarchy, and called the police. He was arrested on the spot, and it was Curtius who supposedly bribed Robespierre with three hundred louis to achieve his release.

Although Philipstal may have developed the idea of phantasmagoria, Étienee-Gaspard Robert is the person credited with having perfected the techniques. Robert, who went by his stage name Robertson, attended one of Philipstal's performances in 1793, realized the potential and created his own shows calling them 'fantasmagorie', a combination of optics, magic, and conjuring, accompanied by sounds and eerie lighting effects.

Fantasmagorie was produced by a magic lantern. A typical magic lantern in late 1700 or early 1800s was housed in a wooden box of varying heights. They usually had a hinged door or several hinged doors on the side and sometimes a door on the top too. These doors were used to adjust the light sources, such as candles or lanterns that burned whale oil. In addition, a metal chimney might be located on the top to aid air flow or provide an updraft and release of heat.

A barrel lens frame rested outside at the front of the box and near it might be a focus knob for the lens or lenses. The interior of the box was black and housed the light source and concave mirror, which was placed at the back, and directed the light through a small rectangular sheet of glass and projected this image forward to the lens. The reflection produced was then magnified so that 'images could be made to appear like fantastic luminous shapes, floating inexplicably in the air'.[5]

A Parisian journal called *L'Ami des Lois* printed a description of what one spectator experienced at one of Robertson's shows. Robertson had requested audience members to ask for any person they knew to be raised from the dead. One person asked for the radical revolutionary Marat, and after Marat appeared came a second request:

> 'A young man desired to see the apparition of a woman whom he had tenderly loved, and showed her miniature to the magician, who threw upon the brazier some swallow's

feathers, a dozen dried butterflies, and a few grains of phosphorus. We presently saw the phantom of a young woman, with her hair floating over her shoulders, fixing her gaze upon her lover, and regarding him with a tender and melancholy smile.'[6]

Gothic was particularly popular, and Robertson's Gothic shows enthralled the public. They plunged audiences into utter darkness, where for an hour and half, audience members were completely mesmerized. One newspaper account of a fantasmagorie extravaganza in 1801, though not necessarily a show produced by Robertson, described the bizarre types of things that such audiences might see and experience.:

'This spectacle ... is lighted up with flashes of lightning: the decorations are tombs, caverns, and infernal dungeons. The actors are spectres, ghosts, phantoms, goblins, and banchees, and the walking gentlemen hyaenas, tygers, and devils of all colours.'[7]

To create these spectral shows, Robertson used assistants. Eventually, two assistants decided to start their own fantasmagorie show, and Robertson filed a lawsuit to stop them. The case went to trial in 1799 and to defend himself, Robertson had to reveal his secrets. Once they were out, others developed their own fantasmagorie shows, and soon they could be found everywhere.

Philipstal likewise began to produce phantasmagoria shows and ended up in England around 1801. There Gothic was all the rage too, and his phantasmagoria shows were well received. A poster advertising Philipstal's show at the Lyceum on the Strand, promised both optical illusions and mechanical pieces of art. Optical illusions included ghosts, disembodied spirits, and phantoms or apparitions of the dead. Some of the mechanical pieces advertised included rope dancers, a peacock, and a 'beautiful cossack' in a small box that danced after the manner of Cossacks.

Philipstal also promised patrons that he would provide entertainment that had never been 'offered to the eye,' and claimed:

'This Spectrology, which professes to expose the practices of artful impostors and pretended exorcists, and to open the eyes of those who still foster an absurd belief in Ghosts, or

Disembodied Spirits, will, it is presumed, afford also to the spectator an interesting and pleasing Entertainment.'[8]

During a break, Philipstal returned to France, and while there, he talked to Madame Tussaud about joining him and presenting her wax figures. He must have realized that her wax displays would be a superb addition to his own shows and likely suggested to her that her wax exhibitions could not fail. At any rate, Madame Tussaud liked his suggestion and became his junior partner on the road. Unfortunately, the partnership with Philipstal did not make her life any easier. Philipstal's terms were strict and arranged to his advantage, as 'he would take half of her gross earnings'.[9] However, despite these harsh terms, Madame Tussaud agreed, and at the age of forty, she left France, never to return.

Before her departure, Madame Tussaud gave her failing Paris wax business to her husband but kept control of the two houses, the Ivry-sur-Seine and the house located at No. 20 Boulevard Temple, which was still saddled with a mortgage. She also took her 4-year-old son Joseph, and left 2-year-old François, who was called Francis in England (and to differentiate him from his father, shall be referred to from this point forward as Francis), in France in the care of Madame Tussaud's mother, aunt, and François. Francis would join his mother fifteen years later.

PART III

Madame Tussaud Goes to the United Kingdom

1802

London, England

Chapter 15

United Kingdom

'He treats me like a slave.'
Madame Tussaud On Paul Philidor

In 1802, the same year that a feisty and determined Madame Tussaud arrived in London, mainly with her wax figures and stories, a wave of creativity in the art field was in vogue. For instance, the English actor, comedian, and dancer Joseph Grimaldi first performed his white-faced clown character called 'Joey' at the Sadler's Wells Theatre. Romantic poet William Wordsworth's also wrote his sonnet, *Composed upon Westminster Bridge September 3, 1802*, that described London and the Thames. In addition, the first play to be explicitly called a melodrama was performed at the Theatre Royal in Covent Garden. It was Thomas Holcroft's Gothic, *A Tale of Mystery*, which was an unacknowledged translation of the French director René-Charles Guilbert de Pierécourt's, *Cœlina, ou, l'enfant du mystère* (*Coelina, or The Child of Mystery*).

Madame Tussaud added her own creativity to the mix. Besides her steely determination to succeed, she brought with her all the death masks and heads she had inherited or made, some wax faces and busts, and about 30 wooden-limbed leather bodies, Not everything arrived safely, and she was forced to repair some of her wax models and costumes that were damaged during shipment.

Besides those repairs necessary to ensure her livelihood, she quickly discovered that she was not a headline act. Philipstal did not mention her or her wax figures on his advertising bills. In addition, Madame Tussaud had to care for Joseph and find a place to live. The spot she selected as home was located on Surrey Street near the Lyceum Theatre on the Strand.

On the Strand, besides the Lyceum, were other attractions. People could easily see juggling, conjuring, freaks, and menageries. Although the Lyceum Theatre dated to 1765 and had originally opened with art exhibits, it hosted a variety of other entertainments between 1794 and 1809 that included Astley's circus with trained animals, clowns, and acrobats, and scenes painted by Robert Ker Porter. In 1800, Porter painted a 120-foot three-quarter round panorama called the *Storming of Seringapatam*, and, in 1802, he had another panoramic displaying the 'contest between the English and French Forces, on the memorable 21st of March, 1801, at the BATTLE OF ALEXANDRIA; the events of which terminated a war, so much to the glory of the British name, and finally restored to Europe the Blessing of Peace'.[1]

Besides Astley and Porter, Monsieur Henri-Louis Charles was also appearing at the Lyceum in 1802. He was a ventriloquist with a show named 'The Auricular Communications of the Invisible Girl'. Perhaps, Madame Tussaud already knew Charles because Curtius had once hired a ventriloquist, and it may have been Charles who performed for him.

Charles' Lyceum show consisted of an 'Aerostatic Globe' eighteen inches in diameter that was placed in the centre of the room and from which issued a female voice. It was described in an advertisement as follows:

'The Voice of a Living Female is distinctly heard as if originating in its centre, and will answer Questions put by any Person present, or maintain a Conversation, either in Whisper, or in a more audible Tone: the lady will also, if requested, entertain the Company with Specimens of Vocal Music, producing a most peculiar effect. This Living Aerostat, and its incomprehensible Voice, form a most impenetrable puzzle to the inquisitive mind, at the same time that conjecture is equally excited by another singularity attending the Lady of the Balloon, who though herself invisible to the keenest eyes, seems to be in the midst of the assemblage, and sees every thing as passes in the room: she is heard to breathe, and by her answers returned instantaneously to all proper Questions.'[2]

Charles' show was appearing on the second floor of the Lyceum. Beneath him on the first floor was Madame Tussaud's wax exhibition, or to be more precise, 'Curtius' Cabinet of Curiosities'. Madame Tussaud would continue to call her display a cabinet and use Curtius' name until she established her own reputation as a competent businesswoman and wax modeler in 1808.

In the meantime, Madame Tussaud wrote home about twice weekly to her husband, mother, and young son, Francis. Using nearly unreadable handwriting that was somewhat sloppy and severely slanted, she scrawled French sentences occasionally awkwardly constructed with inconsistent grammar and incorrect spelling. Her letters were sporadically boastful and sometimes recalled connections she had made in her travels. Other times, she was homesick. These letters noted she would eventually return home and expressed her longing for the mother she adored and her precious son Francis.

Madame Tussaud would also quickly realize that her relationship with Philipstal needed to end. After her arrival in London, she wrote to her husband that she hoped to be rid of Philipstal in six months but noted that disconnecting herself from him would take time. In fact, she would not be able to buy herself out of her contract until 1804.

In her letters home, she also dismissed Philipstal's abilities. She claimed that her exhibition was what was keeping him afloat. To be fair, Philipstal's shows drew large crowds night after night. Phantasmagoria shows were so popular at the time that the great caricaturist artist James Gillray created several cartoons honouring phantasmagoria, including one titled, *A Phantasmagoria;— scene – Conjuring-up an Armed Skeleton* dated 5 January 1803.

Phantasmagoria was not the only interest in the early nineteenth century. The British public also became fascinated with murder and executions. Newspapers were constantly printing details and there were numerous books published about trials and executions. For instance, one book provided all the gory details about a married schoolmaster named Eugene Aram who murdered his wife's lover, a shoemaker named Daniel Clark. There were also numerous newspaper stories with headlines that read 'Shocking Murder', 'Murder! Murder! Murder!', and 'Atrocious Murder'.

Madame Tussaud knew that murder was a popular topic with the public. She also had an uncanny ability to understand what visitors to her cabinet wanted to see. So, when an Irish soldier in the English army, Colonel Edward Marcus Despard, conspired but failed to assassinate George III, she knew immediately that Despard would bring in a crowd. Even before his execution, she began devising how to obtain a copy of his severed head.

Despard's run of bad luck began long before he was arrested for attempting to assassinate George III. In 1790, he was appointed superintendent of the Bay of Honduras, and while there he married a black woman. Soon after his marriage, he decided that all blacks should have the same rights as white settlers. Such a decision of course resulted in a backlash by white settlers, and he was forced to return to London to explain himself. The result of his explanation was imprisonment at the King's Bench Prison. When he was released, he eventually joined the United Irishmen and began to fight for equal rights for the Irish. When war with France broke out, the United Irishmen went underground and backed the French in an invasion against Ireland. Unfortunately, the invasion failed, and in response, the passage of the Act of Union in 1800 went into effect on 1 January 1801, abolishing the Irish Parliament and creating the United Kingdom of Great Britain and Ireland.

Hoping to reverse the situation in Ireland, Despard conspired with other individuals. Their plan was to encourage other uprisings by assassinating George III, taking over the Bank of England, and seizing the Tower of London. However, in late 1802, one week before the plot was to be enacted, it was discovered. Despard and about twenty others were arrested at a Lambeth pub and jailed.

On 7 February 1803, Despard and six of his co-conspirators were tried for high treason by prosecutor Spencer Perceval. The public was enthralled, and newspapers could not provide enough coverage. Evidence against the conspirators was weak, but the trial became particularly exciting when Horatio Nelson appeared as a character witness for Despard. In the end, however, Despard and his six co-conspirators were found guilty and sentenced to be hanged and beheaded.

On 21 February 1803 at 5am, St. George's bell tolled and continued tolling for about an hour. An hour and half later, the prison bell rang as a signal to unlock the cells of the convicted prisoners. At 7am, all but two of the seven men went to the chapel, Despard being one of the men who stayed behind. When all the men at the chapel had finished, their irons were knocked off and they were bound by their arms and hands and taken to the scaffold.

Seven coffins were placed upon the platform where the drop had been erected. Sawdust was already in place near the block to catch the blood when their heads were severed from their bodies. The block was near the scaffold and about one hundred spectators were situated on the platform. About half past eight, the prisoners were brought to the platform and an orderly procedure followed:

> 'As soon as the cord was fastened round the neck of one, the second was brought up, and so on till the cords were fastened round the necks of all the seven. ... Despard was brought up the last, dressed in boots, a dark brown great coat, his hair unpowdered. He ascended the scaffold with great firmness. His countenance underwent not the slightest change during the fastening of the rope round his neck.[3]

A crowd of 20,000 came to watch the spectacle. Each man was given an opportunity to speak. Afterwards the clergy prayed with the five prisoners who had visited the chapel earlier. A clergyman then shook hands with each prisoner and then the 'most awful silence' prevailed. At seven minutes to nine the signal was given and simultaneously the platform under each man dropped. They were left hanging for about a half hour before they were cut down.

Despard's body was the first to be placed upon the sawdust with his head on a block, which was then severed. The executioner then took Despard's head by the hair, carried it to the edge of the parapet, held it up for spectators to view, and exclaimed, 'This is the head of a traitor – Edward Marcus Despard'.[4] By ten o'clock the executions were over, the bodies were delivered to loved ones or friends, and spectators were traveling home.

After the execution, Madame Tussaud immediately visited Despard's friends. She wanted to obtain a cast of his head, and, luckily, permission was granted so his head became her first cast of a severed head since leaving France. Thereafter, death masks of those executed became a popular part of her exhibits.

That was not all she did. She knew that part of what made a great exhibit was an appropriate setting, and so her display included eerie blue lighting. The English public embraced her exhibit and quickly helped her plans to escape Philipstal because soon after her Despard display debuted, her Lyceum attendance dramatically rose as did her profits.

Madame Tussaud travelled with Nini and without Philipstal to Edinburgh on 27 April 1803. However, before she left England, she wrote her husband a letter dated 25 April 1803 and complained to him that Philipstal treated her as badly as François did. Philipstal would not let her see the books and she had to be happy with whatever he paid her.

Madame Tussaud also saw a solicitor near Manchester Square. François needed to raise money to keep the business afloat in France and so she drew up legal papers giving her husband full power of attorney. At the time, she believed the business in France could be saved. The papers put her in financial jeopardy as they allowed her husband to borrow what he needed but compelled her to support what he borrowed by paying the accrued interest.

The trip had been terrible and even the captain noted that he had never experienced such rough seas. Madame Tussaud survived three days of rolling hell. No one could go on deck, and the churning waters were so violent, they affected even those who did not expect to get seasick. One of the few persons who apparently faced the turbulent seas bravely and did so with little problem was her little Nini or as the crew called him 'Little Bonaparte'.

When the ship reached Edinburgh on 10 May, Madame Tussaud found lodgings with a landlady who spoke French. She also learned Philipstal had not paid to ship her wax figures, yet, he had led her to believe he had paid the costs. The burden now fell upon her and she had no money. That was not her only problem. Because the seas were so rough, she discovered there were 36 figures needing major repairs and most of the other figures were badly damaged. Fortunately, the ventriloquist Charles came to her aid with a temporary loan of £30.

Her arrival left eight days before her cabinet opened on 18 May 1803. That was the same day a horse show was slated to start in Edinburgh, which would thereby allow her to take advantage of the show's extra visitors. Madame Tussaud also thereafter tried to have her cabinet coincide with other events in other cities because then she could take advantage of extra customers.

Madame Tussaud fell in love with Edinburgh. In 1801, its population was stated to be 129,954 but she described it in 1803 as 'little'. It was vibrant, romantic, and charming. The historic Edinburgh Castle dominated the skyline and the whole city was breathtakingly beautiful but more; it was at peace.

Besides its beauty, Edinburgh also served as a haven for French émigrés. In fact, Louis XVI's brother, the Count d'Artois had found sanctuary at the Palace of Holyrood between 1796 and 1799. He would also periodically visit Edinburgh and stay at the palace until 1803. Further, other émigrés from his court would linger in the area until after the Bourbon Restoration in 1814.

Madame Tussaud knew she needed to make money in Edinburgh, and she did. She charged an entrance fee of 2 shillings, which was an exorbitant amount as it was about twice the amount most showmen were charging for a similar exhibit. However, when the horse show ended, she reduced her fee to the more reasonable 1 shilling. She also kept exhaustive records of her daily finances in a notebook. She used one side to record her income and the other side to list expenses. Within two weeks of the Edinburgh show, she reported to her husband that her exhibition was always packed, and, by day eighteen, she recorded that she had earned the substantial amount of £190. Near the end of July, after paying for shipping and advertising costs, she made a profit of £301 12s. (worth today about £22,926). However, she grumbled that half her profits automatically went to Philipstal and wrote to her husband saying, 'I have been forced to accept his accounts as he placed them before me … He treats me like a slave'.[5]

For the first time, Madame Tussaud also published a catalogue that provided a biographical sketch of each wax figure in the cabinet and allowed spectators to navigate the exhibit in an interactive way but at their own speed. The 1803 catalogue was titled *Biographical Sketches of the Characters Comprising the Cabinet of Composition Figures Executed by the Celebrated Curtius of Paris and His Successor.* It served as another clever way to extract money from her customers and she sold it for 6d. Yet, money was not the only reason for producing the catalogue.

Catalogues were informative, and from about 1818 onward, they would be available in every town she visited as they afforded visitors a self-guided tour by providing a layout of the rooms and the location of every wax figure in the exhibit. Moreover, they allowed people to roam the exhibit at their own leisure staying as long or as short a time as they liked. They also allowed Madame Tussaud to stress the educational and cultural value of her exhibits.

One newspaper strongly recommended a visit to Madame Tussaud's in 1819 because of the educational value her exhibit offered. The article stated that a visit should be undertaken by 'preceptors and others having young persons under their care, as a view of the figures will awaken in their minds a desire to open the pages of history and biography, and be the means of their deriving much useful knowledge as well as rational amusement'.[6] Moreover, the historical aspects could be easily demonstrated in catalogues, which also stressed the historical value of the collection and provided detailed or sometimes lengthy biographies of each figure displayed. For instance, in her 1842 catalogue, the first line describing Frederic William III of Prussia stated, 'his late Majesty, who was born 1768, and began his reign in 1797, may be considered as one of the principal agents in the downfal [*sic*] of Napoleon'.[7] Also included in the 1842 catalogue was information about Admiral Nelson said to have 'produced the most important consequences to this country,'[8] Joan of Arc who was 'tried by order of the Duke of Bedford, and ordered to be burnt as a sorceress'[9] and Voltaire, 'a most voluminous author, and may be considered as one of the chief of those writers whose works prepared the public mind for the Revolution'.[10]

For the next few years, Madame Tussaud travelled throughout Ireland and Scotland and avoided England. There were several reasons for this, including the fact that anti-French sentiment was at its height, Napoleon was threatening England, and passage of the Aliens' Act in 1793 regulated immigration into the country. The act also forced all aliens to register upon their arrival and prohibited any foreigners who arrived in England after October 1801 from remaining in the country for more than three months.

From Edinburgh, Madame Tussaud travelled to Glasgow arriving there in time for a show in October 1804. She had since cut off all communication with her husband as it seemed he only wrote to ask for money. She sent him her last letter on 27 June of that same year. Then she was off to Dublin, Ireland, where newspaper advertisements appeared for her exhibition in August, September, and October. Her Dublin exhibition was held at the Shakespeare Gallery on Exchequer Street and was open from eleven o'clock till four and from five till dusk. She was charging 2 shillings as the entrance fee or for 7 shillings a permanent non-transferable ticket could be acquired.

Madame Tussaud also announced that her cabinet was to include one of Dublin's most popular gentlemen. His name was John Philipot Curran, an eminent Irish orator, politician, lawyer, and judge. He may have helped Madame Tussaud or at the very least encouraged Philipstal to come to terms with her, thereby ending her business relationship with him and allowing her to keep all profits thereafter. From Dublin, she travelled the countryside before returning there sometime in 1806. On 24 December, she ran advertisements informing the Dublin public that she had once again commenced her cabinet. This time it was being held at No. 22, New Sackville-Street. Her fee was 1 shilling with the cabinet open ten till four and in the evening from five until ten o'clock.

During these travelling years, her exhibitions slowly evolved. When Madame Tussaud first arrived in England she displayed death heads and French figures that had never been shown in France. These French death heads and figures changed over time, evolving to encompass more British, Scottish, or Irish individuals. Napoleon also became a cornerstone of her exhibition because the English were intrigued to see their enemy. Of course, everyone loved her wax figure of Nini that greeted guests, and people were still intrigued by Marat, Robespierre, and Fouquier-Tinville, the last guillotined heads she modelled in France.

Among the new wax figures that the British, Scottish, and Irish visitors wanted to see were such people as Mary Queen of Scots or Bonnie Prince Charlie. She also presented some new English wax figures for her Sackville

Street cabinet that she advertised. They included full size models of George III, Queen Charlotte, and the Prince of Wales. There was also figures of other famous Englishmen such as Admiral Lord Nelson, the British Whig statesman Charles James Fox, and Fox's arch rival, Tory statesman William Pitt the Younger.

To keep her Dublin patrons interested, just like Curtius had done, Madame Tussaud continually rotated the figures or added new ones. For instance, in August of 1807, she announced that she had two new full-size models for display. These new models were Talleyrand and Abbé Sieyès, two of the men involved in Napoleon's coup. In October, she also added the full-size wax figure of the celebrated songstress Madame Angelica Catalani assuming the character of Cleopatra, which brought customers into direct contact with someone they considered famous but replicated in wax.

Madame Tussaud announced that her final show in Dublin would occur on Saturday, 16 January of 1808. However, such announcements claiming an imminent departure were often a ploy to drum up business and get those viewers who been delaying their visit to hurry in and see her wax figures. If the advertisement increased business, she would often delay her departure, thereby making it seem as if there was high demand to visit her show.

Newspaper advertisements for her cabinet in Belfast began appearing in mid-May. Belfast was a small town with a population of about 25,000 at the time. Her Belfast advertisements bragged that she had received 'great applause' in London and Dublin, and she noted that her cabinet was being held at 92, High Street, which was near the location of the *Belfast Monthly Magazine*, a short-lived publication produced between 1808 and 1814 that focused on subjects related to Ireland and Irishmen.

September was also the month that she received stunning news. Her husband had lost his Paris exhibition and the house on the Boulevard du Temple. They were now in possession of the creditor, Madame Salomé Reiss. The house that had been rented to tenants on the Rue des Fosses du Temple was where François and the family moved and now lived. If Madame Tussaud had been entertaining any thoughts on returning to Paris, she now realized there was nothing left for her there.

After her husband's loss of the waxworks in France, Madame Tussaud focused on making a life for her and little Nini in England. Moreover, 1808 was the same year she no longer advertised her show as 'Curtius's Cabinet of Curiosities'. She had established herself as a competent wax sculptress and business woman, and now she focused on touring and establishing her name throughout Ireland, England, and Scotland. By the end of 1808, she was back in Scotland preparing for her next exhibition, announcing her return to Edinburgh on 19 January 1809 in the *Caledonian Mercury* stating:

> 'Madame Tussaud, just returned, after an absence of five years, begs to present her respects to the Nobility, and Inhabitants in general of Edinburgh, and to assure them, that ever grateful for the liberal patronage with which she was honoured here, and an anxious desire to merit a continuance of their favour, she has been most studious in the Selection of about THIRTY PROPER CHARACTERS, added to her former EXHIBITION; and she hopes the Personages, the delicacy of the Workmanship, and the elegance of Dresses, will meet general approbation.'[11]

During her travelling years, Madame Tussaud and her son did not just travel by sea. They also travelled by land, and she hired a coach to ensure they arrived before her exhibition arrived by caravan. A caravan referred to a large horse-drawn van or pantechnicon that advertised her name in stylish letters on its side. It was the caravan that carried her exhibition goods, such as the wax figures, costumes, decorations, candles, and other necessary materials related to her displays.

On the road, Madame Tussaud continued to faithfully note her expenses in her notebook. Even the occasional splurge was noted. Splurges included a pinch of snuff, a sip of porter, and once a hat costing £1 4s. Otherwise, her expenses were always just for the basics needed to survive or to promote her show. Basics included such things as candles, food, laundry, lamp oil, or wages to pay her staff.

In 1815, to increase profits, Madame Tussaud added an additional attraction to her show. Seventeen-year-old Nini was now advertised as Joseph, and he was busy creating silhouette portraits. Silhouettes were an image of a person, animal, or any solid object, composed of a single colour, and matched the outline of the sitter. Joseph's silhouettes ranged in price from two to five shillings.

Silhouette portraits had acquired their name from Étienne de Silhouette. He had been France's Controller of Finances under Louis XV's Ancien Régime for eight months in 1759. During Silhouette's tenure, he became known for his penny-pinching ways and that resulted in critics coining the term, à la Silhouette. Because silhouette meant cheap and because such artworks could be produced inexpensively, the term silhouette was then applied to this portrait alternative. Silhouettes appealed to the lower classes who could not afford a costly portrait. It allowed them to obtain a likeness of themselves or their loved ones. Joseph accomplished his silhouettes using a magic lantern that cast the sitter's full-size shadow and allowed him to trace a smaller version of that shadow onto a piece of paper. Joseph had learned his silhouette skills from his mother's friend, French-born artist and writer Francis Hérve, the younger brother of Charles Hérve, the inventor of the prosopographus, a silhouette machine that captured a person's likeness as they sat perfectly still.

Silhouettes were a good advertising technique and helped Madame Tussaud to compete effectively with the variety of showmen that were also touring her same route. Among those touring was George Wombell and his menagerie, declared by Wombell to be as varied as Noah's Ark. His menagerie included such exotic creatures as elephants, leopards, llamas, monkeys, ostriches, ocelots, giraffes, tigers, and a gorilla. Wombell was also an extraordinary marketeer and perhaps Madame Tussaud learned a trick or two from him. Once when London's Bartholomew Fair was about to open, Wombell undertook a forced march of his elephant to arrive at its opening on time. Unfortunately, in the process his elephant died. Wombell's rival then began advertising 'The Only Live Elephant in the Fair'. Wombell was not about to be beaten and got creative. He displayed a sign bragging, 'The Only Dead Elephant in the Fair'. Such creative signage helped him handily defeat his rival as his dead elephant was a hit.

Another person on the travelling circuit was Monsieur Godeau who performed 'matchless evolutions' or in other words extraordinary feats on the tightrope. For instance, there was his 'much-admired WOODENSHOE DANCE; at the end of which he … turn[ed] a SURPRISING SOMERSET [*sic*] with the BALANCING POLE'.[12] His finale often included him turning a double somersault while playing a woodwind instrument known as the flageolet.

Madame Godeau also eventually began performing with her husband. In March of 1816, while in Scotland, she supposedly gave her first and last performance by dancing a *pas seul* on the rope fitted with iron fetters. Newspaper ads later showed that her act was not a one-time performance. In fact, Madame Godeau's performance expanded and came to include Monsieur Godeau and their daughter.

Not to be missed was the fire-eater Josephine Girardelli. She was said to be impervious to fire and was first introduced in Portsmouth in 1814 by the famous showman John Richardson. Richardson owned Richardson's

Show and was always on the lookout for a good act that would draw crowds. Richardson knew he'd found a winner when he saw Girardelli perform for the first time. His hand-bill describing her abilities read:

> 'Wonders will never cease! – The Great Phenomena of Nature. Signora Josephine Girardelli (just arrived from the Continent), who has had the honour of appearing before most of the Crowned Heads of Europe, will exhibit the Powers of Resistance against Heat, every day ... She will, without the least symptoms of pain, put boiling melted lead into her mouth, and emit the same with the imprint of her teeth thereon; red-hot irons will be passed over various parts of her body; she will walk over a bar of red-hot iron with her naked feet; will wash her hands in aquafortis; put boiling oil in her mouth! ... Admission 3s.'[13]

Chapter 16

Touring

'The promenade among the illustrious dead and illustrious
living is truly delightful.'

London Observer

The Battle of Waterloo was fought on Sunday, 18 June 1815, and it ended
Napoleon's reign when he was beaten by the British forces commanded
by Field Marshal Arthur Wellesley, 1st Duke of Wellington. Wellington's
win caused his reputation to skyrocket making him one of Britain's
greatest military heroes, while a defeated Napoleon was placed aboard the
Bellerophon off Torbay to be taken into exile. However, before Napoleon
was taken to St. Helena, Madame Tussaud was allowed to obtain a second
likeness of him.

When this was added to her exhibit, Englishmen could not wait to see
their mortal French enemy. In fact, Napoleon became a centrepiece of her
exhibition. Like many of her other figures, Napoleon's wax figure was also
more appealing because he had been modelled from real life. Thus, this
attribute gave her exhibition instant cachet that other wax exhibitors did not
possess.

Madame Tussaud's abilities and skills were another reason people visited
and praised her exhibition. One newspaper published a very complimentary
article in 1829:

'Madame Tussaud's collection of composition figure continues
to attract a constant and increasing influx of visitors. The
grouping attitudes and colouring of the figures are extremely
natural and the costumes are uniformly correct and appropriate.
… It is probably owing to this artist-like attention to the finish,
positions, and art decoration of the figures, even more than to
the extent of the collection, or the selection of the subjects,
that Madame Tussaud's exhibition is admitted to be the most

160

splendid and complete that has ever been brought together. The selection however, is both comprehensive and judicious, embracing the most illustrious individual of modern times; and a great proportion of the models have been taken from life.'[1]

Among the models were several important busts of individuals from the French Revolution. They included the 'sanguinary demagogue' Robespierre, the 'infamous republican' Carrier, and the vindictive public prosecutor Fouquier-Tinville. The three men's likenesses, along with others, would eventually end up in a separate exhibit room that Madame Tussaud would note in her 1823 catalogue as containing 'highly interesting figures & objects in consequence of their peculiarity of their appearance'.[2]

Another reason so many visitors were impressed with Madame Tussaud's exhibit was that she had a way of drawing visitors in by creating an intimate setting. She also made visitors feel as if the wax figures were alive. Visitors believed they were promenading and socializing with real people as indicated by a remark made by one newspaper reporter:

> '[T]he figures seem, by the gas lights, to live, breathe, and have a being; and although they are of course perfectly motionless, the general stillness of the scene is broken and relieved by the movement of the spectators, – between whom and the lifeless figure it is quite impossible, at a cursory glance, to discriminate.'[3]

This inability to discriminate between live people and wax ones was further exemplified by the comments made by one gentleman visitor in 1821. He stated:

> 'In running up stairs, I did not observe the first few figures, but went to the top of the room, and on my return to the bottom, to go out, I observed Madame Tussaud, and after mentioning the excellence of the figures, I expressed a hope that the exhibition had been numerously attended, judge my surprise, after waiting some moments, that I found I had been conversing with an inanimate model, the likes of the artist.'[4]

One Nottinghamshire visitor to Madame Tussaud's wrote a glowing review of her exhibit in 1819. To demonstrate the 'marked superiority' of her exhibit, he used words such as 'matchless,' 'striking,' 'grand and 'imposing'. He also stated:

> '[Madame Tussaud's exhibition] far exceeds any thing of the kind ever before seen in this town. Instead of a number of unmeaning sallow faces, sitting in rows behind benches covered with green cloth, as is often the case in exhibitions of this kind, the room presents a scene of the utmost gaiety. We are astonished on entering it, to behold a vast number of full length figures standing, sitting, and lying, in various attitudes, in different parts of the room, many of them arrayed in splendid attire, and the whole bearing the appearances of real life. Indeed, a stranger must be some time in the room, before he can ascertain, which are the figures and which the spectators.'[5]

To further increase the authenticity of her displays, Madame Tussaud often arranged her wax figures in a dramatic tableau or still life that related a story or an event. For instance, there was the 'execrable wretch' Marat sitting in his bath tub having just been assassinated by Corday. George IV's coronation that occurred on 19 July 1821 also memorialized a moment in time as the coronation turned scandalous after George IV rejected his wife and prevented her from entering Westminster because he feared she would cause a scene. Madame Tussaud made sure to preserve this piece of history, excluding Queen Charlotte's shenanigans of course.

The French monarchy also fascinated the English as Madame Tussaud's figures of Louis XVI, Marie Antoinette, and their son the Dauphin, were of great interest. The royal couple were depicted sitting on a sofa with the Dauphin standing beside them. English patrons had read all about them, imagined their lives, and even mourned their deaths. Thus, with the accompanying model of the guillotine, it made the horror of the king and queen's death all the more palpable to viewers.

Other authentic details later involved Napoleon's exhibits. After his defeat at Waterloo, Major von Keller confiscated Napoleon's military carriage as 'his own booty'. After its seizure, it was either bought by the British government or given to the Prince Regent. William Bullock then bought it from the Prince Regent. Bullock displayed it at his exhibition in Piccadilly at the Egyptian Hall and then took it on tour throughout England,

Ireland, and Scotland. After the tour, it was sold at an auction to a gentleman who planned to show it in America, but when that fell through, it was used to satisfy a debt and became the property of a coach maker, who in turn sold it to Madame Tussaud in 1842.

Supposedly, Joseph was the person who discovered the carriage some time later. It occurred one day as he was leaning over London Bridge watching a carriage being hoisted from a barge. He began a conversation with a gentleman, who revealed, 'I can take you to a place where you can see Napoleon's carriage which he used at Waterloo'.[6] Of course, Joseph was interested and accompanied the man to a carriage shop in Gray's Inn Road. There he discovered the carriage, complete with 'a sleeping bunk, a writing-desk, and stowage for a quantity of baggage'.[7]

On 5 May 1821, Napoleon died and his death allowed Madame Tussaud to update her tableau of him. To do so, she relied on David's painting, 'The Coronation of Napoleon' (*Le Sacre de Napoléon*). She had Napoleon crowning himself while Josephine, his uncle, and others stood nearby and watched.

By 1865, besides Napoleon's carriage, various other relics could also be viewed. There was his camp bedstead used at St. Helena, along with his mattress and pillow on which he died. A tableau also represented Napoleon 'lying in state in his Chasseur uniform, covered with the cloak he wore at Marengo'.[8] Madame Tussaud would also purchase the coronation robes used by Napoleon and the Empress Josephine. There were also busts, pictures, decorations, and a full-length portrait of the Empress Marie-Louise, Napoleon's brother Jerome, and Napoleon's mother, as well as various letters attesting to the authenticity of certain relics on display.

Napoleon remained a popular wax figure after his exile to St. Helena and even after his death. Because he was so popular, Madame Tussaud eventually had two rooms dedicated to him. Some of the figures in these rooms included Field Marshal von Blücher, who lead his army against Napoleon at the Battle of the Nations at Leipzig in 1813 and the Battle of Waterloo in 1815; Frederick William III, king of Prussia; and Joachim Murat, Napoleon's brother-in-law who was also King of Naples.

Madame Tussaud had always stressed her relationships with the upper classes, nobility, and royalty, and, hence, it should be no surprise that her greatest desire was to acquire a genteel clientele. To do so, she was willing to follow them to their winter and summer haunts and to take advantage of their willingness to spend cash. As time passed, she made a concerted effort to target the affluent middle class by touring towns or cities that they frequented. She also took out advertisements, such as the one in the *Bristol Mercury* in August of 1823, that called on ladies and gentlemen and read:

> 'There will be a PROMENADE every Evening, from 6 till 10, accompanied by a full MILITARY BAND, of acknowledged merit. No improper Persons will be admitted.'[9]

This idea of promenading from room to room to study the wax figures accompanied by music, seems to have been a Madame Tussaud invention. Visitors could spend the entire evening in leisurely fashion at her exhibition, and apparently, they loved it. The *Liverpool Observer* noted, 'The promenade among the illustrious dead and illustrious living is truly delightful'.[10]

Madame Tussaud's also stressed her important connections with royalty, including Queen Victoria. This approval from royalty for her collection added to its cache and her status. Thus, she began to list those who had patronized her exhibitions in the past. Included in that list in her catalogue of 1842 were the following visitors:

> 'Their late majesties, Louis XVI and Maria [*sic*] Antoinette, Louis XVIII., and Charles X.; Their late Royal Highnesses the Duke and Duchess of York; His majesty the King of Hanover; His Royal Highness the Duke of Sussex; their Royal Highnesses the Princess Augusta and Sophia; Prince George of Cambridge; his grace the Duke of Wellington; Lords Brougham, Harrowby, Auckland; the foreign ambassadors, etc., etc., etc.'[11]

According to Madame Tussaud's great-grandson Victor, her husband François had arranged for their son Francis to apprentice with a grocer. This was unfortunate as the young Francis dreamed of being an architect. When François discovered the grocery apprenticeship was costly, it fell through and he then obtained employment for Francis working with a billiard table builder. Francis didn't like that either and was unhappy, which likely contributed to his decision to join his mother and brother in London in 1817. However, things did not go according to plan.

When 17-year-old Francis reached Dover, he ran out of money. He was then mistaken for a military deserter and arrested. He might have spent a long time in prison if it had not been for the fact his English was so poor military authorities realized he couldn't have deserted, and they set him free. When he finally reached London, he joined his mother and brother, eventually establishing his permanent residence in London with them, demonstrated by his application for naturalization in 1846 that shows his residence in 1821 as 10 Salisbury Place New Road.

Both Joseph and Francis now worked for their mother like virtual apprentices and did her bidding for no pay. They aided her in any way necessary, and Francis' carpentry skills were likely used to help build wooden legs and arms or improve the exhibits. Although no pay was involved, her sons did get billing as Madame Tussaud's was now called Madame Tussaud and Sons.

There are several harrowing stories about Madame Tussaud's life on the road. The first involves Madame Tussaud surviving a shipwreck in 1821. The ship that seems to fit best with the timeframe and story is a ship where neither Madame Tussaud or her sons appear on the passenger list. It was the *Earl of Moira,* a Dublin packet ship that had 110 passengers on board when it sailed on 8 August 1821.

The *Moira* was scheduled to leave at 5pm but left about 6:30pm because the ship's captain had celebrated the birth of his child and came aboard late, intoxicated. After the ship set sail, when attempting to tack, it missed the stays and struck the Burbo Bank off Liverpool. The collision caused many passengers to go up to the deck where they discovered their captain was drunk. They also reported that he seemed 'bewildered and underdetermined'.

The ship was eventually freed, and the captain then ordered the ship out to deep sea. Many of the passengers objected and pointed to black and threatening clouds in the distance. The captain refused to listen to them and the vessel again missed the stays and became grounded on the Mockbeggar Wharf Bank.

'When the flood tide set in, the vessel being occasionally lifted, struck the bank, and it is probable, from the manner in which she afterwards leaked that her bows were injured by striking against the anchor, which was injudiciously dropped when she grounded, as she did not take cable. The mainsail, kept on her for the purpose of running her on the bank as the tide rose, had only the effect of sinking her deeper in the sand and rendered her situation more fatal.'

'At half-past two, the vessel filled with water fore and aft; the pump having previously been plied, but with no effect. Two fine horses that were in the hold, were now hoisted up, the groom wished to ride one of them to shore, but was persuaded to desist. The horses were washed, or thrown overboard – Previous to this the passengers wished a signal to be made to which the Captain would not agree, declaring there was no danger.'[12]

But there was great danger. The tide was rising, and it brought the vessel on her broadside. Moreover, by four or five in the morning, the water had leaked into the cabins and luggage hold and the sea was breaking over the ship. People were exhausted from a sleepless night. Those on board were attempting to survive by holding onto the rigging or anything solid. Some people were washed away because they were tired, and their dead bodies began to surround the *Moira*.

Signals for help were being given and news of the ship's distress finally reached shore. Sometime after 7am, a Hoylake lifeboat arrived. About thirty-three exhausted and dying passengers dropped into the lifeboat and it would have been swamped if it had not quickly departed. A second boat, captained by Matthew Naill, arrived from Liverpool about an hour later. It took eight survivors. When a third boat arrived, it took another twelve passengers. About eighteen people remained behind. They were picked up by other boats, but the captain was not among the 71 survivors because he went down with his ship.

Madame Tussaud never mentioned the 1821 shipwreck but rumours about her being involved in a shipwreck circulated. For a time, most historians thought it was a tall tale, but what gives credence to the claims appeared in 1924 when a woman named Anna R. Craik published a recollection for descendants of two Lancashire families entitled *Annals of our ancestors: some records and recollections of the families of Fynes-Clinton and Mathews*. In the *Annals*, Craik gives no exact date as to when the incident occurred but states that it must have occurred before 1830. Moreover, Craik claims that a bedraggled Madame Tussaud and party appeared at the door of her great aunt, a Mrs. Farington (written ffarington at the time with the two ffs indicating a capital F) who lived along the Lancashire coast where the shipwreck occurred, and when she heard a knock and then 'voluble French' being addressed to her butler, she went to investigate. It was then that Mrs. Farington learned a shipwreck had occurred. Craik states:

> 'All her [Madame Tussaud's] possessions went to the bottom, except one small box which the unfortunate companions

carried between them when they all started off to walk to Preston, which they were told was the nearest town. Darkness fell upon them and they struggled along in the rain and wind, soaked to the skin and caked with Lancashire mud. They mistook their road and instead of arriving at Preston, they found themselves at the Lodge Gates of Worden. How they got past the lodge I don't know, but they arrived at the house as described and were taken in and housed: supper was got ready and dry clothing, and they turned out to be such charming and interesting people that their stay was prolonged for several days.

'The small box contained miniature models of various historical figures, and Madame Tussaud announced her intention of setting to work at once with fresh life-sized models of those that had been lost.

'Mrs. ffarington took her upstairs to a room where a number of old chests were kept, full of costumes which belonged to the former members of the family, and presented her with a good many of these to clothe her new figures, and to help her to restart her exhibition. In addition to this, Mrs. John Mathews (Mrs. ffarington's stepmother) ... gave her a quantity of valuable old Venetian point lace.'[13]

There are also other stories of Madame Tussaud facing dangers on the high seas. One supposedly occurred on her way to Edinburgh in 1803, another in 1804 while travelling from Waterford to Dublin, and, still another in 1814, when she landed penniless in Cork after her exhibition was reported to be nearly submerged in the Irish Sea.

Another story about Madame Tussaud nearly losing everything occurred near the end of October 1831. However, this story occurred on land. The show was in Bristol at the time and had been there since August. The exhibit was staged at the Assembly Rooms on Prince's Street when riots broke out. The riots erupted because the house of Lords' rejected a Reform Bill that would have done away with some rotten boroughs and given certain industrial towns greater representation in the House of Commons, which included Bristol. Citizens of Bristol were unhappy and decided to demonstrate their unhappiness using violent protests. When the protests began, a local magistrate, who strongly opposed the bill, threatened to imprison rioters but instead, rioters chased him to the Mansion House in

Queen Square where he escaped in disguise. Nevertheless, rioters were able to besiege the mayor and other city officials at the Mansion House.

Most of the rioters were young and formed a group about 500 strong. They looted property, destroyed the gaol, and attacked private homes. The rioters also decided to burn buildings and warned owners where they might strike next. One of the buildings on their list was that housing Madame Tussaud's exhibition. One newspaper reported:

> 'During this awful state of suspense, among others, Madame Tussaud and her family experienced the most painful anxiety. It was stated, among other places, that the assembly rooms were marked out for destruction, containing, at the time, their valuable collection of figures. These, at an imminent risk of injury, were partly removed, as hastily as circumstances would permit. The house in which Madame Tussaud lodged, on the opposite side of the street, was amongst the number which became ignited from the firing of the west side of the square; and we regret to hear that the lady's constitution has received a very severe shock.'[14]

As Madame Tussaud and her sons carried their wax figures to safety, a black servant helped to keep rioters at bay. Also, on the scene was a young artist named William James Muller. Muller captured in a watercolour the wax figures being carried to safety amid rioters and lapping flames.

Some years later, after Madame Tussaud established a permanent spot, Muller's watercolour was displayed in her museum. It remained on display until a fire broke out on 18 March 1925. The 1925 fire was so spectacular that witnesses observed 50-foot multi-coloured leaping flames, and amidst sizzling wax figures, the watercolour was burned along with Napoleon's military carriage, and many of the Napoleon relics Madame Tussaud had collected over the years.

As to the fate of those involved in the Bristol riots of 1831, many people suffered the effects of the fire. Reports claimed that four rioters died and over eighty people were wounded, but many deaths may have been overlooked as indicated by one newspaper that provided the following report on the aftermath a week or so after the riots ceased:

> The opinion we ... gave respecting the destruction of many of the heartless wretches by the fire, which their own hands

had assisted to kindle, has been realised ... [and shows] the reckless fury which hurried them on to irretrievable ruin. ... From the ruins of almost every house on the north side of the square, the crushed and mangled remains of one or more bodies have been taken out. The scenes ... have indeed been revolting to humanity. – Heads without bodies, trunks without members, broken fragments of limbs, and entire bodies reduced to a cinder ... Among the spectators were some who doubted whether it was really so or not; and, among others, some sailors took some pieces in their hands, and, smelling it, pronounced it to be boiled beef. We, however, subsequently saw a limb, the flesh adhering to which, from the similarity in appearance to what we had previously seen scattered on the ruins, left us no doubt of its identity.'[15]

Chapter 17

Permanency

'The only dispenser of permanent reputation.'
Punch on Madame Tussaud

Near the end of 1833, Madame Tussaud and Sons became a tenant at the London Royal Bazaar between Derby Street and Gray's Inn Road. The exhibition was located on the upper floors in an assembly room. The announcement of its opening appeared in *John Bull* on 12 January 1834:

> 'Patronised by the Princess August and Prince George, Madame Tussaud and Sons respectfully announces that their splendid exhibition, unequalled in Europe ... is now open, in the great assembly room of the London Royal Bazaar, Gray's Inn Road, King's Cross. Admittance one shilling. Second room, sixpence. Open from 11 til 4 and from 7 to 10.'[1]

A year or so later, in 1835, Madame Tussaud and Sons relocated and they put down permanent roots in Baker Street. Over the years, the exhibition had become more than simply that; it had museum pieces, quality art, and displays that were much more elaborate and costly than when Madame Tussaud first began touring. It was also expensive to ship the exhibits and arduous and time-consuming to set up and tear down the displays. Additionally, Madame Tussaud's sons had married and established families. Joseph married Elizabeth Babbington from Birmingham in 1822 and they had three children. Seven years later, on 26 November 1829 in St. Peters, Leeds, Yorkshire, Francis married Rebecca Smallpage. Francis and Rebecca would eventually have eleven children. Yet, it was not the complexity of the exhibition, the transportation costs, or even the wives and families that caused Marie Tussaud to finally give up touring; it was her uncanny ability to recreate the head of the singer Maria Malibran.

Maria was an idolized 28-year-old Spanish mezzo-soprano, Parisian by birth and the eldest daughter of a celebrated Spanish tenor, Manuel Garcia, who had an extremely flexible range and powerful voice. Although people may have lauded Garcia, Maria was claimed to be much more talented than him. Contemporaries described her as an extraordinary singer and she became known as the unrivalled 'Queen of Song' in Paris, London, and Milan. However, despite her extraordinary talent she also possessed a stormy personality and dramatic intensity.

It's unclear if her stormy personality resulted in her marrying a man named Malibran or if her father forced her to marry him as he was said to be rather tyrannical. Either way, the marriage was a disaster. Malibran, who was 28 years older than Maria, was a rich merchant, but soon after their marriage, he declared bankruptcy and Maria found herself supporting him. Unhappy with her aged bankrupt husband, Maria became involved with another man, a Belgian violinist, Charles-Auguste de Bériot. De Bériot adored Maria, and Maria adored him back. She left Malibran, lived with de Bériot, and had a son with him. When she was granted an annulment from Malibran in 1836, the same year that she was in the zenith of her glory on stage, she married de Bériot.

Soon after her marriage, Maria unexpectedly collapsed while performing in Manchester at a music festival. She died a week later, on 23 September 1836. The public was stunned, as was her husband. In fact, de Bériot was so inconsolable and distraught that he inexplicably fled to Brussels or Antwerp, and his unexpected flight raised questions about his wife's death and caused the public to wonder if he was somehow involved. Before de Bériot fled, he left a few requests. He was particularly adamant that no cast of Maria's face or head be obtained and ordered that no portrait should be undertaken either. He also demanded 'no *post mortem* examination should be made; and, in short, that the body should not be touched by anyone except during the necessary preparations for interment'.[2]

Years earlier, Madame Tussaud had become adept enough to create a mould of a person's face from a portrait, drawing, or memory. She did not need Maria to create a perfect imitation. As Madame Tussaud was busy creating her wax figure, newspapers were filled with reports about Maria, her death, and de Bériot's sudden flight. In fact, Maria was the only name on people's lips, even after it was determined that her death was due to a fall from a horse that had occurred in July. Everyone wanted to see Maria. According to Madame Tussaud's great-grandson, she decided to take advantage of the publicity associated with Maria and she did so 'with all speed' placing her wax figure in the exhibit. Maria's wax figure was so popular that Madame Tussaud saw her profits double.

It was then that she realized she no longer needed to tour. People would come to her and she could make it so. Her 'exhibition would command perennial success by being constantly brought up to date through the adding of the portraits of people whose names were on everybody's lips'.[3] Displaying the most popular person thereafter became a trademark of Madame Tussaud and Sons.

In 1849, *Punch*, a British weekly magazine of humour and satire established in 1841 by Henry Mayhew and engraver Ebenezer Landells, noted this penchant for changing figures based on public popularity and wrote about Madame Tussaud's 'melting moods' (changing out one figure for another). The weekly magazine also noted that Madame Tussaud's made a lasting and permanent impression on the public and that the first and best way for a person to achieve fame was to appear in wax at Madame Tussaud's:

> '[T]he only efficient dispenser of permanent reputation; and the glory of a sovereign, the triumphs of a warrior, the wisdom of a statesman, the genius of an author, or even the utmost atrocity of criminal, would be insufficient as a passport to fame, if Madame Tussaud's wax failed to own the soft impeachment, and hand down to posterity the virtues, the achievements, or the villainies, by which the parties in question have brought notoriety.'[4]

Madame Tussaud was not just in the business of making people famous or infamous. Her dream of providing educational and cultural benefits to the country's youth was also realized after she settled into her permanent location. This was indicated by an article that appeared in the *Morning Chronicle* in January of 1835:

> 'Let any one compare the figures by this artist with those which in our youth we were wont to gaze on, with wonder and astonishment, in Westminster Abbey and Fleet-street; let any do so, and they must acknowledge that Madame Tussaud has raised the art which she professes to a pitch which can hardly be expected to be surpassed, and which probably no one but herself has ever attained, and which must be seen to be credited. Here neither expense nor troubles have been spared to render the collection at once instructive and amusing; and Madame has evidently kept

in view the desire to make it so to youth in particular, who in an hour may, by looking at various characters, gain more insight in character and biography than by months of study.'[5]

The location that became Madame Tussaud's permanent spot was on the west side of Baker Street, called the Baker Street Bazaar. The bazaar was something that *Punch* called the perfect 'Beehive of industry'. London's Baker Street was a fashionable district close to retail shops. Moreover, with improved roads, a railway, and eventually an underground system, patrons were practically delivered to Madame Tussaud's door. Thus, the location could not be beaten.

Baker Street was a popular spot in other ways. William Pitt the Elder lived on Upper Baker Street next to Regent's Park in the 1700s. The famous Welsh tragedienne actress Sarah Siddons also resided on Upper Baker Street until her death on 8 June 1831. There was also the English novelist, poet, playwright, and politician Edward Bulwer who was born in a little house at No. 31 Baker Street on 25 May 1803.

The three-storey building that housed Madame Tussaud's exhibit had originally been the King Street Barracks, and, according to Madame Tussaud's great-grandson, Life Guards had marched from the barracks on their way to Waterloo. This bit of history was made more interesting when one of the first visitors to Madame Tussaud's new location was Wellington himself. He visited on 26 August, and afterwards was frequently observed strolling from room to room, particularly spellbound by the wax figures of Queen Victoria and his enemy Napoleon.

Wellington, whom Madame Tussaud had modelled from a bust in 1812, was not the only person fascinated with Madame Tussaud and Sons. From the moment the Baker Street exhibition opened, it was a hit and constantly filled with patrons. During the early years, the hours were from 11am to 5pm and from 7pm to 10pm. To ensure entrance, 'when the place was closed, seats were provided in the vestibule, and it was no uncommon sight to see from fifty to a hundred persons waiting for the reopening of the doors at 7pm'.[6]

The exhibition was on the upper two floors, with the first floor being reserved for the sale of horses and carriages. To obtain entrance to Madame Tussaud's, patrons entered on the ground floor through a hall that lead to a wide staircase. Upstairs, patrons were greeted and paid their fee. Everyone paid. There were no exceptions. A bonneted Madame Tussaud took the money as she sat behind the cashier desk. As usual, the tiny woman was dressed in an austere, matronly style that became her trademark.

When the exhibition at Baker Street opened, so too did the 'Chamber of Horrors'. One description of the room claimed that it was cold, damp, and dimly lit. The walls were dark roughly painted boards, the floor of heavy planks, and the ceiling painted red. The Chamber of Horrors housed some of the victims of the French Revolution and a slew of murderers. Besides Despard, there was William Corder, who committed what came to be known as the Red Barn Murder in 1827.

Corder was twenty-four when he shot his lover, 26-year-old Maria Marten. Marten was the daughter of a mole-catcher, and she and Corder had begun a relationship in March of 1826. At the time, Corder was well-known for being a ladies' man and a fraudster, on one occasion, selling his father's pigs as his own. Another fraud occurred when Corder passed some bad cheques, and he also helped a local thief named Samuel 'Beauty' Smith steal a pig.

Of course, Corder's father punished him, but no sort of punishment seemed to induce him to behave, so his father finally shipped him off to London. Shortly after Corder's arrival in London, one of his brothers drowned, and his father recalled him to help on the farm. However, misfortune again occurred because within 18 months of his return, Corder's father and remaining three brothers died. This left Corder and his mother to run the farm.

After Corder began a relationship with Marten, he hid the relationship because he did not want any of his relatives to know, becoming even more emphatic that no one know about their relationship after Marten gave birth in 1827 to a boy, who then died or was perhaps murdered. Although Corder didn't want anyone to know about the relationship, Marten wanted to legitimize their relationship, and, so, apparently, Corder ultimately agreed to marry her.

He proposed that they meet at the Red Barn and elope. In addition, he told Marten that because authorities were going to prosecute her for having given birth to a bastard child, she needed to avoid suspicion by dressing in men's clothing. Thus, the last Marten was seen was wearing men's clothes and heading to the barn.

Soon after Marten disappeared, so did Corder. When he reappeared, he claimed that Marten was living nearby in either Ipswich, Great Yarmouth, or somewhere else. Corder also claimed that they had married, but he insisted that he could not bring her home because his relatives would be upset about their marriage. As no one heard anything from her, pressure began to build, and people began pressing Corder telling him that Marten had to at least write. He had yet another excuse as to why she couldn't write. He said she had a sore hand and could not hold a pen. As he continually had an excuse and refused to produce his wife, Marten's stepmother became suspicious. In the meantime, Corder fled to London. There he advertised for a wife and met and married Mary Moore. He and Moore then began running a boarding house.

While Corder was living in London, Marten's stepmother had a dream. In her dream she saw Corder kill Marten and convinced her husband to conduct a search of the barn. The search occurred on 19 April 1828 by Marten's father and two other men. A report on the search was given at trial:

> 'They began to poke down in the straw to see if they could find any thing. The straw was thick ... At the second or third time of rolling it off, ... the earth seemed to have been disturbed ... and something that appeared to be flesh stuck to the spike. ... They cleared the earth away till they came to the body. They then cleared towards the head part, and found a handkerchief that appeared to be tied round her neck. ... They then cleared towards the feet. The body was lying down, but not stretched out. It occupied about three feet and a half. The legs were drawn up, and the head was bent down a little into the earth. ... The body was then taken from the hole.'[7]

Marten's badly decomposed body had been found and her father reported, 'When they turned the mouth up ... it looked like my daughter's Maria Marten'.[8] After the discovery, authorities were notified, and an investigation conducted. An officer named James Lee of Lambeth tracked Corder to his house in London and arrested him in his drawing room. Corder was returned to Suffolk to stand trial. One newspaper reported on his capture:

> 'In company with a local officer, Lee, the police-officer, apprehended the prisoner at Ealing, who, on his apprehension, denied having known Maria Martin. He thrice denied having known her. Lee searched the house ... Pistols were also found in the house by Lee, and a sword, which had been compared with the hole in the stays, and the hole in the left side of the body. It had been sharpened for the prisoner before he left Polstead and seen in his possession there.'[9]

At trial, Marten's stepmother related her prophetic dream about Corder killing Marten and her father told jurors about discovering his daughter's body in the barn. Her 10-year-old brother testified that he saw Corder before the murder near the barn carrying a loaded pistol. The brother also testified that later he saw Corder leaving the barn carrying a pickaxe, as did a neighbour. In addition, the Polstead constable, John Baalam, also testified. He denied that he ever wrote a letter or threatened to arrest Marten for having a bastard child and claimed that Corder made it up to entice Marten to the barn.

With so much evidence against him, Corder began to lose confidence and finally admitted he had been at the barn. However, he claimed Marten had committed suicide. He also maintained that after leaving the barn, he heard a shot and ran back, only to discover Marten dead with one of his pistols lying next to her. Despite Corder's claims, when the jury adjourned to determine the verdict, they did not believe him and found him guilty of murder. The guilty verdict came as no surprise to one newspaper:

> 'Any one who has read the trial, the summing up of the Judge, and above all, the defence of the prisoner, must be convinced that there never was a case so clearly proved by circumstantial evidence. ... Since his conviction, Corder has remained in a state of the utmost despair. There does not appear, indeed, to be one circumstance attending his committal, trial, and conviction, that can afford him the smallest consolation. He committed the murder without any ostensible object, he has denied the deed all along, and, in order to save appearances, has been driven to the utmost falsehood and deceit, which have only the more confirmed every one of the certainty of his guilt. His very friends seem to have deserted him. His mother has not visited him since his conviction ... His wife has seen him occasionally and took her last farewell yesterday.'[10]

As Corder sat in jail, the clergy pressed him to confess his crime. Corder agonized over doing so but finally did. Nonetheless, in his confession, he claimed Marten's murder was an accident. He maintained that they argued and that he accidentally shot her in the right eye while she was changing out of her disguise.

Corder's case was so well publicized, when he was executed on 11 August 1828, 10,000 spectators attended his execution. His execution was also reported on by many newspapers. One newspaper reported that spectators for his execution poured in from all quarters arriving in gigs, chaises, carts, and wagons, and that some vehicles were stuffed with as many as fourteen people.

When the execution got underway, Corder's arms were fastened and he appeared faint when brought to the scaffolding. He might have fallen to the ground, if he had not been supported by the constables. Before he was hanged, he repeatedly asked for God's forgiveness under his breath, and his last words were, 'I deserve my fate – I have offended my God – may he have mercy on me'.[11]

Two other murderers that ended up in Madame Tussaud Chamber of Horrors were William Burke and William Hare. Burke and Hare teamed up over a ten-month period in 1828 to commit a series of sixteen murders in Edinburgh. The Scottish historical novelist, playwright and poet, Sir Walter Scott, took a keen interest in the case, as did Madame Tussaud. So, when she modelled Scott's face, the two must have had some interesting and lively discussions about Burke and Hare and their murder spree.

Burke was probably the older of the two men. He had been born in 1792 in Ulster province in Urney, Ireland, to middle-class parents. He had married but deserted his wife after fighting with her father. When he left, he moved to Scotland, found lodgings near Falkirk, and worked as laborer on the Union Canal. He then bigamously married Helen McDougal, whom he affectionately called Nelly, and, in 1827, they moved to Edinburgh where he eventually worked as a cobbler.

Hare's year of birth ranges from 1792 to 1804. Like Burke, he was born in Northern Ireland in the province of Ulster and worked on the Union Canal before he moved to Edinburgh in the mid-1820s. He found lodgings in Edinburgh at a house in Tanner's Close that was run by a man named Logue. Logue was married to a woman named Margaret Laird, and when Logue died, Hare married Margaret and helped her to run the lodging house.

To make ends meet, Burke and Nelly went to work helping to bring in a harvest in Penicuik. Hare also went to work there and met Burke. Hare was a hard-drinking, quarrelsome, and amoral person whereas Burke was described as friendly, industrious, and someone who always carried his Bible, so it was somewhat surprising the two men bonded and became good friends, but they did. Because of their friendship, after the harvest, Burke and Nelly moved to Tanner's Close.

Hare's lodging house had eight beds with lodgers paying 3d. each, and sometimes two or three lodgers slept in the same bed. Hare had one lodger who was an army pensioner named Donald, and while living at Hare's, he died from dropsy on 29 November 1827. His death occurred before his pension cheque arrived, and, therefore, Hare bemoaned his financial loss to Burke.

Because corpses were so difficult to come by, medical schools began offering financial compensation for corpses. Hare and Burke had heard about these compensations that anatomists paid and conceived the idea to sell Donald's corpse for dissection. They surreptitiously removed Donald's corpse from the coffin and weighted it down with tanning bark so no one would know they had taken it.

After dark, they carried Donald's corpse to Edinburgh University where they met Doctor Robert Knox, who was also curator of the College of Surgeons' museum. Knox was willing to buy the corpse to use for dissection in his anatomy lectures. Moreover, Knox or one of his assistants hinted that other corpses would also be welcomed. The price fixed for Donald's corpse was £7 10s, which in today's value is over £636. Thus, the two men realized they had just discovered a gold mine.

When another of Hare's lodgers named 'Joseph the miller' became ill, the men became impatient and decided to help fate along. They plied Joseph with whisky, forcibly restrained him, and suffocated him, though some historians believe that Joseph was not the first person killed but rather a woman named Abigail Simpson.

To ensure that a corpse would not be injured or damaged, the pair soon devised a successful *modus operandi* to achieve their murders. Burke would sit on or lay across the victim's chest to prevent the person from moving or crying out. Hare would then cover or compress the person's nose, mouth, and neck so that the person could not breath, a technique that later became known as 'Burking'.

Over time, the men became bolder, and 'when they wanted money, they would say they would go and look for a shot; that was the name they gave them when they wanted to murder'.[12] It was also reported that when they first began delivering the murdered bodies, they always did so under darkness. However, the men came to believe that they would never be caught, grew more brazen, and started delivering bodies in broad daylight. One newspaper reported:

> 'When they carried the girl [named] Paterson to Knox's, there were a great many boys in the high School Yards, who followed Burke … crying, "They are carrying a corpse," but they got her safely delivered [without incident].'[13]

Hare and Burke eventually had a falling out and Burke and Nelly moved in with Burke's cousin, Broggan, who lived a few streets away from Hare and also operated a lodging house. But the breach between the two murderers did not last long. They repaired their friendship and began killing again.

Hare and Burke's undoing came about because of a couple named Gray. They were a husband and wife who began lodging with Broggan. They became suspicious that something untoward was happening at the lodging house. They then discovered the body of Margaret (or Margery) Campbell Docherty under a bed covered by straw and notified authorities.

After Burke and Hare were arrested, wild and exaggerated stories circulated in the press. Anyone missing was alleged to be their victims. Hampered by a lack of evidence, prosecutors offered Hare immunity. As Hare could not testify against his wife, Margaret could not be charged, and, therefore, Hare agreed to testify against Burke and Nelly.

Burke and Nelly faced three murder charges. During the trial, it was reported that although Nelly knew about the murders, she did not participate in them. In addition, the trial began on Christmas Eve, which probably caused jurors to want to reach a quick verdict. They did, because on Christmas Day, Burke was found guilty of the murders and Nelly was released.

After the trial, Margaret, Hare, and Nelly were recognized in public. In separate incidents, angry mobs attacked Margaret and Hare, and soon after they disappeared never to be seen again. As for Nelly, she was also attacked several times, but as to her final disposition there are conflicting stories. An Edinburgh broadside reported in 1829 that after some mill workers recognized her, they attacked and killed her, but other reports claim she moved to Australia.

The clergy encouraged Burke to give a full confession of the murders before his execution. He did, but primarily blamed Hare for the murders. Burke was hanged on 28 January surrounded by a crowd of some 25,000 people. The public was informed that his corpse was to be publicly dissected and that a limited number of tickets would be distributed. The dissection occurred at Old College, in the university's anatomy theatre, but because there were so many people interested in seeing his body, a minor riot ensued. Thus, accommodations were made to allow groups of 50 people to pass through the theatre after the dissection was complete.

Madame Tussaud attended Burke's trial and modelled him during it. Hare was modelled by her sons while he was imprisoned at the Edinburgh prison, and later it was learned someone else made a mask of Hare during the trial. Madame Tussaud's sons also later acquired another copy of Burke's shaven head that was completed within three hours of his death by someone else. As there was hardly anyone in Britain who had not heard about Hare and Burke's story of murdering for profit, Madame Tussaud's exhibit of them proved extremely captivating and was a profit generator for her and her sons.

Although Despard, Corder, and Burke and Hare may have been extremely popular in Madame Tussaud's 'Chamber of Horrors', the room was not initially called such. Apparently, the room holding these 'violated bodies' and macabre relics was at first known as the 'Adjoining Room'. People then began calling the room the 'Dead Room' because of its sombre blackness, although sometimes it was also referred to as the 'Black Room'. It officially became the 'Chamber of Horrors' in 1843, and although some people credit *Punch* for coining the term, it was Madame Tussaud who first used it in an 1843 advertisement.

The suite of rooms that housed Madame Tussaud's exhibit at Baker Street was about 243 feet long by 48 feet wide. The exhibition was lit by 800 lamps and had plenty of spots for people to sit and rest comfortably. There was also a balcony that housed the orchestra who played in the evening. Besides the Chamber of Horrors, there was, of course, the Napoleon Rooms that had been established in March 1843 and the Great Room described as being 'richly adorned by a radiant combination of arabesques, artificial flowers, and mirrored embellishments'.[14]

The Great Room was also described as an exhibition unto itself and it was the heart of the attraction. It housed magnificent engravings, expensive paintings, and fantastic bronzes. It had panelled walls of plate glass, rich, luxurious draperies, and burnished gilt ornaments in Louis XVI style. It was surrounded on all four sides by statues and sculptures with a scene and a combination of figures placed in the centre of the room.

Another section, known as the Hall of Kings, included such royal figures as Henry VIII, Mary Queen of Scots, and the Hanoverians. Coronations played a large part in the displays in the Hall of Kings. In fact, by 1840, the wax King George IV was decked out in the coronation robes worn by the real George IV at his coronation in 1821. The robe had been rumoured to have cost £18,000, and if it did, the Tussauds obtained it for a steal, as they paid a mere £300.

The decision to stay in a permanent location ultimately paid off for Madame Tussaud and Sons. According to one twenty-first century historian, their average weekly profits more than doubled within a few years. 'In 1833, when they were still touring, average weekly takings were £45, by 1837, they stood at £102 a week'.[15]

Chapter 18

Memoirs and Memories

'At times she is very ill.'
Francis Tussaud of his Mother

In 1838, Madame Tussaud was again able to model another sitting Queen. This queen was English rather than French and she had succeeded to the English throne in 1837. Queen Victoria's coronation was held on 28 June 1838. The ceremony at Westminster Abbey cost a staggering £79,000 (amounting in 2017 with inflation to be £8,137,000).

It was a glorious day with fine weather when the procession began. The route, which was nearly circular, was extended so that the enormous number of spectators could see the Queen. It started from Buckingham Palace and Hyde Park and travelled to Piccadilly, St. James's Street, Pall Mall, Charing Cross and Whitehall. The *Gentleman's Magazine* reported on the magnificent procession:

> 'To meet in some degree the general wishes expressed for a Coronation more stately than the last, the exterior cavalcade was increased in splendour and numbers, and a much more extended line of approach was adopted. It was thus brought to resemble, still more closely than on the former occasion, the procession through the metropolis which was formerly considered a necessary part of the solemnities of the Coronation, but which was last performed by King Charles the Second. The main difference was that the modern procession was not through the city of London, but through that of Westminster, a city now much larger, and far more magnificent, than ancient London.'[1]

Unprecedented crowds witnessed the event. In fact, it has been estimated that 400,000 visitors came to London to see Queen Victoria's coronation. Reports claimed there was 'scarcely a house or a vacant spot along the whole line from Hyde Park Corner to the Abbey, that was unoccupied with galleries or scaffolding'.[2] The weekly *Carlisle Journal* provided a full page of coverage on the event. They noted that along the route people stayed in open spots throughout the night to obtain a good spot to see the procession, and the following morning people arrived early:

'[A]s early as five o'clock [spectators sallied forth] … by six o'clock the space between the statues of Charles I and the front of the National was filled as far as it could be with convenience, but before nine it was crowded to a degree which rendered ingress or egress impossible. The appearance of the whole area, extending as far as the east end of Cockspur street, the west end of the Stand, and west to the Admiralty, was one of the most imposing kind. At the west side of Trafalgar square the Union Club had erected two galleries, which were filled with an elegant assemblage of beauty and fashion. In the distance … were other galleries as attractively occupied. In a word, every front story of every house in the whole line teemed … and the throng continued from that time without intermission … until every nook and corner and housetop, and whatever other lodgment could be obtained for human foot, was crowded to overflowing; … Even the housetops up to the chimney-pots were crowded in every place which could command a view of the expected pageant. By nine o'clock the whole area already described was filled or covered from the basement to the roof with a living mass. … We do not exaggerate when we say, that in the space between the east end of Pallmall, the front of St. Martin's church, and the west end of the Strand, and the Admiralty, there were not less than 200,000 persons assembled.'[3]

The *Carlisle Journal* also described in length the scene at Westminster Abbey. The Archbishop of Canterbury administered the Coronation Oath and the Queen was anointed in front of the altar as the Archbishop declared, 'Be thou anointed'. The crowning followed, and when the glittering diamond crown encrusted with pearls, sapphires, and emeralds was placed on Victoria's head, loud and hearty acclamations rent the air from the loyal crowds who loved and adored their new queen. Moreover, repeated shouts arose, 'God save the Queen' followed by blaring trumpets, beating drums, and the firing of guns.

A few months later, Madame Tussaud's display captured the enthusiasm of the event in a beautiful replica of the scene. A perfect papier-mâché imitation of Westminster Abbey's interior was shown, and Queen Victoria, who had visited Madame Tussaud's in 1833 and allowed Madame Tussaud to model her from life in 1836, was displayed in the middle with her crown, orb, and sceptre. In addition, the Queen also added to the authenticity of Madame Tussaud's wax scene by ordering an exact replica of her coronation robes and a duplicate of Sir George Hayter's coronation painting to be delivered to Madame Tussaud's and Sons.

The year 1838 was also the year that Hérve, the man who had taught Joseph the art of silhouettes, published *Madame Tussaud's Memoirs and Reminiscences of France*. Hérve had been commissioned earlier by a British general to create several portraits of the leaders of the Greek War of Independence. He also published in 1837, the two-volume *A Residence in Greece and Turkey, with Notes of the Journey Through Bulgaria, Servia, Hungary and the Balkan* that contained his impressions during his journey and were accompanied by his own original drawings.

Although Hérve was not a trained historian, he was fascinated by Madame Tussaud's tales. He meticulously recorded them and added events of interest related to the French Revolution, thereby creating what he claimed on the title page to be 'an abridged history of the French Revolution'. Yet, the *Memoirs* possessed little information about Madame Tussaud and appeared to be more of an attempt to craft a certain image of her for public consumption than to tell her life story.

Reviews of Hérve's book were often critical. For instance, the *New Yorker* referred to the *Memoirs* as 'a light, gossiping work made up of sketches of character and anecdotes of the times, compiled from the personal reminiscences of Madame Tussaud'.[4] Others critical of the book focused on the veracity of Madame Tussaud's statements claiming they were inaccurate. One reviewer stated:

'Mr. Herve proved himself a lively and versatile writer by his "Residence in Greece and Turkey," and has really made the Memoirs and Reminiscences of Madame Tussaud the text of a good deal of spirited gossip about the French Revolution … To be sure the publication has somewhat the appearance of its editor being a partner in the Bazaar Exhibition … where the ancient lady has so long and prosperously … displayed her literal powers of personification in wax and modelling.'[5]

Despite the criticism, the book propelled Madame Tussaud's celebrity to new heights. It also brought her husband François out of the woodwork. He sent a letter to an intermediary in London in 1841 pretending not to know his wife's address and asked the intermediary to show his letter to Madame Tussaud.

To say the least, Madame Tussaud was unhappy that François had attempted to contact her. She knew that if he was interested, his interest strictly involved money, and she was thoroughly displeased. Through the intermediary, she informed François that she owned nothing. She also stated that she had given everything to her sons and that it was her sons who had been functioning as the chief modelers since 1830.

The letter from their father to their mother did not sit well with Joseph or Francis either. They jointly wrote an uncompromising note back to their father dated 27 August 1841. Despite its clumsy French, they noted the exhibition was their property and made it clear they were supportive of their mother:

> 'Madame Tussaud and ourselves, not wishing to have any correspondence with you, believe that you have lived a sufficiently long time on support. Moreover having reached middle-age we believe this position and action is necessary. We hope, nonetheless, that Providence may do something for you, and that the Eternal God will be able to pardon your scandalous behavior.'[6]

The curt letter from Joseph and Francis deterred François for a time. However, three years later when another letter arrived, the boys agreed to provide their father some help. That was because François pleaded 'old age … infirmity, and incapacity to manage his own affairs'.[7]

Joseph and Francis also travelled to France to see what could be done. Madame Tussaud had forbidden Joseph to talk to his father. An archivist at Madame Tussaud's tells what happened next:

> 'Joseph obeyed his mother till his curiosity overcame him. He went with Francis to the house in the Rue Fossés du Temple, and without being detected, peeped over a screen at his father. He saw no monster, but a harmless-looking old gentleman sitting in his chair.'[8]

Whatever agreement was reached between father and sons did not last long. Back in London, Joseph and Francis soon wrote another angry letter to their father:

'Since you have enjoyed a life-interest in our mother's property, and she has received no profit from this property for so many years, she can in no way grant what you are seeking of her, seeing that, as we have already told you, this would naturally harm our interests. Therefore enjoy the life-interest as you please for the rest of your days.'[9]

Madame Tussaud and her sons were deeply concerned about François' continuing claims and his desire to obtain her enterprise in England. His letters sometimes stated that he wanted to visit her, and when he pressed his relationship as her husband, she fell ill. Moreover, she knew that because she was still a French citizen and married to François, French law left her defenceless and vulnerable if he pressed his claims.

That wasn't her only worry. There was also the problem that François was several years younger than her. If she died first, he could claim everything. Therefore, to ensure she and her sons were protected against any claims by François, 'Articles of Partnership' between her and her sons were signed on 3 July 1844.

Over the years, François was not the only person who attempted to take advantage of Madame Tussaud. Her great-grandson related a humorous story about the lengths that one woman devised to gain free admission into the exhibition as Joseph watched. It all began when Joseph noticed a buxom and portly matron at the pay station. She wore an enormous skirt that was further enlarged by her crinoline. However, it was not her enormous skirt that caught his attention but rather 'the shuffling of her feet was accompanied by an unaccountable sound of pattering'.[10]

Curious, Joseph kept a close eye on the buxom matron, and once inside, at her first opportunity, she hid from view, 'cautiously raised her crinoline ... [and to his amazement] out stepped two little boys'.[11] Joseph did nothing, but thereafter when he told the story, he said 'the expression on her face at the success of her subterfuge was one of radiant satisfaction'.[12]

Although some people took advantage of Madame Tussaud, Queen Victoria helped to increase Madame Tussaud's coffers when she married Prince Albert of Saxe-Coburg and Gotha. Prince Albert was the Queen's first cousin, and Victoria's ambitious uncle, King Leopold I of Belgium is the one who first considered the two might make a perfect match. Leopold I arranged through Victoria's mother (his sister) for Albert to visit and meet Victoria. Others favoured another match, but Prince Albert impressed Victoria:

> 'Albert … is extremely handsome; his hair is about the same colour as mine; his eyes are large and blue, and he has a beautiful nose and a very sweet mouth with fine teeth; but the charm of his countenance is his expression, which is most delightful; *c'est à la fois* full of goodness and sweetness, and very clever and intelligent.'[13]

Victoria was as pleased with Prince Albert on his second visit as she had been on his first. The second visit occurred on 10 October 1839, and five days later, as protocol required, Queen Victoria made her position clear and proposed to him. Prince Albert's acceptance was revealed in a letter she wrote to her Uncle Leopold:

> 'My Dearest Uncle: This letter will, I am sure, give you pleasure, for you have always shown and taken such a warm interest in all that concerns me. My mind is quite made up; and I told Albert this morning of it. The warm affection he showed me on learning this gave me great pleasure. He seems perfection, and I think I have the prospect of great happiness before me. I love him more than I can say, and shall do everything in my power to render this sacrifice (for such in opinion it is) as small as can be.'[14]

On 10 February 1840, Albert and Victoria married at the Chapel Royal of St. James's Palace. Prince Albert was decked out in a British field marshal's uniform. He entered first to strains of Handel's 'See, the Conquering Hero Comes' and following behind him was 20-year-old Victoria. She wore a white silk dress trimmed in Honiton lace, a diamond necklace with matching earrings, and a sapphire brooch, a gift from Albert.

There could not have been a happier bride. She demonstrated her happiness writing the following enthusiastic notation in her diary:

> 'I NEVER, NEVER spent such an evening! MY DEAREST DEAREST DEAR Albert sat on a footstool by my side, and his excessive love and affection gave me feelings of heavenly love

and happiness I never could have hoped to have felt before! He clasped me in his arms, and we kissed each other again and again! His beauty, his sweetness & gentleness, — really how can I ever be thankful enough to have such a *Husband*! Oh! This was the happiest day of my life!'[15]

Madame Tussaud was nearly as happy as Victoria when her wax tableau of the queen's marriage appeared on exhibit. Madame Tussaud showed Prince Albert placing the ring on the finger of his beloved Victoria, and the wax queen's wedding gown was an exact duplicate of the real one. Madame Tussaud was also happy to announce that their duplicate satin gown cost £1000.

Queen Victoria's patronage and approval was also important to Madame Tussaud. The wax figures of the queen that graced Madame Tussaud's allowed the British to feel a close connection to their queen, even after Albert's death and after Victoria's self-imposed seclusion. English royalty also had a pull that French royalty never did. Thus, the royal wax figures of Great Britain became one of Madame Tussaud's most profitable attractions.

Soon after the wedding display of Albert and Victoria went on display at Madame Tussaud's, a man named Francis Birch went to see it. An assistant named Mary Ann Jones was sitting in the upper end of the show room and noticed Birch. Birch was in front of the display and 'inside the railing, which was put up in order to prevent the spectators from brushing against, or by any other conduct injuring, the objects presented to their view'.[16]

The assistant realized something was wrong and went to the display as Birch walked away. Jones then noticed that the wedding ring was missing. Jones went immediately to Madame Tussaud, who sent for a constable. The constable, on questioning Birch, asked him why he had taken the ring. Birch denied that he had it or that he had taken it, and, when searched, the ring was not found in his possession. The judge therefore determined that there was not sufficient evidence to justify detaining him, and he was discharged.

Another story of crime at Madame Tussaud's involves two pickpockets. One was Thomas Daldy (whose alias was Nobby Bill). He appeared at Madame Tussaud's respectably dressed but was quickly arrested by a plain clothes officer named Allen for attempting to rob a widow of her purse inside the exhibition in January of 1850. Daldy wasn't the only pickpocket operating at Madame Tussaud's as another pickpocketing incident happened a few months later. On 12 March 1850, an article appeared in the *Morning Post* about a woman named Margaret Flynn who had been arrested for pickpocketing female patrons inside Madame Tussaud's museum. Allen also apprehended her, and just like Daldy, Flynn was found guilty and sentenced to serve time.

Of course, not every unusual character who visited Madame Tussaud's was a criminal. One interesting story involves a Norfolk farmer who went to London in 1849 and after visiting the cattle show, decided to visit the wax museum. He paid his money at the door and entered to find he was the only visitor. He wandered around and was astonished by the wax effigies. After a time, he saw some ladies and children arrive and as he stood in front of one of the displays, he said to one woman that some of the royal figures were grim looking. Then according to the farmer, the following ensued:

> '[The lady smiled, and answered,] "I perfectly agree with you; they are". My attention was soon arrested by hearing one of the party, pointing to a figure, mention Lord Nelson, when, proud of having been born in the same county with the illustrious sailor, I could not help exclaiming, "Ah, he was from my neighbourhood;" upon which one of the ladies advancing, said to me, "Then you are from Norfolk; pray can you tell me anything about poor Mrs. Jermy, in whose melancholy fate I so deeply sympathise?" … "No, madame, for I have been some days from home".'[17]

Scarcely did the conversation end, when Madame Tussaud suddenly appeared. She asked the farmer how he had gained entrance. He told her he paid his money at the door and entered. Apparently, however, the exhibition was to have been closed for a private party and astonishingly the woman the Norfolk farmer was talking to was no ordinary woman. It was Queen Victoria who had come with the royal children and their attendants.

Over the years, Madame Tussaud became as important as the figures that graced her salons. After she established her reputation as a competent wax modeler, people were as curious about her as her wax figures, and she was often seen greeting guests while standing among them. Moreover, there were many people who wanted to be a part of Madame Tussaud's wax museum and were willing to sit for her.

Among those who willingly modelled for Madame Tussaud was Charles Kean, who had played Hamlet to rave reviews at Drury Lane in 1838, the same year that Madame Tussaud was living at 24 Wellington Road, St John's Wood. After Kean sat for Madame Tussaud in March of 1844, he was so excited about his wax figure, he told everyone that his effigy would soon be gracing her exhibition.

It wasn't just Kean who was enthusiastic about Madame Tussaud's exhibition. In 1844, the famous American showman P.T. (Phineas Taylor) Barnum visited London, and when he saw the extent of Madame Tussaud's exhibit, he was astonished. Barnum had begun working for the first American circus when he was a boy, and, by 1841, he was managing Barnum's American Museum in New York City. To increase patronage, he added exotic animals, included elements of a freak show, and improved existing exhibits.

Barnum was also always looking for ways to improve his museum, and his visit to Madame Tussaud's was a surprise. Kings, queens, princes, princesses, and celebrities graced her rooms and were displayed so spectacularly, he wanted to buy her whole enterprise lock, stock, and barrel. He planned to transport the entire enterprise back to New York. Unfortunately, for Barnum, the deal fell through at the last moment as Madame Tussaud had no intention of leaving London.

Over the years, the animosity felt by Madame Tussaud and her sons to François had lessened. This friendlier attitude resulted in François receiving some financial aid by December 1845. However, that same year, he once again pestered his wife for more money as he was suffering from eye and leg problems. His health continued to deteriorate over the next few years until on 12 November 1848, he made out his will. He left 500 francs to a woman named Madame Bertrand, who had served as his long-time companion and looked after him.

Four days later, on 16 November, when François passed away, there was little left of his wife's dowry. His funeral was held at the Church of St. Elizabeth at 195 rue du Temple. Madame Tussaud must have felt relief because François' death allowed her to completely severe her ties to Paris and no longer worry about his efforts to squander the legacy that she intended to leave to her sons.

The year 1848 was also the year Madame Tussaud turned eighty-seven. She remained mentally feisty, but age had caught up with her and each passing day she grew thinner and feebler. Francis had written a letter to his father before his death that mentioned his mother's worsening health:

'At times she is very ill and she suffers from asthma which allows her no rest at night … Her legs are bad like yours, and she has bunions that hurt her when she walks.'[18]

Chapter 19

Legacy

'I implore you, above all things, never to quarrel.'

Madame Tussaud

It was an ordinary day, a Monday, on 16 April 1850 when Madame Tussaud died; at half past nine in the evening, she took her last breath. Her sons were sitting next to her bedside at the time. Although Madame Tussaud's favourite saying to her grandsons had long been, 'Beware, my children, of the three black crows — the doctor, the lawyer, and the priest,'[1] those were not the last words she spoke to her sons. She gave them sound advice, 'I implore you, above all things, never to quarrel'.[2]

Madame Tussaud's words were heeded by her sons, but more importantly, her life made an impact on them and on the future generations that were not sitting at her bedside. For instance, John Theodore never met his great-grandmother as she had died eight years before he was born, but in tribute to her, he wrote:

'In figure she was small and slight, and her manner was vivacious. Her complexion was fresh, her hair dark brown with never more than a sprinkling of grey, and her soft brown eyes were keen and alert when her interest was aroused. She was a great talker, her conversation was replete with reminiscences, and, moreover, she was blessed with a faultless memory. Austere in her habits of life, exacting in her likes and dislikes, she showed a ready sympathy with those in distress, and, above all, she was generous to a fault.'[3]

What no one mentioned at Madame Tussaud's passing was that although everyone seemed to know her, no one really *knew* her; she was enigmatic. What she thought, how she felt, what emotions she experienced were things she never shared. What people knew of her they gleaned from observing her talkative, vivacious, and determined nature. She carved out a life and a legacy for herself and her children in a foreign country, but she did so by revealing little of herself while recording the lives of others in wax.

Five days before she died, Madame Tussaud suffered a final illness. Fancesco Galassi from the Institute of Evolutionary Medicine at the University of Zurich, Switzerland, noted in 2016 that Madame Tussaud's illness was 'suggestive of an infection, such as pneumonia, which is common today with patients with chronic obstructive pulmonary disease'.[4] He also noted that pulmonary disease accounts for many of her symptoms — asthma, weakness, and varicose veins — that she suffered prior to her death.

Her death was briefly highlighted in newspapers. London's *Morning Post* wrote that she had 'been a servant to the British public for 48 years',[5] and they noted that she had exhibited her collection of wax figures at many principal cities throughout Great Britain and Ireland. The *Waterford News* in Ireland published a similar report lauding her skilful abilities in wax. The *Illustrated London News* published one of the most informative obituaries about her life and included her obituary among their 'eminent persons recently deceased'. They referred to her as the 'famous exhibitor of the greatest collection of wax-work ever known',[6] included a drawing of her, and provided a brief history of her life.

Because the praises for Madame Tussaud were so modest at her death, one London reporter wrote the following:

> 'Why is Madame Tussaud to leave this mortal stage "unwept, unhonoured, and unsung?" ... We shall see another TITIAN, another VANDYKE, or another REYNOLDS before another TUSSAUD ... She is entitled to this passing tribute at our hands; for, had she lived and died in Paris, she would at the very least have obtained the honour of a necrological notice from M. Janin, with a monument in Père la Chaise, where a chosen body of *flaneurs* would periodically assemble to scatter *immortelles* upon her grave.'[7]

Madame Tussaud's death also did not interrupt business. Her sons were busy planning a new addition that would honour Queen Victoria's husband, Prince Albert. There was also to be a new Hall of Kings. These changes and additions would be costly but with Albert's Great Exhibition of 1851 that was staged in London's Hyde Park, visitors to London would include a stop at Madame Tussaud's worthy exhibit, thereby allowing her sons to recoup all their costs.

MADAME TUSSAUD: HER LIFE AND LEGACY

A visitor to the museum several years after Madame Tussaud's death noted that little had changed. The visitor wrote that the Duke of Wellington is still 'lying in repose, under a splendid canopy of purple velvet and gold cloth, on a tented couch, and covered with the mantle of the Order of the Garter. ... There were several fine paintings in the room, the best of which is "Wellington visiting the relics of Napoleon".'[8]

By the late 1850s, other figures created by Madame Tussaud also remained unchanged and untouched by time. For instance, Queen Victoria looked as she did years before in 1838 when she was crowned, and everything pertaining to Napoleon that had been used by him remained in the same exact state as when he was alive. The Chamber of Horrors still held murderers, conspirators, highwaymen, and robbers. Moreover, the guillotine continued to have a commanding spot in the room with a large model of a prisoner's cell at the Bastille shown behind it.

There was also Madame de Saint Amaranthe whom Curtius had modelled after her execution. She was a salon hostess (*salonnière*) executed for her royalist sympathies and considered one of the most beautiful women in Paris. Madame Tussaud had brought this reposing wax figure with her when she came from France in 1802. The model Curtius did of her was known as 'Sleeping Beauty' when Madame Tussaud toured in Great Britain. In 1851, Madame de Saint Amaranthe was displayed lying on a couch at Baker Street with a wax Madame Tussaud standing at her head.

Madame Tussaud alleged in her 1823 catalogue that Robespierre had become enamoured of Madame de Saint Amaranthe:

'and endeavoured to persuade her to become his mistress; but she, as virtuous as she was beautiful, rejected his solicitations, with scorn and indignation. Robespierre, who never wanted a pretext for destroying anyone who had given him offence, brought Madame St. Amaranthe before the Revolutionary Tribunal, and at the age of 22, in all the bloom of youth and loveliness this victim of virtue was hurried into eternity.'[9]

Whether Madame Tussaud's claims about Robespierre and Madame St. Amaranthe are true remain to be seen, but the same claims were printed in Madame Tussaud's 1876 catalogue.

Over the years, the first 'Sleeping Beauty' of Madame de Saint Amaranthe was replaced with another figure modelled by Curtius in 1765. This figure was Louis XV's famous mistress Madame du Barry. The wax Madame du

Barry is claimed to be the oldest figure at Madame Tussaud's museum today and was originally designed with an inflatable bladder that appeared to show her breathing. Like the original 'Sleeping Beauty,' Madame du Barry is shown reclining, one arm above her head.

As to the Chamber of Horrors, after Madame Tussaud's death, it remained filled with all sorts of criminals. In 1860, it was overhauled and expanded, and, in 1865, the most popular figure was James Bloomfield Rush. He had been convicted of murdering his wife, his mother, his father-in-law, his son, and a Mr. Jermyn in 1849. Madame Tussaud and Sons claimed Rush had 'seduced many young women ... [and] committed forgeries of the blackest dye'.[10] Rush was so notorious his deeds were commemorated not only in writing but also in pottery and wax, and he remained on display at Madame Tussaud's wax museum until 1971.

Despite the popularity of Rush and Madame Tussaud's Chamber of Horrors, not everyone was fan. *Punch* stated:

> 'Good Madame Tussaud, devoting art to homicide, turns to the pleasantness of profit for the abomination of blood. With her so much murder is so much counted money; and – knowing the susceptibility of a British public – it must be owned she sets forth her wares with a wise eye to business. Every day in the newspapers MADAME TUSSAUD offers to the heads of families and their littles ones, – "RUSH THE murderer, taken from life, at Norwich, during his trial, in his usual dress!" Every morning do we behold the miscreant gibbetted in the newspaper column, with the intelligence that the wretch is the last new tenant of the Chamber of Horrors, to be seen for only an extra sixpence. The ordinary exhibition, composed of kings and queens, philosophers and so forth, is one shilling; murderers, sixpence more. Blood, like condiments at a meal, must be paid for extra.'[11]

Regardless of *Punch's* critique, the Chamber of Horrors remained and was enhanced during the nineteenth century, revamped in 1996, and closed in 2016 because of complaints from families whose young children were terrified. However, in the Victorian Era, Madame Tussaud's added a couple of new husband and wife murder teams. The oldest of these was the murdering husband and wife team named Stewart. John Stewart and his wife Catherine Wright had their wax figures taken by Madame Tussaud three hours after their execution in August of 1829. They were convicted of poisoning and robbing a sea captain. John had apparently been robbing and murdering his victims long before, which was noted in Madame Tussaud's 1865 catalogue along with a claim that he had dispatched nine other individuals in this heartless way.

George and Maria Manning were a murdering couple who operated in the late 1840s. They had been convicted of premeditation in the murder of Maria's lover, a Mr. Patrick O'Connor, a well-to-do money lender who owned stock in a railway. The couple invited O'Connor to dine with them, murdered him, and then stole his money and railway shares. Their crime was considered so despicable, they were executed together. Charles Dickens attended their execution and noted the levity that surrounded the immense crowd who witnessed them hanged.

Another murdering couple in the Chamber of Horrors lived in France. They were named Dumollard. According to Madame Tussaud's catalogue of 1876, the Dumollards were fiends. Between 1855 and 1861, they supposedly decoyed 'young women, under the pretence of getting them situations … [and] in this manner … they despatched seventeen or eighteen'.[12] The bearded Mr. Dumollard was hanged and Mrs. Dumollard was sentenced to the galleys for life.

Curtius' workshop of headless bodies and eerie heads that may have once caused a 6-year-old Marie wonderment was now part of Madame Tussaud's legacy. Her sons would keep her legacy alive and well at Baker Street until their deaths: Joseph died in 1866 and Francis passed away in 1873. After Francis' death, Francis' oldest son, Joseph Randall Tussaud, became chief modeler.

In 1884, an important decision was made by Joseph Randall to leave the Baker Street location. He decided to move the museum around the corner to Marylebone Road. Part of the reason for the move was that the Baker Street facility lacked space and was cramped. Moreover, the lease at the Baker Street site had soared in price. The owners also would not give a price nor negotiate until the last minute. So, when the price for the lease was finally announced, Joseph Randall decided a move was in order.

The new landlord on Marylebone Rd was a property estate founded in 1715 by Edward Harley, 2nd Earl of Oxford and Earl of Mortimer that became known as the Howard de Walden Estate. Later, the freehold was bought and the existing building, the Gothic Granary, was demolished. In its place a new substantial and modern red building, surmounted by six glass domes and seven exhibition halls, was built to house Madame Tussaud's museum.

LEGACY

The move to the new building was not particularly easy. It took a week of preparation and several sleepless nights, to transport the figures without causing attention. The move was accomplished by Whiteley's and involved much forethought:

> Each figure was primarily beheaded, the hands removed, and the body ticketed to match, it was then well wrapped in an ample cloth, and packed standing upright in large furniture vans, which came and went between the old home in Baker Street and the new one in Marylebone Road from ten at night till four in the morning Friday and Saturday ... till all had taken up their new quarters.'[13]

The opening of the Marylebone location was slated for Bastille Day, 14 July, and it opened with much fanfare. The new building was described as having a 'handsome frontage; a row of fine iron and gilded railings, with a noble entrance gate, enclosing a well-designed little garden, stocked with flowers, leading to a lofty door through which is reached the imposing entrance hall of the new palace of waxen effigies'.[14] Inside in the spacious hall was mosaic pavement and white marble staircase, a relic of Kensington House that had originally cost £20,000. London's *Morning Post* noted the colossal four caryatides at the entrance hall and the two flights of stairs that led to the salons, with the left side featuring an orchestra. Newspapers also reported that the new building allowed more room for the figures and that the excellent collection could be 'seen to tenfold advantage in its new premises'.[15] However, not everything was perfect. One reporter who visited on opening day noted that the celebrated Napoleon collection was not arranged in its 'Imperial Saloon'.

The move initially proved financially beneficial. Records at Marylebone Rd showed receipts initially quintupled, and Madame Tussaud's grandsons claimed in 1885 that as many as 10,000 visitors came a day. However, with a cousin's half share having been bought out in 1881 and the price of the building falling soon after its purchase, Joseph Randall found the business was underfunded, and, in 1885, he retired. An advertisement appeared in the *London Gazette* stating that the partnership was dissolved by mutual consent on 23 September 1885 and that Francis Curtius and Victor Francis Tussaud assumed all debts.

A limited partnership was formed in 1888 hoping to attract new capital. It was dissolved a year later in 1889 because of arguments between family shareholders, and Tussaud's was sold for £173,000 to three businessmen, who set up a limited company and then turned it into a private company in 1908.

Some employees stayed with the new owners, as did some of the members of the Tussaud family. However, some Tussauds left perhaps because of bitterness over the purchase. Among those who stayed at Tussaud's was Madame Tussaud's great-grandson, John Theodore (son of Joseph Randall), and he was appointed artistic adviser.

Despite the many changes of ownership in the late 1800s, the process of wax modelling remained much same. John Theodore noted that 'modelling of the features of celebrated people stamps the memory of the artist with a deep and abiding impression'.[16] He also maintained that he liked to accomplish the modelling within four sittings, 'the first two to obtain the general appearance, the third to model the precise features, and the last to capture the expression, although he sometimes completed the head after a single sitting'.[17]

When the move was made to Marylebone Rd, it also appeared that behind the scenes, little had changed from the early days when Curtius was alive. A reporter who visited the new location in 1884 noted that he was privileged enough to be admitted into the modeler's workshop.

> 'I almost fancied myself in the dissecting room of some hospital, or in the larder of some fabulous giant, who, after prowling about with his "fee-fi-fo-fum," had not only smelt the blood of an Englishman, but had slain and dismember many, reserving heads, arm, legs and hands, for future consumption. A row of heads arranged on a green baize table looked very ghastly, and I thought it would be difficult to prevent a confusion of members in such a general resurrection … before the public admittance.'[18]

At the new location, most of the old displays remained. For instance, there was the Napoleon collection, the Hall of Kings, and the Chamber of Horrors. Madame Tussaud was also not to be missed. She was there not only in spirit but also in wax. Visitors could see her and imagine her interesting stories and lively character. The tiny but feisty woman was dressed in her quaint, black bonnet and austere, neat dress, just like years earlier when she patiently sat, greeted customers, and collected their entrance fee.

Bibliography

Books:

ABBOTT, John S. C. *The French Revolution of 1789 as Viewed in the Light of Republican Institutions v. 1,* New York: Jefferson Press, 1887.

ABBOTT, John S. C. *The Life of Marie Antoinette, Queen of France,* London: Sampson Low, 1850.

ABBOTT, John S. C. *History of Joseph Bonaparte: King of Naples and of Italy,* New York: Harper, 1899.

ADAMS, John. *A View of Universal History, from the Creation to the Present Time: Including an Account of the Celebrated Revolutions in France, Poland, Sweden, Geneva &c. &c. Together with an Accurate and Impartial Narrative of the Late Military Operations; and Other Important Events v. 3,* London: G. Kearsley, 1795.

AMBROSE, Tom. *Godfather of the Revolution: The Life of Phillipe Égalité Duc d'Orléans,* London: Peter Owens Publisher, 2008.

ANDRESS, David. *The Terror: The Merciless War for Freedom in Revolutionary France,* New York: Farrar, Straus and Giroux, 2006.

BAIRD, Julia. *Victoria: The Queen: An Intimate Biography of the Woman Who Ruled an Empire,* New York: Random House Publishing Group, 2016.

BERRIDGE, Kate. *Madame Tussaud: A Life in Wax,* Harper Collins, 2008.

BIRÉ, Edmond. *The Diary of a Citizen of Paris During 'the Terror' v. 2,* London: Chatto & Windus, 1896.

BLANC, Louis. *History of the French Revolution of 1789 v. 1,* Philadelphia: Lea & Blanchard, 1848.

BLIND, Mathilde. *Madame Roland,* Boston: Roberts Brothers, 1886.

CARLYLE, Thomas. *The French Revolution,* New York: P. F. Collier, 1897.

CASTLE, Terry. *The Female Thermometer: Eighteenth-Century Culture and the Invention of the Uncanny,* New York: Oxford University Press, USA, 1995.

CHALLICE, Annie E. *Heroes, Philosophers, and Courtiers of the Time of Louis XVI,* London: Hurst and Blackett, 1863.

CHAPMAN, Pauline. *Madame Tussaud in England: Career Women Extraordinary*, London: Quiller Press, 1992.

CHATEAUBRIAND, François R. (v. d.). *Memoirs of Chateaubriand v. 1*, London: Henry Colburn, 1848.

CHURCH, Roy A., and GODLEY, Andrew. *The Emergence of Modern Marketing*, London: F. Cass, 2003.

CONWAY, Moncure D., and COBBETT, William. *The Life of Thomas Paine: With a History of His Literary, Political, and Religious Career in America, France, and England*, New York: G.P. Putnam's sons, 1909.

COOPER, Bransby B. *The Life of Sir Astley Cooper, Bart: Interspersed with Sketches from His Note-books of Distinguished Contemporary Characters v. 1*, London: J.W. Parker, 1843.

CRAIK, Anna R. *Annals of our Ancestors: Some Records and Recollections of the Families of Fynes-Clinton and Mathews (Eure of Witton),* Edinburgh: R. & R. Clark, 1924.

CRAIK, George L., and MACFARLANE, Charles. *The Pictorial History of England: Being a History of the People, as Well as a History of the Kingdom v. 8*, London: Charles Knight, 1842.

CROKER, John W. *Essays on the Early Period of the French Revolution*, London: John Murray, 1857.

CROKER, John W. *History of the Guillotine*, London: J. Murray, 1853.

DE BERTRAND DE MOLEVILLE, Antoine-François. *Annals of the French Revolution v. 4,* London: T. Cadell, Jun. and W. Davies, 1800.

DE LA BRETONNE, Nicolas-Edme Restif. *Les nuits de Paris*, Paris: Hachette, 1960.

DICK, Leslie. *The Skull of Charlotte Corday and Other Stories,* New York: Scribner, 1995. *Dictionary of Conversation and Reading, 52 vols*. 18. W. Duckett, 1832.

DRYER, George H. *History of the Christian Church: The advance of Christendom, 1880-1901,* Cincinnati: Jennings & Pye, 1903.

DUNOYER, Alphonse. *The Public Prosecutor of the Terror, Antoine Quentin Fouquier-Tinville*, New York: G. P. Putnam's sons, 1913.

FLEICHSMANN, Hector. *La guillotine en 1793 d'après des documents inédits des Archives Nationale,* Paris: Librairie des Publications Modernes, 1908.

FREMONT-BARNES, Gregory. *Encyclopedia of the Age of Political Revolutions and New Ideologies, 1760-1815,* Westport, Connecticut: Greenwood Press, 2007.

BIBLIOGRAPHY

FROST, Thomas. *The Lives of the Conjurors*, London: Tinsley, 1876.

FROST, Thomas. *The Old Showmen, and the Old London Fairs*, London: Tinsley Brothers, 1875.

GREENE, Richard G. *The International Cyclopedia: A Compendium of Human Knowledge. 15 vols. v. 3,* New York: Dodd, Mead, 1890.

GREGORY, George. *The Elements of a Polite Education; carefully selected from the letters of the late Earl of Chesterfield, to his son,* London, 1807.

HAMMERSLEY, R., ed. *Revolutionary Moments: Reading Revolutionary Texts*, London: Bloomsbury Publishing, 2015.

HERVÉ, F.E., ed. *Madame Tussaud's Memoirs and Reminiscences of France, Forming an Abridged History of the French Revolution*, London: Saunders and Otley, 1838.

LA ROCHETERIE, Maxime d. *The Life of Marie Antoinette,* New York: Dodd, Mead, and Company, 1906.

LANE, Jason. *General and Madame de Lafayette*, Lanham: Taylor Trade Publishing, 2003.

LATHAM, Edward. *Famous Sayings and Their Authors: A Collection of Historical Sayings in English, French, German, Greek, Italian, and Latin,* Swan Sonnenschein, 1906.

LENOTRE, G., and HAVELOCH, H. *Tragic Episodes of the French Revolution in Brittany: With Unpublished Documents*, London: D. Nutt, 1912.

LENOTRE, G., and MAY, J.L. *The Daughter of Louis XVI: Marie-Therese-Charlotte de France, Duchesse D'Angouleme,* London: J. Lane, 1908.

LESLIE, Anita, and CHAPMAN, Pauline. *Madame Tussaud: Waxworker Extraordinary,* London: Hutchinson & Co., 1978.

LIVINGSTON, Luther S., and ROGERS, Bruce,. *Franklin and His Press at Passy: An Account of the Books, Pamphlets, and Leaflets Printed There, Including the Long-lost 'Bagatelles'*, New York: Grolier Club, 1914.

LONG, George. *France and Its Revolutions: A Pictorial History, 1789-1848,* London: C. Knight, 1850.

LOWELL, E. J. *The Eve of the French Revolution*, Houghton, Mifflin and Company, 1892.

Madame Tussaud and Sons' Exhibition. Biographical and Descriptive Sketches of the Distinguished Characters which Compose the Unrivalled Exhibition and Historical Gallery of Madame Tussaud and Sons, London: G. Cole, 1865, 1866, 1876.

MARTIN, Henri. *A Popular History of France from the First Revolution to the Present Time v. 1*, Boston: C. F. Jewett Publishing Company, 1877.

MATHIEZ, Albert. *The Fall of Robespierr,* London: Williams and Norgate, Ltd., 1927.

MAUGRAS, Gaston, Croze-Lemercier, Pierre comte de. *Memoirs of Delphine de Sabran, Marquise de Custine*, London: W. Heinemann, 1912.

MAXWELL-SCOTT, Monica. *Madame Elizabeth de France, 1764-1794,* London: E. Arnold, 1908.

MERCIER, Louis-Sébastian. *Paris: Including a Description of the Principal Edifices and Curiosities of that Metropolis 1,* 1817.

MILLINGEN, John G. *Recollections of Republican France, from 1790 to 1801 v. 1*, London: H. Colburn, 1848.

MORRIS, Anne. C., ed. *The Diary and Letters of Gouverneur Morris: Minister of the United States to France, Member of the Constitutional Convention, etc. 1,* New York: Charles Scribner's Sons, 1888.

NATHAN, Isaac, and MALIBRAN, Maria,. *Memoirs of Madame Malibran de Beriot.* 3rd, London: Joseph Thomas, 1836.

NORRIS, Joseph P. *The Death Mask of Shakespeare*, Philadelphia: Franklin Printing House, 1884.

O'DANIEL, William. *Ins and Outs of London,* London: S. C. Lamb, 1859.

O'LEARY, Margaret. *Forging Freedom: The Life of Cerf Berr of Médelsheim*, Bloomington: iUniverse, 2012.

PEARSON, Roger. *Voltaire Almighty: A Life in Pursuit of Freedom*, New York: Bloomsbury Publishing, 2005.

PHILP, Robert K. *The Dictionary of Useful Knowledge: Vol. III*. G-N, London: Houlston and Wright, 1861.

PILBEAM, Pamela. *Madame Tussauds: And the History of Waxworks*, London: Carnegie Publishing, 2003.

PRICHARD, James C. *A Treatise on Insanity and Other Disorders Affecting the Mind,* Philadelphia: Haswell, Barrington, and Haswell, 1837.

Reed, T.B., ed. *Modern Eloquence.* v. 4, Philadelphia: Dorian and Company, 1903.

REIGNY, Louis-Abel B. *Histoire de France, Pendant Trois Mois, Ou Relation exacte, impartiale, & suivie des événemens qui ont eu lieu à Paris, à Versailles & dans les Provinces,* Paris: Belin, 1789.

RICHARDSON, C. F. *Good Literature v. 4*, American Book Exchange, 1883.

ROACH, Mary. *Stiff: The Curious Lives of Human Cadavers*, New York: W. W. Norton, 2004.

ROSENBLUM, Robert. *Transformations in Late Eighteenth Century Art,* Princeton, New Jersey: Princeton University Press, 1967.

BIBLIOGRAPHY

SAINT-AMAND, Imbert *Famous Women of the French Court,* New York: C. Scribner's Sons, 1897.

SANSON, H., ed. *Memoirs of the Sansons, from Private Notes and Documents, 1688-1847. 2 vols. v. 1,* London, 1876.

SCHAMA, Simon. *Citizens: A Chronicle of the French Revolution,* New York: Alfred A. Knopf, 1989.

SCHWARTZ, Vanessa R. *Spectacular Realities: Early Mass Culture in Fin-de-Siècle Paris,* Berkeley: University of California Press, 1998.

SCHWARTZ, Vanessa R., and Przyblyski, Jeannene M. *The Nineteenth-century Visual Culture Reader,* New York: Routledge, 2004.

SMUCKER, Samuel M. *Memorable Scenes in French History,* New York: Miller, Orton & Co., 1857.

STEPHENS, H.M., ed. *The Principal Speeches of The Statesmen and Orators of the French Revolution 1789-1795,* Oxford: Clarendon Press, 1892.

STEPHENS, Henry M. *A History of the French Revolution v. 2,* New York: C. Scribner's Sons, 1891.

STRACHEY, Lytton. *Queen Victoria,* New York: Harcourt, Brace and Company, 1921.

SYDNEY, William C. *The Early Days of the Nineteenth Century in England, 1800-1820 v. 1,* London: G. Redway, 1898.

THIERS, Aldophe. *The History of the French Revolution v. 1-2,* Philadelphia: Carey and Hart, 1847.

THORNBURY, Walter. *Old and New London: Westminster and the Western Suburbs,* London: Cassell, Petter, & Galpin, 1891.

TUSSAUD, John T. *The Romance of Madame Tussaud's,* New York: George H. Doran Company, 1920.

TUSSAUD, Marie. *Biographical and Descriptive Sketches of the Distinguished Characters which Compose the Unrivalled Exhibition of Madame Tussaud and Sons,* London, 1842.

TUSSAUD, Marie. *Biographical and Descriptive Sketches of the Whole Length Composition Figures and Other Works of Art, Forming the unrivalled Exhibition of Madame Tussaud, etc,* London: J. Bennett, 1823.

VIGÉE-LEBRUN, Louise-Elisabeth, and STRACHEY, Lionel. *Memoirs of Madame Vigée LeBrun,* New York: Doubleday, Page & Company, 1903.

VON DER TRENCK, Baron Frederick. *The Life of Frederick Baron Trenck, Carefully Abridged from His Own Memoirs,* Gainsborough: H. Mozley, 1812.

WALTON, Geri. *Marie Antoinette's Confidant*, Barnsley: Pen and Sword, 2016.

WARWICK, Charles F. *Mirabeau and the French Revolution,* Philadelphia: George W. Jacobs, 1908.

WORMELEY, Katharine P. *The Ruin of a Princess*, New York: The Lamb Publishing Company, 1912.

Publications:

Aberdeen Press and Journal, 'Our Ladies' Column', July 26, 1884.

All the Year Round v. 2, London, 1872.

Archives of Dermatology 147, no. 5 **Coto-Segura, C., Coto-Segura, Pablo and Santos-Juanes, Jorge**, 'The Skin of a Revolutionary', (2011): 539.

Bell's New Weekly Messenger, 'Marylebone', June 28, 1840.

Bentley's Miscellany v. 30, London: Richard Bentley, 1851.

Blackburn Standard, 'Curiosities of a Revolution in France.' June 7, 1848. 678.

Bristol Mercury, 'Splendid Promenade', August 18, 1823.

Caledonian Mercury, 'Advertisements & Notices', January 19, 1809.

Caledonian Mercury, 'Advertisements & Notices', March 25, 1816.

Caledonian Mercury, 'Edinburgh', January 27, 1787.

Caledonian Mercury, 'Paris, August 12', August 20, 1792.

Carlisle Journal, 'Coronation of Queen Victoria', July 7, 1838.

Chepstow Weekly Advertiser, 'The Tussaud Family and Their Colossal Waxworks', April 11, 1885.

Chester Chronicle, 'Festival Dedicated to the Supreme Being', June 27, 1794.

Chester Chronicle, 'Honours Paid to Voltaire!' June 3, 1791.

Chester Chronicle, 'Madame Elizabeth', June 6, 1794.

Chester Chronicle, 'Paris - Thursday Noon', August 10, 1792.

Chester Chronicle, 'Wednesday Night's Mail', July 23, 1790.

Chester Courant, 'Curtius's Curiosities', March 28, 1797.

Chester Courant, December 5, 1797.

Dublin Morning Register, 'The College of Surgeons', January 8, 1830.

Dundee Evening Telegraph, 'Letters to the Ladies', July 26, 1884.

Eclectic Magazine v. 24, 1851.

Essex Herald, 'Confessions of Burke, Authenticated by His Own Signature', February 17, 1829.

Fraser's Magazine v. 7, 1868.

BIBLIOGRAPHY

Gentleman's Magazine v. 10; v. 164, 1838.

Godey's Magazine v. 74-75, Philadelphia: Godey Company, 1867.

Hereford Times, 'Gleanings', January 20, 1849.

Hull Advertiser and Exchange Gazette, 'Portrait of Robespierre', September 6, 1794.

Illustrated London News, 'Obituary of Eminent Persons Recently Deceased', April 20, 1850.

Ipswich Journal, 'Parisian Intelligence', April 16, 1791.

Jackson's Oxford Journal, 'Execution of Favras', February 27, 1790. 1922.

John Bull, 'Patronized', January 12, 1834.

Kentish Gazette, 'Foreign Affairs', January 2, 1801.

Kentish Gazette, 'Paris, April 7, Mirabeau!' April 15, 1791.

Liverpool Mercury 'Letters to the Editors', May 4, 1821.

London Evening Standard, 'Trial of William Corder', August 8, 1828.

London Literary Gazette and Journal of Belles Lettres, Arts, Sciences, Etc, 1826.

London Quarterly Review, 1835.

London Times, 'Execution of Louis XVI. King of the French', January 25, 1793.

London Times, 'France: Imprisonment of the King and Queen, and the Late Massacre', September 12, 1793.

London Times, 'France', September 10, 1792.

Manchester Courier and Lancashire General Advertiser, 'Madame Tussaud's Collection', June 20, 1829.

Monthly Review, or, Literary Journal, 1772 and 1838.

Morning Chronicle, 'London', April 18, 1850.

Morning Chronicle, 'Novel Exhibition - Lyceum, Strand. Phantasmagoria', October 30, 1801.

Morning Chronicle, 'Police Intelligence', January 26, 1835.

Morning Post, 'Death of Madame Tussaud', April 17, 1850.

Morning Post, 'Loss of the Earl Moira Packet', August 14, 1821.

Morning Post, 'Lyceum - Now Open', June 28, 1802.

Morning Post, 'Madame Bonaparte', August 18, 1801.

Morning Post, 'Madame Tussaud's New Building', July 14, 1884.

New Zealand Herald, 'Relics of Buonaparte', May 9, 1925.

Newcastle Courant, 'News from France', July 30, 1791.

Norfolk Chronicle, 'Curtius's Grand Cabinet of Curiosities', January 9, 1795.

Nottingham Review and General Advertiser for the Midland Counties, September 24, 1819.

Observer 'Exhibitions', August 15, 1802.

Peterson's Magazine 'The Princess de Lamballe', 1891.

Proceedings of the Bunker Hill Monument Association at the Annual Meeting, Boston: Bunker Hill Monument Association 1870.

Punch, 1849.

Salisbury and Winchester Journal 'Execution of Colonel Despard &c.', February 28, 1803 *The Nation v. 56.* 1893.

Scots Magazine; Or, General Repository of Literature, History, and Politics v. 56, 1794.

Sheffield Independent, 'Riots at Bristol', November 19, 1831.

Staffordshire Advertiser, 'London', May 23, 1795.

Stamford Mercury, 'Lincoln County Hospital', August 27, 1819.

Supplements to the Courant: For the Year 1858 v. 23, 1858.

Sussex Advertiser 'Conduct Since Condemnation and Execution of William Corder', August 18, 1828.

Telegraph, 'Heart of the dauphin gets royal burial 200 years on', December 21, 2003.

The New-Yorker v, 8, 1839.

Notes

Chapter 1 – Boiling Point

1 Francis E. Hervé, ed., Madame Tussaud's Memoirs and Reminiscences of France, Forming an Abridged History of the French Revolution (London: Saunders and Otley, 1838), 23.

2 John Stevens Cabot Abbott, *The Life of Marie Antoinette, Queen of France* (London: Sampson Low, 1850), 62.

3 Ibid.

4 Margaret O'Leary, *Forging Freedom: The Life of Cerf Berr of Médelsheim* (Bloomington: iUniverse, 2012), 257.

5 George Long, *France and Its Revolutions: A Pictorial History, 1789-1848* (London: C. Knight, 1850), 3.

6 Bunker Hill Monument Association, *Proceedings of the Bunker Hill Monument Association at the Annual Meeting* (Boston: The Association, 1870), 50.

7 Louis-Sébastian Mercier, *Paris: Including a Description of the Principal Edifices and Curiosities of that Metropolis* 1 (1817), 248.

8 Louise-Elisabeth Vigée-Lebrun and Lionel Strachey, *Memoirs of Madame Vigée LeBrun* (New York: Doubleday, Page & Company, 1903), 24.

9 F. E. Hervé, ed., 58–59.

10 Ibid., 88.

11 Louis-Abel Beffroy de Reigny, Histoire de France, Pendant Trois Mois, Ou Relation exacte, impartiale, & suivie des événemens qui ont eu lieu à Paris, à Versailles & dans les Provinces (Paris: Belin, 1789), 24–25.

12 David McCallam, "Waxing Revolutionary: Reflections on a Raid on a Waxworks at the Outbreak of the French Revolution," French History White Rose University Consortium, accessed August 14, 2017, http://eprints.whiterose.ac.uk/629/1/mccallamd1.pdf, 21.

13 Geri Walton, *Marie Antoinette's Confidant* (London: Pen and Sword, 2016), 142.

14 François René (vicomte de.) Chateaubriand, *Memoirs of Chateaubriand* v. 1 (London: Henry Colburn, 1848), 208.

Chapter 2 – Marie and Dr Curtius

1 F. E. Hervé, ed., 4.

2 Patrice Portier, "Anne-Marie GROSHOLTZ Marie Tussaud," http://gw.geneanet.org/papor17?lang=en&p=anne%20 Marie&n=grosholtz&oc=2.

3 Bransby Blake Cooper, *The Life of Sir Astley Cooper, Bart: Interspersed with Sketches from His Note-books of Distinguished Contemporary Characters* v. 1 (London: J.W. Parker, 1843), 352.

4 William Connor Sydney, *The Early Days of the Nineteenth Century in England, L800-1820* v. 1 (London: G. Redway, 1898), 140.

5 Charles Dickens, ed., *All the Year Round* v. 2 (London: Charles Dickens, 1872), 235.

6 *Dublin Morning Register,* "The College of Surgeons," January 8, 1830, 3.

7 Thomas N. Haviland and Lawrence C. Parish, "A Brief Account of the Use of Wax Models in the Study of Medicine," *Journal of the History of Medicine and Allied Sciences* 25, no. 1 (January 1970): 57.

8 F. E. Hervé, ed., 7.

9 Maxime de La Rocheterie, *The Life of Marie Antoinette* (New York: Dodd, Mead, and Company, 1906), 171.

10 Anne C. Morris, ed., *The Diary and Letters of Gouverneur Morris: Minister of the United States to France, Member of the Constitutional Convention, etc.* 1 (New York: Charles Scribner's Sons, 1888), 22–23.

11 *The Monthly Review, or, Literary Journal* v. 45 (Griffith, 1772), 514.

12 E. J. Lowell, *The Eve of the French Revolution* (Houghton, Mifflin and Company, 1892), 158.

13 A. C. Morris, ed., 34.

14 George Gregory, *The Elements of a Polite Education; carefully selected from the letters of the late Earl of Chesterfield, to his son* (London, 1807), 266–67.

Chapter 3 – The Resort of Talented Men

1 F. E. Hervé, ed., 7.

2 Ibid., 73.

3 Ibid., 15.

4 *The London Literary Gazette and Journal of Belles Lettres, Arts, Sciences, Etc* (London: H. Colburn, 1826), 374.

5 F. E. Hervé, ed., 125–26.

6 Madame Tussaud's London, "Behind the Scenes - How a Wax Figure is Made," accessed September 8, 2017, https://www.madametussauds.com/media/1632898/behind-the-scenes-how-a-wax-figure-is-made.pdf.

7 James Cowles Princhard, *A Treatise on Insanity and Other Disorders Affecting the Mind* (Philadelphia: Haswell, Barrington, and Haswell, 1837), 295.

8 Luther Samuel Livingston and Bruce Rogers, *Franklin and His Press at Passy: An Account of the Books, Pamphlets, and Leaflets Printed There, Including the Long-lost 'Bagatelles'*. (New York: Grolier Club, 1914), 6.

9 F. E. Hervé, ed., 13.

10 John Theodore Tussaud, *The Romance of Madame Tussaud's* (New York: George H. Doran Company, 1920), 66–67.

11 Annie Emma Challice, *Heroes, Philosophers, and Courtiers of the Time of Louis XVI* (London: Hurst and Blackett, 1863), 154.

12 *Caledonian Mercury,* "Edinburg," January 27, 1787, 3.

13 Kate Berridge, *Madame Tussaud: A Life in Wax* (Harper Collins, 2008), 52.

14 R. Pearson, 390.

Chapter 4 – Mounting Tensions

1 Samuel M. Smucker, *Memorable Scenes in French History* (New York: Miller, Orton & Co., 1857), 88.

2 Ibid.

3 G. Walton, 19.

4 John Adams, *A View of Universal History, from the Creation to the Present Time: Including an Account of the Celebrated Revolutions in France, Poland, Sweden, Geneva &c. &c. Together with an Accurate and Impartial Narrative of the Late Military Operations; and Other Important Events* v. 3 (London: G. Kearsley, 1795), 387–88.

5 Ibid., 388.

6 G. Walton, 94.

7 Robert Kemp Philp, *The Dictionary of Useful Knowledge: Vol. III. G-N* (London: Houlston and Wright, 1861), 1196.

8 Thomas Carlyle, *The French Revolution* (New York: P. F. Collier, 1897), 110.

9   Edward Latham, *Famous Sayings and Their Authors: A Collection of Historical Sayings in English, French, German, Greek, Italian, and Latin* (Swan Sonnenschein, 1906), 172.

10 Louis Blanc, *History of the French Revolution of 1789* v. 1 (Philadelphia: Lea & Blanchard, 1848), 556.

11 Ibid., 558.

12 Ibid., 560.

13 Ibid., 561.

14 Ibid., 562.

15 Ibid.

16 Madame Tussaud and Sons' Exhibition, *Biographical and Descriptive Sketches of the Distinguished Characters which Compose the Unrivalled Exhibition and Historical Gallery of Madame Tussaud and Sons* (London: G. Cole, 1866), 36.

17 F.E. Hervé, ed., 96.

18 *Hull Advertiser and Exchange Gazette,* "Portrait of Robespierre," September 6, 1794, 4.

Chapter 5 – Prisoners of the People

1   J. S. C. Abbott, 131.

2   *Dictionary of Conversation and Reading,* 52 vols. 18 (W. Duckett, 1832), 372.

3   Pamela Pilbeam, *Madame Tussauds: And the History of Waxwords* (London: Carnegie Publishing, 2003), 35.

4   J. S. C. Abbott, 141.

5   *Bentley's Miscellany* v. 30 (London: Richard Bentley, 1851), 311.

6   Imbert de Saint-Amand, *Famous Women of the French Court* (New York: C. Scribner's Sons, 1897), 27.

7   *Jackson's Oxford Journal,* "Execution of Favras," February 27, 1790, 1922, 1.

8   Aldophe Thiers, *The History of the French Revolution* v. 1-2 (Philadelphia: Carey and Hart, 1847), 134.

9   F. E. Hervé, ed., 115.

10 Walter H. Bidwell, ed., *The Eclectic Magazine* v. 24 (New York, 1851), 335–36.

Chapter 6 – Celebrations

1   F. E. Hervé, ed., 116–17.

2   Ibid., 333.

3   *Chester Chronicle,* "Wednesday Night's Mail," July 23, 1790, 2.
4   Ibid.
5   Ibid.
6   *Chepstow Weekly Advertiser,* "The Tussaud Family and Their Colossal Waxworks," April 11, 1885, 4.
7   von der Baron Trenck, Frederick, *The Life of Frederick Baron Trenck, Carefully Abridged from His Own Memoirs* (Gainsborough: H. Mozley, 1812), 77.
8   John Stevens Cabot Abbott, *The French Revolution of 1789 as Viewed in the Light of Republican Institutions* v. 1 (New York: Jefferson Press, 1887), 192.
9   Maxime de La Rocheterie, *The Life of Marie Antoinette; Translated from the French* (1906: Dodd, Mead, 1893), 112.
10 Charles Franklin Warwick, *Mirabeau and the French Revolution* (Philadelphia: George W. Jacobs, 1908), 395.
11 *Ipswich Journal,* "Parisian Intelligence," April 16, 1791, 4.
12 *The Kentish Gazette,* "Paris, April 7, Mirabeau!," April 15, 1791, 4.

Chapter 7 – Setting the Stage

1   John Wilson Croker, *History of the Guillotine* (London: J. Murray, 1853), 14.
2   Ibid., 10.
3   Ibid., 11.
4   Henry Sanson, ed., *Memoirs of the Sansons, from Private Notes and Documents, 1688-1847,* 2 vols. v. 1 (London, 1876), 257.
5   F. E. Hervé, ed., 135.
6   G. Walton, 165.
7   John Wilson Croker, *Essays on the early period of the French revolution* (London: John Murray, 1857), 150.
8   *Newcastle Courant,* "News from France," July 30, 1791, 5990, 2.
9   *Chester Chronicle,* "Honours Paid to Voltaire!," June 3, 1791, 2.
10 Antoine-François de Bertrand de Moleville, Antoine-François, *Annals of the French Revolution* v. 4 (London: T. Cadell, Jun. and W. Davies, 1800), 229.
11 Ibid., 227–29.
12 George L. Craik and Charles MacFarlane, *The Pictorial History of England: Being a History of the People, as Well as a History of the Kingdom* v. 8 (London: Charles Knight, 1842), 676.
13 G. Walton, 181.
14 F. E. Hervé, ed., 219–20.

Chapter 8 – War with Austria and September Massacres

1 *Chester Chronicle,* "Paris - Thursday Noon," August 10, 1792, 4.
2 F. E. Hervé, ed., 233.
3 Jason Lane, *General and Madame de Lafayette* (Lanham: Taylor Trade Publishing, 2003), 180.
4 *Caledonian Mercury,* "Paris, August 12," August 20, 1792, 3.
5 F. E. Hervé, ed., 243.
6 C. F. Richardson, *Good Literature* v. 4 (American Book Exchange, 1883), 79.
7 Virginia G. Sully, "The Princess de Lamballe," *Peterson's Magazine* 100, no. 4 (1891): 322.
8 *London Times,* "France: Imprisonment of the King and Queen, and the Late Massacre," September 12, 1793, 2.
9 J. T. Tussaud, 91.
10 K. Berridge, 140.
11 de la Bretonne, Nicolas-Edme Restif, *Les nuits de Paris* (Paris: Hachette, 1960), 247–53.
12 *London Times,* "France," September 10, 1792, 1.
13 F. E. Hervé, ed., 248.
14 C. F. Warwick, 228–29.

Chapter 9 – The End of the Monarchy

1 F. E. Hervé, ed., 177–78.
2 G. Walton, 204.
3 *The London Times,* "Execution of Louis XVI. King of the French," January 25, 1793, 2.
4 Katharine Prescott Wormeley, *The Ruin of a Princess* (New York: The Lamb Publishing Company, 1912), 258.
5 Joseph Parker Norris, *The Death Mask of Shakespeare* (Philadelphia: Franklin Printing House, 1884), 2–3.
6 Mathilde Blind, *Madame Roland* (Boston: Roberts Brothers, 1886), 311–12.
7 Covadonga Coto-Segura, Pablo Coto-Segura, and Jorge Santos-Juanes, "The Skin of a Revolutionary," *Archives of Dermatology* 147, no. 5 (2011): 539.
8 Robert Rosenblum, *Transformations in Late Eighteenth Century Art* (Princeton, New Jersey: Princeton University Press, 1967), 84.
9 Leslie Dick, *The Skull of Charlotte Corday and Other Stories* (New York: Scribner, 1995), 23.

10 Edmond Biré, *The Diary of a Citizen of Paris During 'the Terror'* v. 2 (London: Chatto & Windus, 1896), 197–98.

11 *Chester Courant, "–,"* December 5, 1797, 1.

12 Ibid.

13 Mary Roach, *Stiff: The Curious Lives of Human Cadavers* (New York: W. W. Norton, 2004), 199–200.

14 *Supplements to the Courant: For the Year 1858* v. 23 (Hartford: Day & Clark, 1858), 7.

15 Tom Ambrose, *Godfather of the Revolution: The Life of Phillipe Égalité Duc d'Orléans* (London: Peter Owens Publisher, 2008), 241.

16 Ibid., 246.

Chapter 10 – The Beginning of Terror

1 Rachel Hammersley, ed., *Revolutionary Moments: Reading Revolutionary Texts* (London: Bloomsbury Publishing, 2015), 93.

2 Ibid., 95.

3 Moncure Daniel Conway and Cobbett William, *The Life of Thomas Paine: With a History of His Literary, Political, and Religious Career in America, France, and England* (New York: G.P. Putnam's sons, 1909), 89.

4 John Gideon Millingen, *Recollections of Republican France, from 1790 to 1801* v. 1 (London: H. Colburn, 1848), 209.

5 Ibid.

6 Richard Gleason Greene, *The International Cyclopedia: A Compendium of Human Knowledge,* 15 vols. v. 3 (New York: Dodd, Mead, 1890), 488.

7 *Blackburn Standard,* "Curiosities of a Revolution in France," June 7, 1848, 678, 4.

8 Gregory Fremont-Barnes, *Encyclopedia of the Age of Political Revolutions and New Ideologies, 1760-1815* (Westport, Connecticut: Greenwood Press, 2007), 184.

9 *The Scots Magazine; Or, General Repository of Literature, History, and Politics* v. 56 (Edinburgh: A. Chapman, 1794), 278.

10 F. E. Hervé, ed., 387–88.

11 Hector Fleichsmann, *La guillotine en 1793 d'après des documents inédits des Archives Nationales* (Paris: Librairie des Publications Modernes, 1908), 290.

12 F. E. Hervé, ed., 292.

13 Ibid., 293–94.

14 Gaston Maugras, Pierre comte de Croze-Lemercier, *Memoires of Delphine de Sabran, Marquise de Custine* (London: W. Heinemann, 1912), 154.

15 Monica Maxwell-Scott, *Madame Elizabeth de France, 1764-1794* (London: E. Arnold, 1908), 93–95.

16 K. P. Wormeley, 32.

17 *Chester Chronicle,* "Madame Elizabeth," June 6, 1794, 991, 2.

18 F. E. Hervé, ed., 404–5.

19 Simon Schama, *Citizens: A Chronicle of the French Revolution* (New York: Alfred A. Knopf, 1989), 419.

Chapter 11 – Peak and Fall of Robespierre

1 George Herbert Dryer, *History of the Christian Church: The advance of Christendom, 1880-1901* (Cincinnati: Jennings & Pye, 1903), 43.

2 *Chester Chronicle,* "Festival Dedicated to the Supreme Being," June 27, 1794, 4.

3 Ibid.

4 Thomas B. Reed, ed., *Modern Eloquence,* v. 4 (Philadelphia: Dorian and Company, 1903), 1756–57.

5 Ibid., 1757–58.

6 Albert Mathiez, *The Fall of Robespierre* (London: Williams and Norgate, Ltd., 1927), 110.

7 David Andress, *The Terror: The Merciless War for Freedom in Revolutionary France* (New York: Farrar, Straus and Giroux, 2006), 310.

8 F. E. Hervé, ed., 403.

9 S. Schama, 837.

10 Henry Morse Stephens, *A History of the French Revolution* v. 2 (New York: C. Scribner's Sons, 1891), 382.

11 *Fraser's Magazine* v. 7 (London: Longmans, Green & Company, 1868), 292.

12 Henri Martin, *A Popular History of France from the First Revolution to the Present Time* v. 1 (Boston: C. F. Jewett Publishing Company, 1877), 598.

13 Henry M. Stephens, ed., *The Principal Speeches of The Statesmen and Orators of the French Revolution 1789-1795* (Oxford: Clarendon Press, 1892), 294.

14 *The London Quarterly Review* (New York: Theodore Foster, 1835), 304.

15 F. E. Hervé, ed., 423.

16 *The London Quarterly Review*, 305.

Chapter 12 – The End of Terror

1 G. Lenotre and H. Haveloch, *Tragic Episodes of the French Revolution in Brittany: With Unpublished Documents* (London: D. Nutt, 1912), 307.

2 Vanessa R. Schwartz, *Spectacular Realities: Early Mass Culture in Fin-de-Siècle Paris* (Berkeley: University of California Press, 1998), 95–96.

3 Anita Leslie and Pauline Chapman, *Madame Tussaud: Waxworker Extraordinary* (London: Hutchinson & Co., 1978), 81–82.

4 Ibid., 80.

5 K. Berridge, 162.

6 Alphonse Dunoyer, *The Public Prosecutor of the Terror, Antoine Quentin Fouquier-Tinville* (New York: G. P. Putnam's sons, 1913), 139.

7 Staffordshire Advertiser, "London," May 23, 1795, 2.

8 Ibid.

9 Kim Willsher, "Heart of the dauphin gets royal burial 200 years on," *The Telegraph*, December 21, 2003.

Chapter 13 – Becoming Madame Tussaud

1 A. Leslie, and Pauline Chapman, 91.

2 J. T. Tussaud, viii.

3 F. E. Hervé, ed., 466.

4 Ibid., 466–67.

5 J. H. Richards, *The Nation* v. 56 (New York: J.H. Richards, 1893), 47.

6 G. Lenotre and J. Lewis May, *The Daughter of Louis XVI: Marie-Therese-Charlotte de France, Duchesse D'Angouleme* (London: J. Lane, 1908), 220.

7 J. H. Richards, 47.

8 *Norfolk Chronicle,* "Curtius's Grand Cabinet of Curiosities," January 9, 1795, 1351, 2.

9 *Chester Courant,* "Curtius's Curiosities," March 28, 1797, 3338, 3.

10 John Stevens Cabot Abbott, *History of Joseph Bonaparte: King of Naples and of Italy* (New York: Harper, 1899), 59.

11 Ibid., 60–61.

Chapter 14 – New Directions

1 F. E. Hervé, ed., 491.

2 *Kentish Gazette,* "Foreign Affairs," January 2, 1801, 3.

3 Ibid.

4 Vanessa R. Schwartz and Jeannene M. Przyblyski, *The Nineteenth-century Visual Culture Reader* (New York: Routledge, 2004), 102.

5 Terry Castle, *The Female Thermometer: Eighteenth-Century Culture and the Invention of the Uncanny* (New York: Oxford University Press, USA, 1995), 146.

6 Thomas Frost, *The Lives of the Conjurors* (London: Tinsley, 1876), 163.

7 *Morning Post,* "Madame Bonaparte," August 18, 1801, 2.

8 *The Morning Chronicle,* "Novel Exhibition - Lyceum, Strand. Phantasmagoria," October 30, 1801, 1.

9 K. Berridge, 176.

Chapter 15 – United Kingdom

1 *Morning Post,* "Lyceum - Now Open," June 28, 1802, 1.

2 *The Observer,* "Exhibitions," August 15, 1802, 555, 3.

3 *Salisbury and Winchester Journal,* "Execution of Colonel Despard &c.," February 28, 1803, 2.

4 Ibid.

5 Roy A. Church and Andrew Godley, *The Emergence of Modern Marketing* (London: F. Cass, 2003), 10.

6 *Stamford Mercury,* "Lincoln County Hospital," August 27, 1819, 3.

7 Marie Tussaud, *Biographical and Descriptive Sketches of the Distinguished Characters which Compose the Unrivalled Exhibition of Madame Tussaud and Sons* (London, 1842), 5.

8 Ibid., 9.

9 Ibid., 18.

10 Ibid., 5.

11 *Caledonian Mercury,* "Advertisements & Notices," January 19, 1809, 1.

12 *Caledonian Mercury,* "Advertisements & Notices," March 25, 1816, 1.

13 Thomas Frost, *The Old Showmen, and the Old London Fairs*, 2nd (London: Tinsley Brothers, 1875), 235–36.

Chapter 16 – Touring

1 *Manchester Courier and Lancashire General Advertiser,* "Madame Tussaud's Collection," June 20, 1829, 2.

2 Marie Tussaud, *Biographical and Descriptive Sketches of the Whole Length Composition Figures and Other Works of Art, Forming the unrivalled Exhibition of Madame Tussaud, etc* (London: J. Bennett, 1823), 33.

3 *Manchester Courier and Lancashire General Advertiser*, 2.

4 *Liverpool Mercury,* "To the Editors," May 4, 1821, 6.

5 *Nottingham Review and General Advertiser for the Midland Counties*, September 24, 1819, 3.

6   *New Zealand Herald,* "Relics of Buonaparte," May 9, 1925, 5.

7   Ibid.

8   Madame Tussaud and Sons, *Biographical and Descriptive Sketches of the Distinguished Characters which Compose the Unrivalled Exhibition and Historical Gallery of Madame Tussaud and Sons* (London: G. Cole, 1865), 30.

9   *Bristol Mercury,* "Splendid Promenade," August 18, 1823.

10   R. A. Church, and Andrew Godley, 16.

11   M. Tussaud, 1.

12   *Morning Post,* "Loss of the Earl Moira Packet," August 14, 1821, 2.

13   Anna R. Craik, *Annals of our Ancestors: Some Records and Recollections of the Families of Fynes-Clinton and Mathews (Eure of Witton)* (Edinburgh: R. & R. Clark, 1924), 88–89.

14   *Sheffield Independent,* "Riots at Bristol," November 19, 1831, 1.

15   Ibid.

Chapter 17 – Permanency

1   *John Bull,* "Patronized," January 12, 1834, 1.

2   Isaac Nathan and Maria Malibran, *Memoirs of Madame Malibran de Beriot*, 3rd (London: Joseph Thomas, 1836), 24–25.

3   J. T. Tussaud, 118–19.

4   *Punch* v. 16 (Punch Publications Limited, 1849), 33.

5   *Morning Chronicle,* "Police Intelligence," January 26, 1835, 4.

6   J. T. Tussaud, 119.

7   *London Evening Standard,* "Trial of William Corder," August 8, 1828, 1.

8   Ibid.

9   *London Evening Standard,* "Trial of William Corder," August 8, 1828, 1.

10   *Sussex Advertiser,* "Conduct Since Condemnation and Execution of William Corder," August 18, 1828, 4.

11   Ibid.

12   *Essex Herald,* "Confessions of Burke, Authenticated by His Own Signature," February 17, 1829, 4.

13   Ibid.

14   Walter Thornbury, *Old and New London: Westminster and the Western Suburbs* (London: Cassell, Petter, & Galpin, 1891), 419.

15   P. Pilbeam, 103.

Chapter 18 – Memoirs and Memories

1 Sylvanus Urban, *The Gentleman's Magazine* v. 10; v. 164 (London: William Pickering; John Bowyer Nichols and Son, 1838), 188.

2 Ibid.

3 *Carlisle Journal,* "Coronation of Queen Victoria," July 7, 1838, 4.

4 H. Greeley and P. Benjamin, *The New-Yorker* v. 8 (New York: H. Greeley & Company, 1839).

5 *The Monthly Review* (London: R. Griffiths, 1838), 244.

6 Pauline Chapman, *Madame Tussaud in England: Career Women Extraordinary* (London: Quiller Press, 1992), 71.

7 Ibid., 73.

8 Ibid.

9 Ibid., 73–74.

10 J. T. Tussaud, 341.

11 Ibid., 342.

12 Ibid.

13 Lytton Strachey, *Queen Victoria* (New York: Harcourt, Brace and Company, 1921), 51.

14 Louis Antoine Godey, *Godey's Magazine* v. 74-75 (Philadelphia: Godey Company, 1867), 446.

15 Julia Baird, *Victoria: The Queen: An Intimate Biography of the Woman Who Ruled an Empire* (New York: Random House Publishing Group, 2016), 146.

16 *Bell's New Weekly Messenger,* "Marylebone," June 28, 1840, 7.

17 *Hereford Time,* "Gleanings," January 20, 1849, 6.

18 Rosella Lorenzi, "Madame Tussaud's Mysterious Cause of Death Has Just Been Revealed," Seeker.com, accessed October 7, 2017, https://www.seeker.com/madame-tussauds-mysterious-cause-of-death-has-just-been-revealed-2131854492.html.

Chapter 19 – Legacy

1 *Chepstow Weekly Advertiser*, 4.

2 J. T. Tussaud, 359.

3 Ibid., 356–57.

4 R. Lorenzi.

5 *Morning Post,* "Death of Madame Tussaud," April 17, 1850, 6.

6 *The Illustrated London News,* "Obituary of Eminent Persons Recently Deceased," April 20, 1850, 13.

7 *Morning Chronicle,* "London," April 18, 1850, 4.

8 William O'Daniel, *Ins and Outs of London* (London: S. C. Lamb, 1859), 345.

9 M. Tussaud, 24.

10 Madame Tussaud and Sons, 36.

11 *Punch, or the London Charivari* v. 16-19 (London: Punch Publications Limited, 1850), 83.

12 Madame Tussaud and Sons, *Exhibition Catalogue Containing Biographical and Descriptive Sketches of the Distinguished Characters which Compose Their Exhibition and Historical Gallery* (London, 1876), 41.

13 *Dundee Evening Telegraph,* "Letters to the Ladies," July 26, 1884, 2.

14 *Aberdeen Press and Journal,* "Our Ladies' Column," July 26, 1884, 2.

15 *Morning Post,* "Madame Tussaud's New Building," July 14, 1884, 4.

16 J. T. Tussaud, 172.

17 P. Pilbeam, 180–85.

18 *Aberdeen Press and Journal,* 2.

Index